Nursing and Informatics for the 21st Century – Embracing a Digital World, 3rd Edition, Book 4

Nursing and Informatics for the 21st Century – Embracing a Digital World, 3rd Edition is comprised of four books which can be purchased individually at www.routledge.com:

Book 1: Realizing Digital Health – Bold Challenges and Opportunities for Nursing – ISBN: 9780367516888

Book 2: Nursing Education and Digital Health Strategies – ISBN: 9781032249728

Book 3: Innovation, Technology, and Applied Informatics for Nurses – ISBN: 9781032249803

Book 4: Nursing in an Integrated Digital World that Supports People, Systems, and the Planet – ISBN: 9781032249827

Nursing and Informatics for the 21st Century – Embracing a Digital World, 3rd Edition, Book 4

Nursing in an Integrated Digital World that Supports People, Systems, and the Planet

Edited by

Connie White Delaney, PhD, RN, FAAN, FACMI, FNAP
Charlotte A. Weaver, PhD, MSPH, RN, FHIMSS, FAAN
Joyce Sensmeier, MS, RN-BC, FHIMSS, FAAN
Lisiane Pruinelli, PhD, MS, RN, FAMIA
Patrick Weber, MA, RN, FIAHSI, FGBHI

Foreword by Deborah Trautman, PhD, RN, FAAN
President and Chief Executive Officer,
American Association of Colleges of Nursing

Foreword by Kedar Mate, MD
President and CEO,
Institute for Healthcare Improvement

Foreword by Howard Catton
Chief Executive Officer,
International Council of Nurses

A PRODUCTIVITY PRESS BOOK

First published 2022
by Routledge
605 Third Avenue, New York, NY 10158

and by Routledge
2 Park Square, Milton Park, Abingdon, Oxon, OX14 4RN

Routledge is an imprint of the Taylor & Francis Group, an informa business

ISBN: 9781032249841 (hbk)
ISBN: 9781032249827 (pbk)
ISBN: 9781003281047 (ebk)

DOI: 10.4324/9781003281047

Typeset in Garamond
by Deanta Global Publishing Services, Chennai, India

Dedication for Connie White Delaney

Responding to the urgent and powerful invitation for community, partnership and collaboration, this *Nursing and Informatics for the 21st Century—Embracing a Digital World,* 3rd Edition is dedicated to all individuals, organizations and informaticians who are co-creating futures, health and healthcare. May these co-created informatics anchored futures radiate the brain of intellect and wisdom, the brain of heart and compassion, and the action brain of impact, voice, caring and awakening.

Dedication for Charlotte A. Weaver

Reflecting these painful times, this dedication goes out to all our frontline nurses and fellow healthcare workers who have taken care of us all around the globe at the risk of their own lives and well-being. We owe you.

Dedication for Joyce Sensmeier

To my husband and life partner, who has faithfully supported my informatics journey, encouraging me to take risks along the way and congratulating me on every success. Thank you for believing in me.

Dedication for Lisiane Pruinelli

To those who battle every day for a better world … 'I don't write a book so that it will be the final word; I write a book so that other books are possible, not necessarily written by me.'—Michel Foucault

Dedication for Patrick Weber

For the sake of the population, the empowerment of nurses worldwide is the best effort to improve disease prevention and promote good health. Thank you to my co-editors and all the authors for their work on this book series.

Contents

Foreword

When the nation's nursing school deans voted to endorse *The Essentials: Core Competencies for Professional Nursing Education* in April 2021, new competency expectations for tomorrow's nurses came into focus. Driven in part by the need to ensure consistency among graduates of entry-level and advanced-level nursing education programs, one area receiving special emphasis across roles is nursing informatics. As we considered how best to prepare professional nurses to thrive in the future, the need for providers to 'use information and communication technologies and informatics processes to deliver safe nursing care to diverse populations in a variety of settings' (Essential 8.3) was affirmed as a key competency expectation.

Over the past 20 years, informatics increasingly has been a focus in nursing education, given the rapid rise in the use of technology to guide healthcare delivery and clinical decision-making and the need to critically consider all available data when engaging in evidence-based practice and precision healthcare. Basic informatics competencies are foundational to all nursing practice.

Reaching this point in the evolution of our understanding of informatics would not have been possible without pioneers in the field. The authors of *Nursing and Informatics for the 21st Century—Embracing a Digital World*, 3rd Edition—Connie White Delaney, Charlotte A. Weaver, Joyce Sensmeier, Lisiane Pruinelli and Patrick Weber—stand among the world's leading authorities on health informatics, data science and digital health. Committed to enhancing the scholarship of discovery, these nurse leaders are known internationally for their trailblazing work that has been recognized by such authorities as the Alliance for Nursing Informatics, American Medical Informatics Association, International Academy of Health Sciences Informatics and the Healthcare Information and Management Systems Society. Their pedigrees are undeniable, their thought leadership profound.

The publication of this expansive resource comes at a time when nursing is once again divining its future into the next decade. In addition to the re-envisioned AACN's *Essentials*, which is setting a new standard for nursing education, recent National Academy of Medicine reports on *The Future of Nursing* and *Implementing High Quality Primary Care* point the way forward for nursing practice, research priorities and interprofessional engagement. All these paths demand a greater understanding and reliance on informatics as a driver of innovation and impact. Further, healthcare's move to address pressing social needs, including a shared desire to achieve health equity, gain insight into the social determinants of health, expand consumer access to data and attend to global health concerns are all considered within the context of digital technologies and applied data science as part of this new book series.

Nursing and Informatics for the 21st Century—Embracing a Digital World, 3rd Edition will be of great interest to nurses and other health professionals in the US and globally who are eager to learn more about leveraging automated systems and emerging science to sustain health and improve healthcare delivery. This book series serves as an important resource for practice leaders, nurse researchers, systems analysts, healthcare consumers and graduate students looking to explore opportunities for innovation that develop at the nexus of nursing science, emerging technologies, critical thinking and patient-centered care.

As we look to a future with nursing education that is more competency-based, informatics will be front and center. For faculty wishing to keep pace with the latest thinking on contemporary nursing education and practice, this essential resource will help to inform your understanding about the value and reach of informatics and may also generate new ideas for developing experiential learning opportunities using artificial intelligence, telehealth, simulation and other leading-edge technologies. These emerging tools and practices are transforming nursing roles as well as the skills and knowledge needed to manage care remotely. This comprehensive work will help lead conversations to inspire future generations of nurses to explore how best to leverage nursing informatics in their research, practice and leadership roles.

Deborah Trautman, PhD, RN, FAAN
President and Chief Executive Officer
American Association of Colleges of Nursing

Foreword

Walk onto any clinical service unit in a modern hospital, and you will realize that clinical practice today is a fully socio-technological phenomenon—entirely reliant both upon a nurse's compassion and upon our technology's capacity to supply information and services just in time. Technologies are no longer working their way into health and healthcare—they are already integral to both. But the promise of these incredibly exciting digital therapeutics, diagnostics and monitoring systems depends on, just as more conventional medicines have for decades, the human systems required to implement them. This interface—between nurses and the digital information that can make care more effective, efficient, and reliable—is at the heart of 21st-century nursing informatics.

Years ago, the field of quality improvement in healthcare started with a simple premise—we could work on those human processes to take the fruits of clinical science—medications, new diagnostic assays, vaccines—and more reliably deliver them to patients to create lasting health effects. It is time for a complementary agenda—quality and reliability sciences must now be applied to improve the delivery of proven digital therapies and diagnostics. Just as we created reliable workflows that delivered antibiotics that would prevent sepsis deaths, so too must we create workflows that will leverage new data sources and technologies to improve the way we care for patients. Digital will change healthcare just as antibiotics have, but neither will achieve impact without implementation methods that ensure that the 'medicine' gets to the patient.

This is crucial because of the incredible potential of technology and data to improve care and outcomes. Consider how good artificial intelligence (AI)-guided diagnosis and triage have become: for some clinical conditions, AI now gets diagnostic and treatment accuracy over 90% right compared to clinicians in urgent care environments. These technologies won't replace the nurse or the physician, but they can radically affect the capacity of a clinician to see patients. If much of the time-consuming fact-finding, differential diagnosis, care plan documentation, and charting can be done by an AI-guided automated assistant, nurses can spend much more time caring for patients.

Realizing technology's transformative potential in nursing requires a comprehensive understanding of how to turn data into information; information into knowledge; knowledge into wisdom; and wisdom into applied practice. This book series is essential to such an understanding. This new edition is a detailed and exhaustive exploration of the myriad contexts, approaches, challenges and success stories of how effective informatics can improve every dimension of health, including the fiercely urgent dimensions of needing to improve access to care and ensuring health equity.

For those new to the field of informatics, this series contains an illuminating history of the rapid and profound changes in digital health over the past decade. And for those with deep experience in the field, there are chapters detailing both what's happening at the cutting-edge and what the future holds. Anyone who wants to improve nursing practice in the modern era needs to read this book series and heed its calls to action.

Kedar Mate, MD
President and CEO
Institute for Healthcare Improvement

Foreword

As the COVID-19 pandemic has so painfully shown us, it is hard to accurately predict the future. While the temptation is to spend time and effort on futurology—it can be hard to resist—our time is probably better spent on trying to prepare flexibly for what is coming next and, in some way, help to shape it.

What seems certain is that digital health will feature in our futures and that nurses are in a prime position to take advantage of the benefits it can bring. In fact, as we have seen, recent developments in digital health are some of the few positives to have come out of the pandemic.

Finding ways to deal with the pandemic brought about a rapid increase in access to digitally enhanced care, whether it be through the use of video-conferencing for consultations and telehealth or through increased access to massive amounts of data that were previously buried and heavily guarded in the depths of healthcare organizations' information technology systems. The issue now is understanding the data and using it meaningfully to improve services and reduce costs.

While only a year or so ago it would have been correct to say the future is digital, we can now say that, in many parts of the world, digital health is already here and that it looks like it's here to stay. We can see it in the development of nurse-led models of care and how the use of data and new equipment is changing the traditional, paternalistic models of care to more responsive ones that are personalized, faster, sustainable and more affordable.

The biggest challenge ahead will be to expand access to nursing informatics to all nurses, wherever they are so that they can provide equitable access to state-of-the-art care to people everywhere.

This is especially important as the world deals with and recovers from the COVID-19 pandemic. Nurse-led models of care, underpinned by access to data, are a big part of the solution as we strengthen our health systems for the post-pandemic world to come.

I am delighted to write this foreword for what is likely to be a very influential book series about nursing and informatics and how nurses can maximize the impact of digital health for the benefit of patients and their families and the health systems that they work in.

In the past, information technology has promised so much but often failed to deliver on its potential. If it is to fulfil its promise, it must be an enabler for people to be empowered, and it must improve access to services, the quality and efficiency of those services, and the patient's care and health outcomes.

For this to happen, the people on the receiving end of care need to be at the centre of the systems that are developed, and nurses must be involved in all stages of their design, development and implementation. In the past, we have seen how the ill-thought-out introduction of some systems has taken nurses away from direct care, to the detriment of their patients and the annoyance of the nurses.

Nurses do not want to spend hours in front of computer screens, as they have been required to in the past. They do not want to spend their time inputting data into counterintuitive systems that do not meet their requirements. What they want is quick and easy access to the information they need at their fingertips, in people's homes, at the nurses' station on wards, at the bedside and in the clinics where they work, in real time while they are interacting with their patients.

We see the power of technology and data-driven change across the globe, from low- to high-income settings, from the use of Apps on mobile phones to the adoption of sophisticated information systems and algorithms. But underlying it all is the continuing need for a highly skilled and educated nursing workforce. Whatever the future holds in terms of information technology, artificial intelligence and robotics, they will always be used in support of the compassion, the relationships and the dynamic human factors that only nurses can provide.

This *Nursing and Informatics for the 21st Century—Embracing a Digital World*, 3rd Edition shows the path ahead for our profession to become fully digitally enabled. I am sure it will prove to be an indispensable guide along the way.

Howard Catton
Chief Executive Officer
International Council of Nurses

Preface

While we commit to living in the 21st century and maintaining our open minds and hearts to the needs, wishes and wisdom that will inform our future, we have found the pace of change to be challenging in preparing this book series. Every day, new technologies and partnerships are in the social news media, and healthcare systems announce new digital health programs that push care out into the hands of patients and into the home. Additionally, these new care modalities and technology changes are occurring simultaneously with national and international policy mandates to address social injustices and inequities, equality in access to care, and planetary health. Tremendous innovation has transpired since the publication of this book's second edition in 2010. In that space of time, medical sensing devices and mobile technologies have become ubiquitous, permeating every aspect of our lives. Concurrently, the synergistic effect of new technologies and tools such as cloud data storage, application programming interfaces, artificial intelligence and machine learning are game changers in advancing digital health. Together with legislation and regulatory changes, the proprietary limitations of electronic health record (EHR) systems have been upended. The voice of the consumer and insistence on patient-centered, connected and readily accessible care have never had greater velocity, urging our unremitting attention.

Thus, in planning this third edition, we abandoned the previous framework of presenting an 'international snapshot of current state' on EHR adoption and nursing. Technology changes and new applications that extract data, apply AI systems, dashboards, and suggest care protocols made a primary EHR framework irrelevant. Increasingly, economics and policy mandates push healthcare systems to embrace a preventative, wellness and population health focus that requires new thinking toward advanced technology applications that extend services into clinics, community and the home. In the United States, reimbursement linked to Alternative Payment Models (APM) and 'value-based purchasing' with dependency on quality metrics require healthcare systems to collaborate with community resources and post-acute care providers. All collaboration, local to world-wide, demands exchanging and sharing information, as well as actively engaging individual patients and their families. A plethora of digital/mobile applications have emerged to fill this evolving 'non-acute care/non-EHR' space. As chapters from geographic areas spanning the globe describe, economic imperatives, mandates to deliver equal access to care in rural as well as metro areas, and the need to incorporate social determinants of health into care delivery have also driven the adoption of digital health solutions. Therefore, this third edition focuses on these new technologies and the care delivery models they make possible: thus, we gave this work the subtitle *'Embracing a Digital World.'*

Kristine Mednansky, Senior Editor from Taylor & Francis Group, LLC, asked us to consider a new edition, based on feedback from the readers of our previous works. Our full gratitude goes to Ms Mednansky for this series' existence. Her voice was the key driver for creating this work, the *Nursing and Informatics for the 21st Century*, 3rd Edition. Ms Mednansky ensured that this current work would meet the needs of readers in a variety of formats: electronic, print, and the option to purchase either an individual chapter or an entire book. Moreover, readers will note another major difference in the look and feel of the previous hardcover book: this work has been converted to a four-book series to deliver a resource that is more easily consumed. Our hope is that with this flexibility in access and usability, the work embodied in this collection of contributing authors will be widely read and extensively shared. We look forward to receiving your feedback on this novel approach.

This work is organized into a series of four books, each with 11 chapters: (1) Realizing Digital Health–Bold Challenges and Opportunities for Nursing; (2) Nursing Education and Digital Health Strategies; (3) Innovation, Technology, and Applied Informatics for Nurses; and (4) Nursing in an Integrated Digital World that Supports People, Systems, and the Planet. Each book in the series includes international contributors with authors from Africa and South Africa, Brazil, Belgium, Canada, China, England, Finland, Germany, Italy, Norway, the Philippines, South Korea, Sri Lanka, Switzerland, Taiwan, and the United States, as well as authors of additional exemplars from China, India and the West Balkan countries. Throughout this series, the wisdom of leading-edge innovators is interwoven with digital health applications, global thought leaders and multinational, cooperative research initiatives, all against the backdrop of health equity and policy-setting bodies, such as the United Nations and the World Health Organization.

We begin Book 1 of the series by introducing the paradigm of digital health, and its underlying technologies, offering examples of its potential use and future impacts. This introduction is followed by an in-depth look at the ethical considerations in digital health that nurses and informaticists need to understand, authored by an international team of nursing informatics leaders from Finland, Canada and England. The growing movement in consumerism and patient engagement is described in a collaborative research initiative between academia–government–industry. This chapter is bolstered by numerous exemplars, all illustrating the importance of the engaged patient enabled by new digital technologies with the goal of making possible comprehensive access to individuals' digital health information, regardless of system or location. Several chapters focus on the underlying need for terminology and data standards to capture the data necessary to enable new science and knowledge discoveries. Subsequent chapters outline the critical and urgent role that nurse executive leaders' play in advancing digital health, as well as the knowledge and skills needed to take advantage of new digital technologies. We follow with chapters on the role(s) of nursing informatics leaders in large, US health systems, as well as a global perspective from Brazil, Italy and the Philippines. To provide a clear understanding of the challenges facing the United Nations and World Health Organizations' goals for health equity and equality, we include a critical examination of South Africa's healthcare delivery system, technologies and nursing's role across these structural segments. We close Book 1 with a look at the information sharing needed to support true team care spanning multiple settings and systems.

Book 2 is dedicated to a deep examination of nursing education's best practices, strategies, and informatics competencies. The chapters included in Book 2 span nursing education and learning for applied critical thinking, including the use of technology, content, skills versus tools, the use of 'smart' systems for care delivery and the role of critical thinking as essential to nursing care delivery. These concepts are understood as a paradigm shift that must be incorporated into nursing and healthcare education. Best practices for workforce and degree-level education are presented in a description of Emory's Academic/Practice partnership focusing on disruption through nurse innovation enabled by all nurses and students having access to big data. This book closes with a review of innovative methodologies being used in simulation labs across the globe, including some uses of virtual and augmented reality simulations.

Book 3 defines the foundations of artificial intelligence (AI), machine learning (ML) and various digital technologies, including social media, the Internet of Things, telehealth and applied data analytics, all with a look toward the future state. The Applied Healthcare Data Science Roadmap is presented as a framework aiming to educate healthcare leaders on the use of data science principles and tools to inform decision-making. We focus particular attention on the cautions, potential for harm, and biases that artificial intelligence technologies and machine learning may pose in healthcare, with the role of advocate and protector from harm falling under the nurse's role. Book 3 concludes by outlining four case studies featuring innovations developed by nurses in response to COVID-19, which highlight the creative use of technologies to support patients, care providers and healthcare systems during the global pandemic.

We continue with a focus on the theme of enabling digital technologies in Book 4 as they are used to address planetary health issues and care equity across developing countries. Throughout the development of this series, the world has struggled with the core issues of equity in access to care, needed medical equipment and supplies and vaccines. Sustainability and global health policy are linked to the new digital technologies in the chapters that illustrate healthcare delivery modalities, which nurse innovators are developing, leading and using to deliver care to hard-to-reach populations for better population health. Social media use in South Korea for health messaging, community initiatives and nursing research are presented with additional references to other Asian countries. A US description of consumer engagement with patient ownership of all their medical records data is presented with the underlying technologies explained in simple, understandable terms. Additionally, we tapped experts to highlight the legal statutes, government regulations and civil rights law in place for patients' rights, privacy and confidentiality, and consents for the United States, the United Kingdom and the European Union. The next chapter in Book 4 is written by two participants of the 'Future of Nursing 2020–2030' task force who deliver an optimistic message. These authors recognize the work that needs to be done around health equity and equality and review nursing's role responsibilities to effect these changes. Their optimism comes from all the opportunities that social policy and enabling digital technologies make possible for nursing. The authors outline how these changes in care delivery models, the patient/provider role and dependence on digital tools all present opportunities for new nursing roles, access to expansive data resources for research with the exponential growth of our science base and for entrepreneurship.

We conclude this book series with a chapter written by the editors in which we envision the near future. We explore the impact that digital technologies will have on: a) how care is delivered, including expanding care settings into community and home; b) virtual monitoring; and c) the type and quantity of patient-generated data and how it is used to advance knowledge and care excellence. Ultimately these changes highlight the numerous ways that nursing roles and skill sets related to digital health are needed to support the global goal of equal access to health and care. We emphasize the necessity for partnering. We send the message that nursing, along with our transdisciplinary partners, is being called to lead and create unparalleled transformation of healthcare to person-centered, connected and accessible care anchored in digital health.

Acknowledgement

We share our deep gratitude with all of the persons, including care providers, researchers, educators, business and corporate leaders, and informatics experts in all settings, for requesting an update to the second edition of *Nursing and Informatics for the 21st Century*. Together, you recognized the value and synergy of nursing and informatics, the core function of informatics in shaping nursing, health and healthcare, and the reciprocal learning that a global perspective offers us. Thank you to Taylor & Francis Group, LLC, and especially Kristine Mednansky, Senior Editor, for giving us the opportunity to produce this third edition as a totally new body of work in this post-EHR era. But most especially, for your creativity and flexibility as we presented a book double our original plan. Thus, this third edition is presented as a four-book series enveloping *Nursing and Informatics for the 21st Century*. We are deeply humbled by the dedication, work and creativity of our contributing authors, many of whom formed teams that expanded across continents to be able to capture the fullest coverage and latest information. The contributors bring state-of-the-art knowledge, coupled with real-world practice and education. It is the integration of nursing and informatics knowledge and practice that will sustain our health, communities and planet. Last, we would be remiss not to say a deep thank you to Midori V. Green, our project manager par excellence, who kept us organized and on track through her diplomacy and hard work and without which we would not have made our deadlines.

In gratitude,

Connie White Delaney
Charlotte A. Weaver
Joyce Sensmeier
Lisiane Pruinelli
Patrick Weber

Editors

Connie White Delaney, PhD, RN, FAAN, FACMI, FNAP serves as Professor and Dean at the University of Minnesota School of Nursing and is the Knowledge Generation Lead for the National Center for Interprofessional Practice and Education. She served as Associate Director of the Clinical Translational Science Institute—Biomedical Informatics, and Acting Director of the Institute for Health Informatics (IHI) in the Academic Health Center from 2010 to 2015. She serves as an adjunct professor in the Faculty of Medicine and Faculty of Nursing at the University of Iceland, where she received the Doctor Scientiae Curationis Honoris Causa (Honorary Doctor of Philosophy in Nursing) in 2011. She is an elected Fellow in the American Academy of Nursing, American College of Medical Informatics, and National Academies of Practice. Delaney is the first Fellow in the College of Medical Informatics to serve as a Dean of Nursing. Delaney was an inaugural appointee to the USA Health Information Technology Policy Committee, Office of the National Coordinator, and Office of the Secretary for the U.S. Department of Health and Human Services (HHS). She is an active researcher in data and information technology standards for nursing, healthcare. Delaney is past president of Friends of the National Institute of Nursing Research (FNINR) and currently serves as Vice-Chair of CGFNS, Inc. She holds a BSN with majors in nursing and mathematics, MA in Nursing, PhD Educational Administration and Computer Applications, postdoctoral study in Nursing & Medical Informatics and a Certificate in Integrative Therapies & Healing Practices.

Charlotte A. Weaver, Ph.D., MSPH, RN, FHIMSS, FAAN is a visionary senior executive, now retired after 40+ years of experience in nursing informatics, patient safety and quality, evidence-based nursing practices and healthcare automation in acute, ambulatory and post-acute care. She created a breakthrough in the nursing educational curricula by introducing learning using an electronic health record (EHR) in virtual environments and pioneered the corporate-level, Chief Nurse Officer role. She also has Board Director experience in the public/non-profit healthcare sectors. With 15+ years of experience at the chief executive level in the corporate HIT industry and healthcare delivery organizations with Board-reporting responsibilities, her fields of specialization include EHR, health IT policy, post-acute care delivery in home health and hospice provider organizations. Dr. Weaver serves on a number of academic, healthcare systems and healthcare technology company Boards. She is a fellow in the American Academy of Nursing and the Health Information Management Systems Society (HIMSS). She is a frequent presenter at national and international conferences and has published extensively as a writer and editor. Dr. Weaver has a PhD in Medical Anthropology from the University of California, Berkeley and San Francisco, an MSPH in Epidemiology and a BA in Anthropology from the University of Washington, and a Nursing diploma from St Elizabeth's School of Nursing. She was a post-doctoral fellow at the University of Hawaii.

Joyce Sensmeier MS, RN-BC, FHIMSS, FAAN is the Senior Advisor, Informatics for HIMSS, a non-profit organization focused on reforming the global health ecosystem through the power of information and technology. In this role, she provides thought leadership in the areas of clinical informatics, interoperability and standards programs and initiatives. Sensmeier served as Vice President, Informatics at HIMSS from 2005 to 2019. She is president of IHE USA, a non-profit organization whose mission is to improve our nation's healthcare by promoting the adoption and use of IHE and other world-class standards, tools and services for interoperability. An internationally recognized speaker and author of numerous book chapters and articles, Sensmeier achieved fellowship in the American Academy of Nursing in 2010.

Lisiane Pruinelli PhD, MS, RN, FAMIA is Assistant Professor and co-director of the Center for Nursing Informatics in the School of Nursing and Affiliate Faculty at the Institute for Health Informatics, University of Minnesota. She is a Fellow of the American Medical Informatics Association and a University of Minnesota School of Nursing Global Health Scholar. She serves as the co-chair of the Nursing Knowledge Big Data Science Initiative, co-chair for the Data Science and Clinical Analytics workgroup, and as an advisor board member for the International Medical Informatics Association—Student and Emerging Professional interest group. Previously, she served as a co-chair for the Midwest Nursing Research Society Nursing Informatics workgroup. With more than ten years of clinical experience in both transplant coordination and information systems development and implementation, she is part of a new generation of nursing informaticians focused on applied clinical informatics. Her expertise is in applying innovative nursing informatics tools and cutting-edge data science methods to investigate the trajectory of complex disease conditions suitable for clinical implementations. Her work aims to identify the problems and targeted interventions for better patient outcomes. Dr. Pruinelli grew up in Brazil, moved to USA in 2012 and brings an international and diverse perspective to her everyday work and life. She earned a PhD degree from the University of Minnesota School of Nursing in 2016, and a Master's of Sciences (2008), a Teaching Degree in Nursing (2002) and a Bachelor of Nursing Sciences (2000) degree from the Federal University of Rio Grande do Sul, Porto Alegre, Brazil.

Patrick Weber, MA, RN, FIAHSI, FGBHI is Founder, Director and Principal of Nice Computing, SA in Lausanne, Switzerland. He holds a MA degree in healthcare management and is a Registered Nurse with a diploma degree in nursing. Weber has been an active leader in the European health informatics field for over 30 years, serving as his country's representative to IMIA-Nursing for over a decade and has held numerous board-level positions in IMIA-Nursing as well. Weber is an active member and leader in the European Federation for Medical Informatics (EFMI) and has held numerous leadership positions including treasurer, vice president, president and past president over the past decades.

He has served as the vice president of MedInfo 2019 at International Medical Informatics Association (IMIA) and vice president Europe, and is currently the IMIA Liaison Officer to WHO, Geneva. Within his own country, Weber leads the expert group for Swiss DRG quality control for medical coding and is President of the Oliver Moeschler Foundation leading pre-hospitalization healthcare emergencies. He is EFMI Leader of EU H2020 projects such as CrowdHealth, FAIR4Health and HosmartAI. He is the co-editor of *Nursing Informatics for the 21st Century: An International Look at Practice, Trends and Future*, first and second editions; *Nursing Informatics 2016 eHealth for All: Every Level Collaboration – From Project to Realization*; and *Forecasting Informatics Competencies for Nurses in the Future of Connected Health*. Weber is a founding member of the International Academy of Health Sciences Informatics and a member of the Board of the Swiss Medical Coding Association.

Contributors

Whende M. Carroll, MSN, RN-BC, FHIMSS, Director, Clinical Optimization, Contigo Health

Chiyoung Cha, PhD, RN, Assistant Professor, College of Nursing & System Health, Ewha Womans University

Charlene H. Chu, PhD, RN, GNC(c), Assistant Professor, Lawrence S. Bloomberg Faculty of Nursing, University of Toronto; KITE-Toronto Rehabilitation Institute, University Health Network

Aaron Conway, PhD, RN, Assistant Professor, Lawrence S. Bloomberg Faculty of Nursing, University of Toronto

Connie White Delaney, PhD, RN, FAAN, FACMI, FNAP, Professor and Dean, University of Minnesota School of Nursing

Christoph Ellßel, PhD, LLM, Director, Competence Center on the Future of Aging at the Catholic University of Applied Sciences Munich

Daniel Flemming, PhD, RN, Professor of Nursing and Social Work Informatics, Department of Nursing, Catholic University of Applied Sciences Munich

Carlos Alberto Faerron Guzmán, MD, MSc, Planetary Health Alliance-Harvard University; Planetary Health Alliance, University of Maryland, Baltimore; Centro Interamericano para la Salud Global

Marcus D. Henderson, MSN, RN, PhD Student, Johns Hopkins University School of Nursing; Lecturer, Department of Family and Community Health, University of Pennsylvania School of Nursing

Meihua Ji, PhD, MSN, RN, School of Nursing, University of Pittsburg and Capital Medical University Beijing

Lindsay Jibb, PhD, RN, Assistant Professor, Lawrence S. Bloomberg Faculty of Nursing, University of Toronto

Oommen John, MD, MBA, The George Institute for Global Health India

B. Kavitha, RNRM, MA, MHSc, MSc Nursing, MSc Health Informatics, Health Informatics Supervisor GKNM Hospital

Elaine Zacharakis Loumbas, JD, Health, Privacy & Technology Attorney, Zacharakis Loumbas Law, LLC

Ranige Maheshika Madhuwanthi, B.Sc (Hons) Nursing, RN, Nursing Officer, University Hospital-Kothalawala Defence University, Sri Lanka

Rohana Basil Marasinghe, PhD, MPhil, MBBS, Professor and Head of Department of Medical Education, Faculty of Medical Sciences, University of Sri Jayewardenepura and President Health Informatics Society of Sri Lanka (HISSL)

Karen A. Monsen, PhD, RN, FAMIA, FNAP, FAAN, Professor and Director, Center for Nursing Informatics and Director, Omaha System Partnership, University of Minnesota School of Nursing

Lisa A. Moon, PhD, RN, LHIT, CCMC, Founder/CEO, Advocate Consulting, OneSelf Technology LLC

Ivana Ognjanović, PhD, BS, CS, MA, University of Donja Gorica

Suhyun Park, MSN, RN, PhD Candidate, University of Minnesota School of Nursing

Marisol Peters, MS, PMP, CISM, Chief Operations Officer, NationalNoteGroup Capital Funds

Carolyn M. Porta, PhD, MPH, RN, SANE-A, FAAN, FNAP, Professor, University of Minnesota School of Nursing

Teddie Potter, PhD, RN, FAAN, FNAP, Clinical Professor and Director of Planetary Health, University of Minnesota School of Nursing

Lisiane Pruinelli, PhD, MS, RN, FAMIA, Assistant Professor, School of Nursing and Affiliate Faculty, Institute for Health Informatics, University of Minnesota

Charlene E. Ronquillo, PhD, RN, Assistant Professor, School of Nursing, University of British Columbia Okanagan

Suptendra Nath Sarbadhikari, MBBS, PhD, The George Institute of Global Health India

Joyce Sensmeier, MS, RN-BC, FHIMSS, FAAN, Senior Advisor, Informatics, HIMSS

Victoria L. Tiase, PhD, RN-BC, FAMIA, FNAP, FAAN, Director of Research Science, NewYork-Presbyterian Hospital; Assistant Professor, Weill Cornell Medicine

Andre Uhl, PhD, MA, BA, Fellow, Planetary Health Alliance-Harvard University

Vivian Vimarlund, PhD, School of Engineering and Technology, Linköping University

Charlotte A. Weaver, PhD, MSPH, RN, FHIMSS, FAAN, PIH Health Board Member, Retired Healthcare Executive, formerly Sr. Vice President and Chief Clinical Officer, Gentiva Health Services

Patrick Weber, MA, RN, FIAHSI, FGBHI, Founder, Director and Principal, Nice Computing, SA

Ying Wu, PhD, RN, Dean and Professor, School of Nursing, Capital Medical University Beijing

Introduction

In this book, we weave together the leading-edge innovators in digital health applications, global thought leaders and multinational, cooperative research initiatives against the backdrop of health equity and policy-setting bodies, such as the United Nations and the World Health Organization. We open the book in Chapter 1 with Potter and colleagues' introduction to the concept of planetary health as a global expansion of social determinants of health (SDOH) that in its extreme threaten health for all in the form of extinction. It is important to note that almost all chapters in Book 4 acknowledge social determinants of health as a key focus in healthcare across the globe. Linked to SDOH are the themes of health equity in access to care and equality in care treatment. Health equity and equality are addressed by Marasinghe and Madhuwanthi in Chapter 2 using Sri Lanka as their exemplar. Health equity and equality are also discussed by Weber and colleagues in Chapter 3 with China, India and the Western Balkan countries as exemplars. In contrast to Tiase and Henderson's chapter (Chapter 10) on the future of nursing with the 2021 report's emphasis on nursing's explicit role responsibility to ensure equity and equality, the authors in Chapters 2 and 3 call out an absence of the health policies in their respective countries for nursing's involvement or role.

Sensmeier and Carroll's Chapter 4 on the empowering potential for the use of a 'unique nurse identifier' gives us a glimpse of how the nursing profession could move forward in areas of research, capturing the value of nursing in quantitative terms, and in support of chargeable, independent practice.

Game-changing technologies, such as application program interfaces (API), HL7 FHIR® (fast healthcare interoperability resources) data interoperability standard, artificial intelligence and machine learning are presented by Cha and Park (Chapter 5), Moon (Chapter 6) and Chu and colleagues (Chapter 9). Cha and Park present the power of social media for health communications, patient communities, wellness initiatives, nursing research and teaching. The authors give examples from tech savvy Asian countries, including South Korea, Taiwan, China and Japan. Moon (Chapter 6) walks us through the US regulatory policies in the Cures Act and Medicare's interoperability rule that give consumers access to and ownership of their medical records data. Moon describes, in simple to understand explanations, the underlying technologies that in combination with the regulatory changes are fueling an emerging wave of consumers as active participants and partners in their care. Chu and colleagues (Chapter 9) present several applied research and development initiatives based on mobile technologies, AI and patient-centered design methodologies that are in process across Canada. All the above authors speak to the impact and implications of these new enabling technologies for nursing role functions as mentors, advocates and protecting from harm, but Chu and colleagues add the function of 'explainers' with implications for nurses needing to have high levels of digital health literacy. Equally, the authors emphasize continuing education needs for our nursing workforce, faculty and schools of nursing curricula. Implications for nurses in the informatics field are a major theme in all the above chapters.

Chapters 7 and 8 address the legal, ethical and regulatory requirements for consent, privacy and confidentiality for both the European Union and the United States. In Chapter 7, Zacharakis Loumbas and Peters discuss the challenging tasks facing healthcare professionals and organizations that must safeguard and protect patient data and detail case examples of successful cybersecurity attacks with the painful consequences for the involved organizations. Flemming and Ellßel in Chapter 8 cover the rigorous framework for privacy rights established through the General Data Protection Regulation at the EU level (GDPR 2016) for a European perspective and developed at a national level to cover data use, cybersecurity protections and system maintenance requirements. Two participants of the 'Future of Nursing 2020–2030' task force deliver an optimistic message for nursing's future in Chapter 10. Tiase and Henderson recognize the challenging work that needs to be done around health equity and equality and review nursing's role responsibilities to effect these changes. Their optimism comes from the opportunities that social policy changes and enabling digital technologies make possible for nursing. The authors walk us through how these changes in care delivery models, the patient/provider role and dependence on digital tools present avenues for new nursing roles, access to expansive data resources for research with exponential growth of our science base and entrepreneurship.

We conclude this book series with a chapter written by the editors in which we envision the near future. We explore the impact that digital technologies will have on: a) how care is delivered, including expanding care settings into community and home; b) virtual monitoring; and c) the type and quantity of patient-generated data and how it is used to advance knowledge and care excellence. Ultimately these changes highlight the numerous ways that nursing roles and skill sets related to digital health are needed to support the global goals of equal access to health and care. We emphasize the necessity for partnering. We send the message that nursing, along with our transdisciplinary partners, is being called to lead and create unparalleled transformation of healthcare to person-centered, connected and accessible care anchored in digital health.

Connie White Delaney
Charlotte A. Weaver
Joyce Sensmeier
Lisiane Pruinelli
Patrick Weber

Chapter 1

UN Sustainable Development Goals and Planetary Health: Alignment with Nursing Informatics

Teddie Potter, Carlos Alberto Faerron Guzmán,
Karen A. Monsen, Carolyn M. Porta and Andre Uhl

Contents

DOI: 10.4324/9781003281047-1

Introduction

In 2015, the United Nations launched the Sustainable Development Goals (SDGs) with the bold and optimistic intent to eradicate poverty, protect the planet and promote global peace and prosperity by 2030. The COVID-19 pandemic, however, has impacted the timeline and has illuminated the interconnection of human and natural systems. Likewise, it has increased our awareness that we cannot have health and well-being when massive disparities and disruptions of Earth's natural systems persist.

To appreciate what is meant by planetary health, we start with a brief review of the historical events that shaped what would become disciplines, initiatives, partnerships, policies and efforts broadly characterized as 'public health,' 'global health' and 'One Health.'

Public, Global, Planetary and One Health Defined

Public health as a discipline took shape as we increased our knowledge and understanding of infectious agents, the environmental factors that contributed to human disease, infection, illness or death, and the sociopolitical factors that influenced threats to health. When physician John Snow, the 'father' of epidemiology (the incidence, distribution and control of disease), strongly advocated for the link between something unseen in the water supply and the cholera deaths taking place around the Broad Street Pump in London in 1854, he challenged long-standing beliefs about causes of illness and death (Snow, 1855). When his actions led to the outbreak ending, he ushered in a new era of understanding and discovery with a focus on public health and prevention (Tulchinsky, 2018).

Formal colleges and schools of public health emerge some 50 years later in the early 1900s. Charles-Edward Amory Winslow, Yale's first Chair of the Department of Public Health, defined the field of public health and his definition continues to stand the test of time:

> Public health is the science and the art of preventing disease, prolonging life, and promoting physical health and efficiency through organized community efforts for the sanitation of the environment, the control of community infections, the education of the individual in principles of personal hygiene, the organization of medical and nursing service for the early diagnosis and preventive

treatment of disease, and the development of the social machinery which will ensure to every individual in the community a standard of living adequate for the maintenance of health.

(Winslow, 1920, p. 30)

In contrast, global health focuses on the health of the population in each country. Koplan et al. (2009) from the Consortium of Universities for Global Health (CUGH) defines global health as 'an area for study, research, and practice that places a priority on improving health and achieving health equity for all people worldwide' (p. 1995). Velji and Bryant (2011) offer a definition of global health that will resonate with many:

> The concept of global health reaches beyond the rich-poor dichotomy and geographic boundaries and borders to the forces that separate the powerful, free, privileged populations from the population that is powerless and unfree. In its acceptance of human diversity, global health is an expression of support for the human rights enshrined in the WHO constitution, charters, and declarations and in the instruments of governance of several other nation-states.

(Velji & Bryant, 2011, p. 307)

A decade later, Salm et al. (2021) conducted a review of articles that had been published between 2009 and 2018 and included one or both terms 'global health' and 'public health.' They identified 33 definitions of global health, characterized by attention to worldwide improvements to health, operationalized principles of justice and ethical frameworks, and influence on political decision-making and resource allocations. Salm and colleagues' review demonstrates the ongoing emergent nature of 'global health' as a construct representing broad and diverse efforts and perspectives focused on advancing the health of populations around the globe. Additionally, global health carries a commitment to addressing a broader array of health threats and inclusion of numerous disciplines engaged in solving those threats.

In 2007, the American professional associations of medicine and of veterinary medicine came together to summarize the concept of *One Health*. Asokan (2015) reports that this combined task force defined One Health as 'a system approach which includes disciplines of human medicine, veterinary medicine, and other related scientific health disciplines working locally, nationally, and globally to attain optimal health for people, animals, and our environment' (Asokan, 2015, p. 3). Those involved in advancing the health of humans, animals and the environment while addressing the aspects of each, and the interplay among these, often characterize their work and teams as 'One Health.' Zoonoses, infections spread from animals to humans, are often the focus of One Health's related research and education. Some countries in Africa and Asia (e.g., Cameroon, Rwanda) have adopted One Health's national platforms, encouraging respective ministries of health, wildlife and livestock to work together to address infectious zoonotic threats to health and to mitigate outbreak risks.

History demonstrates consistent growth in understanding, appreciating and addressing the complex and multifaceted interplay of risks, protections, threats and resources surrounding human, animal and environmental health. Borders quickly become irrelevant when facing situations such as zoonotic threats, environmental emergencies or regional instabilities. Global, multi-disciplinary and multisectoral cooperation, whether formal or organic, has much potential to mitigate risks and to prevent severe consequences to the health of individuals, communities, nation-states and the globe.

Planetary Health

Public health, global health and One Health all discuss the root causes of illness and disease: planetary health points to the upstream human behaviors that disrupt the planet's natural systems, thereby disrupting human health for generations to come. The 2018 Canmore Declaration defines planetary health as:

> The interdependent vitality of all natural and anthropogenic eco-systems; this vitality includes the biologically defined ecosystems (at micro, meso and macro scales) that favor biodiversity; it includes the more broadly defined human-constructed social, political, and economic ecosystems that favor health equity and the opportunity to strive for high-level wellness; this definition also includes the business ecosystems that influence sustainable and health-promot-ing local and global commerce.

(Prescott et al., 2018, p. 3)

In summary, planetary health is a natural extension of and synergistic with previous and current 'initiatives' to promote health and well-being of all.

The United Nations Sustainable Development Goals

It is undeniable that health is important to everyone, and that the health of planet Earth is critically important and interconnected with human and animal health. The United Nations Sustainable Development Goals (SDGs) comprise a framework that enables every nation-state to track and evaluate progress (or regression) in their progress toward achieving 17 goals of health and well-being (Figure 1.1).

Since 2015, efforts at local, country, continent and global levels have comprehensively promoted health, equity, education, justice, peace and partnership, with attention toward physical, social, economic and political challenges and opportunities (United Nations, n.d.).

Progress has been made on some of the SDGs; however, more progress is needed and the 2020 severe acute respiratory syndrome coronavirus 2 (SARS-CoV-2) pandemic (officially named by the World Health Organization as COVID-19) has hindered progress on many of the goals (United Nations, 2020).

One criticism of the SDGs is an apparent failure to address wealth disparities and overconsumption by a few.

> Basically, the SDGs want to reduce inequality by ratcheting the poor up, but while leaving the wealth and power of the global 1 percent intact. They want the best of both worlds. They fail to accept that mass impoverishment is the *product* of extreme wealth accumulation and overconsumption by a few, which entails processes of enclosure, extraction, and exploitation along the way. You can't solve the problem of poverty without challenging the pathologies of accumulation.
>
> **(Hickel, 2015)**

With a deep grasp of power dynamics and a core domain focused on equity and social justice, planetary health brings a critical awareness to the SDGs that is often missing in other models of health. Planetary health solutions work at the root cause of inequities and challenge human behaviors at the source, including overconsumption of limited resources and disregard for the needs of future generations.

Figure 1.1 United Nations Sustainable Development Goals.

The Urgency of Now

> We are the last generation that can prevent irreparable damage to our planet.

> **President María Fernanda Espinosa**
> **Garcés (United Nations, 2019)**

Not only has the pandemic impacted progress on the SDGs, climate change and other disruptions of the Earth's natural systems are also having significant impacts. According to the United Nations Intergovernmental Panel on Climate Change (IPCC, 2018), if we exceed the 1.5 degree increase in the average global temperatures that is expected to occur between 2030 and 2052, we will very likely set in motion irreversible changes to the planet's life support systems. To remain at or below this 1.5-degree increase, there must be 'rapid and far-reaching' transitions in land, energy, industry, buildings, transport and cities (IPCC, 2018).

It is important to note that climate change is only one of many human caused disruptions of the Earth's natural systems. The *Living Planet Report 2020* (World Wildlife Fund, 2020) found that global species have declined by an unprecedented 69% in less than 50 years. This World Wildlife Fund (WWF) report shows that these losses are mostly the result of reallocated land use for agriculture and that if we can rapidly transform food production and consumption, there may be hope of stopping these species losses. Marco Lambertini, Director General of WWF International, states:

> It's time for the world to agree to a New Deal for Nature and People, committing to stop and reverse the loss of nature by 2030 and build a carbon-neutral and nature-positive society. This is our best safeguard for human health and livelihoods in the long term, and to ensure a safe future for our children.

> **(WWF, 2020, p. 2)**

Loss of land, water and air integrity as well as loss of biodiversity has significant implications for human health.

The Rockefeller Foundation–Lancet Commission on Planetary Health (Whitmee et al., 2015) describes additional indications that human behavior is exceeding planetary boundaries, including water scarcity, land degradation, air, water and land pollution and overexploitation of fisheries. The impacts of unchecked population growth and consumption threaten global health gains that have been made in recent decades. Whitmee and colleagues issue this condemning statement, 'We have been mortgaging the health of future generations to realize economic and development gains in the present' (Whitmee et al., 2015, p. 1973).

Based on data indicating accelerating changes to the Earth's life support system, the 2019 *Lancet* Countdown report issues a wake-up call for all health professionals. The authors warn, 'The life of every child born today will be profoundly affected by climate change. Without accelerated intervention, this new era will come to define the health of people at every stage of their lives' (Watts et al., 2019, p. 1837). The message is clear; we need to act quickly and innovate significant changes if we want to ensure the survival of future generations.

Therefore, there are two tasks facing humanity in the next decade. We need to come to global consensus about the urgent need for change to protect Earth's natural systems to ensure the health of future generations. We also need to radically transform all human systems and institutions to move toward more sustainable models of development and consumption (IPCC, 2018). Myers and Frumkin (2020) offer a hopeful narrative, framing our current situation as an opportunity for a brighter future: 'Our current trajectory leads to ecological collapse and the unraveling of our many gains. Now the eyes of all future generations are upon us, and within a few decades we must chart a new course from extinction to renaissance' (p. 475). Access to current and future data to support decision-making is foundational to impact the SDGs and planetary health.

Planetary Health Provides an Opportunity for Change

Reversing the planetary crisis will require broad societal transformation. Many names have been given to this transformation, including 'The Great Transition' (Raskin, 2006), 'The Great Turning' (Macy, 2009) and 'The Great Reset' (Schwab & Malleret, 2020). In essence, the transformation that is needed will require reimagining and reshaping the core components that make up our societies, including economic systems, food systems, transport systems, energy systems and manufacturing systems, among others. However, and more importantly, a profound shift in the value systems that currently underscore *modern* human civilization is needed. What we value, what we consider fulfilling, our relationship with Nature, how we organize ourselves and make decisions, and how urgent and by what means we decide to eliminate inequities, are all part of the changes needed to reimagine our future.

Approaches to planetary health can best be understood by focusing on three interrelated areas. First, planetary health's starting point focuses on analyzing the current and future health consequences of human caused (i.e., anthropogenic) environmental disruptions. Second, planetary health provides an opportunity and a common foundational language to imagine a future in which natural systems and humans flourish together. Third, planetary health uses an inherently solutions-based approach to chart forward the necessary routes toward a new future (Whitmee et al., 2015; Faerron Guzmán et al., 2021a). All three of these areas have implications for informatics.

Although we characterize planetary health as a distinct field of practice, the field borrows and acknowledges previous scientific movements such as conservation medicine, ecology, eco-health, geo-health and One Health. The field also builds on, recognizes and creates bridges with Indigenous knowledge systems that center their worldviews in the intertwined relationships between humans and Nature (Redvers, 2021).

The following subsections offer some of the lenses, principles and approaches that make up the field of planetary health and which must be operationalized from a data perspective to bridge planetary health and informatics.

Planetary health requires all stakeholders to reorient traditional hierarchical, rigid, colonial and patriarchal power structures that have long been the status quo. Planetary health also overcomes the assumption that less economically developed (i.e., 'Global South') nations/societies have challenges that only high-income countries/societies (i.e., 'Global North') know how to solve. A baseline recognition of dignity and agency of all humans is one of the starting points for planetary health. From there, planetary health seeks to build meaningful reciprocal relationships moving away from a 'working for' (prescriptive/behaviorist) to a 'working with' (constructive/emancipatory) paradigm, as well as shifting mindsets from a deficit-based approach to an asset-based approach.

As part of this process, stakeholders must seek to reach a point of mutual respect and sincere recognition of the contributions of all participants, as well as designing interventions that understand local assets, needs and priorities (e.g., a 'radical listening' approach (Webb, 2018)). An example includes positioning Indigenous *and* Western knowledge paradigms as complementary rather than opposed (Redvers et al., 2020).

Equally important is the creation and maintenance of diverse and broadly inclusive networks. These networks, including virtual, should aim to connect stakeholders, systems and data across distinct disciplines, sectors, geographies and generations. Only through broad and inclusive networks can we aim to coalesce a new vision, create a narrative that is inclusive and focuses on hope and drive effective movements that create sustainable change (Howard, 2020).

The Lens of the Anthropocene—Beyond Anthropocentric and Biologic Health

Planetary health explicitly uses social and environmental determinants of health frameworks (i.e., that incorporate in the analysis of health outcomes elements of policy, governance, gender, place of work, ethnicity, natural resources, and built environment) to understand how health outcomes are interconnected with human-induced changes to Earth's natural systems (Myers, 2017). This planetary health lens 'promotes a social and ecological approach to health promotion and disease prevention, ranging from individual to population-level determinants of human, animal, and ecosystem health' (Faerron Guzmán et al., 2021a, p. 23). Additionally, the planetary health approach moves beyond anthropocentric health models and incorporates animal and ecosystem determinants of health frameworks. For planetary health, using these multitudes of analytical lenses is a crucial tenant to achieve the improvements in well-being not just of humans but also across species and ecosystems (Card et al., 2018).

A Focus on Equity, Justice and Systems Change

As noted earlier in the chapter, many human activities threaten the natural systems that sustain the well-being of humans (Whitmee et al., 2015). However, the impacts are not distributed fairly. Where we live, our socioeconomic status, our race, our gender, among other factors, determine our resilience and vulnerability to the health impacts of anthropogenic (human caused) changes to natural systems (Prescott et al., 2018). For example, although high-income countries are historically responsible for most greenhouse gas emissions, the populations in the 'Global South' will carry the highest burden of consequences from climate change (Burgess et al., 2013). Even within these lower-income nations and regions, some populations such as Indigenous Peoples, will bear an even higher brunt of the impact of climate change due to a greater reliance on the land for food and medicines. It must also be recognized that Indigenous Peoples are at the forefront of resistance and resilience mechanisms to large-scale environmental changes (Redvers et al., 2020). However, the biggest risk is likely held by future generations who will be forced to live in 'inhospitable' environments (Wallace Wells, 2020). Beyond climate change, similar devastating consequences will play out, such as loss of biodiversity, pollution of air, water and soil, and the destruction of our oceans.

Planetary health urges us to understand that some actors are reaping short-term benefits of the disruption of natural systems while others carry the weight of that disruption's consequences. For example, behind every open-pit mining project, there are people around the world benefiting from the minerals extracted from the ground (e.g., not just the investors of the mining project, but also, for example, the end users of the lithium in the batteries that fuel cellphones' screens). Behind every dam that disrupts the ecology of water basins and people's livelihoods that depend on that basin (sometimes thousands of square kilometers large), there are urban environments benefiting from a consistent stream of electricity.

In our current system, we have come to normalize environmental and human sacrifices in the name of development and capital gain. This normalization also extends to hyper-consumption and dysfunctional economic models and results in overt disregard for future generations. Planetary health challenges these 'normals' and seeks to pursue a new form of redistributive, procedural, intergenerational and interspecies justice (Faerron Guzmán et al., 2021a, b).

To achieve these forms of justice and a more equitable future will require a strong focus on the structural power and wealth disparities that currently drive the disproportionate and avoidable consequences of environmental degradation. A more equitable future also calls for expanding human rights frameworks and embracing the understanding that Nature has rights (Prescott et al., 2018). And it will require redefinition and redesign of data, information, knowledge and decision support infrastructures that can serve to strengthen resilience, favor assets-based approaches, increase capacity to anticipate and mitigate risks, and focus on a just transition.

Finally, it must be stated that problems rooted in power disparities cannot be solved by individual changes alone. Although the behavioral changes of individuals (e.g., taking the bus, recycling, eating vegan) are important contributions to the way forward, they can distract us from the deeper structural and institutional-level responsibilities and changes needed for meaningful progress (Howard, 2020; Potter, 2019).

Reimagining the Human–Nature Relationship

Despite overwhelming evidence and knowledge of our interdependence with Earth's natural systems, societies have increasingly become separate from Nature. Multiple rationalizations create this dualistic view, and those include the perception that Nature is at the service (i.e., for domination and exploitation) of humans; the creation of reductionist and objective (i.e., Cartesian) understandings of the natural world; rapid urbanization; separation from food sources; individualism; and the ubiquitousness of digital technology (Zylstra et al., 2014).

Understanding our role within Nature as a species and as individuals is foundational in planetary health science and practice. However, the understanding of our interconnection, as a species, within Nature has been for the most part, an ignored concept. Therefore, planetary health understands the reimagination of this relationship as a central and urgent task. This process demands incorporating cosmovisions (cosmic worldviews), knowledge systems and traditions of cultures (e.g., Indigenous Peoples) that nurture interconnection within Nature. We must also recognize that our relationship with Nature is one of mutualism, reciprocity and symbiosis and that humans are part of and not separate from Nature. Incorporating this ethos will enable us to create and implement true win-win scenarios among humans, Nature and the planet (Redvers, 2021).

Systems Thinking/Complexity

The traditional and predominant approach to our ongoing challenges is based on the belief that to understand and solve a problem, the problem must be broken down into smaller and manageable pieces. Therefore, the institutions created to 'solve problems,' now operate in silos, separate from each other and incapable of creating convergent solution-oriented approaches. The latter is quite evident in the siloed nature of traditional higher education disciplines and the clear trends toward hyper-specialization (Sustainable Development Solutions Network, 2020).

For planetary health, it is essential to take a step back and look at the whole picture. Planetary health builds and relies on approaches that incorporate system thinking (e.g., ecology). By doing so, planetary health attempts to analyze the interaction among elements within a system more than just describing the parts of the system itself. In this process, planetary health examines the interlinkages between human health and environmental health while considering how these interactions happen at different scales (geospatial and temporal) and how they respond to characteristics of complex adaptive systems (e.g., nonlinearity, heterogeneous actors, emerging characteristics, self-organization and feedback loops). In essence, planetary health requires transdisciplinary approaches to understand how human health and well-being emerge from the complex interactions between natural and social systems and address complex phenomena in support of holistic solutions (Whitmee et al., 2015).

Opportunity: Planetary Health Informatics

> Because every individual choice, in your home, in your community, will make a difference for our planet. Act now, and act boldly.
>
> **United Nations Educational, Scientific and Cultural Organization (UNESCO) (2018)**

Biomedical informatics (BMI), a branch of healthcare informatics (HI), 'draws upon the social and behavioral sciences to inform the design and evaluation of technical solutions and the evolution of complex economic, ethical, social, educational, and organizational systems' (American Medical Informatics Association, 2011). Traditionally, BMI has focused on improving the health of individuals and populations, but it is clear from this definition that BMI and HI can play an important role in ensuring that the solutions to our urgent planetary health crises are effective and scalable.

Considering the principles of the Canmore Declaration (Prescott et al., 2018) and awareness that 'everything is connected — what we do to the world comes back to affect us, and not always in ways that we would expect. Understanding and acting upon these challenges calls for massive collaboration across disciplinary and national boundaries to safeguard our health' (Planetary Health Alliance, n.d.), we propose the following definition for *planetary health informatics*:

> Planetary health informatics incorporates tools and techniques that capture the health of human and non-human animals and natural systems; including data standardization, geocoding, interoperability,

quality, granularity, access, and transformation into actionable knowledge to guide the active restoration of planetary health in the context of equity and social justice.

Our definition addresses the complexities of the challenges facing planetary health at individual, community and systems levels. Unique to our work is the intentional synthesis of human and ecosystem goals to elevate win-win outcomes from both perspectives. For example, globally the healthcare industry is responsible for over 4% of carbon dioxide emissions each year. Thus, if global healthcare were a nation, it would be ranked the fifth largest emitter of greenhouse gases (HealthCare Without Harm, 2019, p. 4). Using emissions data together with satellite weather data and clinical data could help identify ways to use real data to create messages that could inform local communities, as well as national and global policymakers in their decision-making. This informatics focus would aim to reduce healthcare costs and its carbon footprint, and lessen the human disease burden, thus facilitating movement toward the UN's SDGs.

Planetary health informatics builds on accurate tracking of climate impacts on human and animal health, as well as natural systems. This multifocus is needed to produce critical information about planet-friendly purchasing and the design and implementation of effective and sustainable supply chains in healthcare. Such a focus is intrinsically transdisciplinary and promotes knowledge sharing that will foster better understanding of the intersectionality of complex planetary systems, including human health systems. Planetary health informatics, by definition, depends on our growing capacity to gather, store and interpret the massive amounts of data being generated across all disciplines to identify, promote and scale the most effective solutions globally.

Of particular interest in this discussion is the application of data science and artificial intelligence to human and planetary data, and the ethical considerations that are inherent within these conversations and initiatives. In many ways, planetary health solutions depend on a heightened level of data transparency and the rapid adoption of breakthrough engineering innovations and infrastructures based on this data. However, the recent rise of technology ethics as a new field of inquiry suggests and re-surfaces recognition that current and emergent technologies are never neutral, but rather shaped by the interests and objectives of the institutions that create and control them. To transform sociopolitical and environmental inequities at the root of planetary health challenges, the field of planetary health informatics requires deeper reflection of what individuals and communities value, the systems that are designed and how they would like to make use of techno-logical and information systems. By integrating a code of ethical principles that honors a community's self-identified needs and values, it is possible to activate innovative practices that prioritize the well-being of people and the planet over technological optimization and productivity.

The key themes of ethical, artificial intelligence (AI) guidelines and stan-dards from intergovernmental, multistakeholder, private sector and civil soci-ety initiatives can serve as a useful reference to develop a holistic approach to planetary health informatics. These guidelines would support the plan-etary health movement's central mission toward equity, justice and systems change as per the following definitions:

Privacy: to ensure a new social contract with end users by fostering lit-eracy for data practices as well as agency over the decisions made with them.

Transparency and Explainability: to ensure processes that enable community oversight for important decisions in the design and imple-mentation phase so that misinformed solutions are prevented.

Fairness and Nondiscrimination: to ensure design practices that center on geographic, cultural and political complexities, instead of technologi-cal optimization.

Safety, Security and **Accountability**: to ensure protocols that account for unintended impacts and misuse of technology, both short term and long term, and provide adequate countermeasures.

Promotion of Community Values: to ensure governance principles that correspond with geographically, culturally and politically relevant core values that prioritize community well-being (Fjeld et al., 2020).

Ethics and justice-oriented planetary health informatics are necessary for sys-tems redesign and transformation. Standardization and effective analyses of transdisciplinary and systems data will support progress on the UN's SDGs and the goal to restore planetary health for future generations.

Clearly there must be expanded, essential and urgent attention to infor-matics. What methods and processes for data generation, storage, retrieval, use and sharing are needed to support the SDGs and planetary health? Are current data and information representation and modeling adequate to represent dimensions of the SDGs and planetary health? Will existing tools and techniques handle planetary health's complex economic, ethical, social, educational, research and organizational systems? Will health-related informatics systems accommodate user/consumer friendly language to support planetary health?

Hope and Urgency

While it is easy to feel overwhelmed with the current situation, planetary health thrives on hope. It is becoming more apparent that the fate of human societies is interconnected with the health of the biosphere; therefore, our values need to be transformed and our systems need to be redesigned to protect the life support systems of the planet. This urgent moment also offers us hope that we can redesign our systems to be more equitable and sustainable. For radical transformation to happen, we need global collaboration, coordination of science-based solutions and effective movements for change.

Informatics provides the tools and techniques to make global coordination and collective action for planetary health possible. Planetary health informatics will inform the design and evaluation of solutions so that the most effective approaches can be deployed rapidly to meet the urgent timelines that are necessary for massive systems transformation in this decade.

References

American Medical Informatics Association (AMIA). (2011). *What is biomedical and health informatics?* [online]. Available at: https://www.amia.org/fact-sheets/what-informatics (Accessed 1 August 2021).

Asokan, G. V. (2015). One health and zoonoses: The evolution of one health and incorporation of zoonoses. *Central Asian Journal of Global Health*, 4(1). https://doi.org/10.5195/cajgh.2015.139

Burgess, R., Deschenes, O., Donaldson, D., & Greenstone, M. (2013). *The unequal effects of weather and climate change: Evidence from mortality in India* [online]. Available at: https://econ.lse.ac.uk/staff/rburgess/wp/WD_master_140516_v3.pdf (Accessed 1 August 2021).

Card, C., Epp, T., & Lem, M. (2018). Exploring the social determinants of animal health. *Journal of Veterinary Medical Education*, 45(4), pp.437–447. https://doi.org/10.3138/jvme.0317-047r

Faerron Guzmán, C. A. et al. (2021a). A framework to guide planetary health education. *The Lancet Planetary Health*, 5(5), pp.e253–e255. https://doi.org/10.1016/S2542-5196(21)00110-8

Faerron Guzmán, C. A. et al. (2021b). *The planetary health education framework* [online]. Available at: https://www.planetaryhealthalliance.org/education-framework (Accessed 1 August 2021).

Fjeld, J., Achten, N., Hilligoss, H., Nagy, A., & Srikumar, M. (2020). *Principled artificial intelligence: Mapping consensus in ethical rights-based approaches to principles for AI* [online]. Available at: https://dash.harvard.edu/handle/1/42160420 (Accessed 1 August 2021).

Health Care Without Harm. (2019). *Health care's climate footprint: How the health sector contributes to the global climate crisis and opportunities for action* [online]. Available at: https://noharm-global.org/sites/default/files/documents-files/5961/HealthCaresClimateFootprint_090619.pdf (Accessed 1 August 2021).

Hickel, J. (2015). *The problem with saving the world* [online]. Available at https://www.jacobinmag.com/2015/08/global-poverty-climate-change-sdgs/ (Accessed 1 August 2021).

Howard, C. (2020). Targeted change making for a healthy recovery. *The Lancet Planetary Health*, 4(9), pp.e372–e374. https://doi.org/10.1016/S2542-5196(20)30200-X

Intergovernmental Panel on Climate Change (IPCC). (2018). *Summary for policymakers of IPCC special report on global warming of 1.5°C approved by governments* [online]. Available at: https://www.ipcc.ch/2018/10/08/summary-for-policymakers-of-ipcc-special-report-on-global-warming-of-1-5c-approved-by-governments/ (Accessed 1 August 2021).

Koplan, J. P., Bond, T. C., Merson, M. H., Reddy, K. S., Rodriguez, M. H., Sewankambo, N. K., & Wasserheit, J. N. (2009). Towards a common definition of global health. *Lancet*, pp.373, 1993–1995. https://doi.org/10.1016/S0140-6736(09)60332-9

Macy, J. (2009). *Joanna Macy: The great turning is a shift from the industrial growth society to a life-sustaining civilization* [online]. Available at: https://www.ecoliteracy.org/article/great-turning (Accessed 1 August 2021).

Myers, S. S. (2017). Planetary health: Protecting human health on a rapidly changing planet. *The Lancet*, 390(10114), pp.2860–2868. https://doi.org/10.1016/S0140-6736(17)32846-5

Myers, S. S., & Frumkin, H. (2020). *Planetary health: Protecting nature to protect ourselves*. Washington, DC: Island Press.

Planetary Health Alliance. (n.d.). *Planetary health* [online]. Available at: https://www.planetaryhealthalliance.org/planetary-health (Accessed 1 August 2021).

Potter, T. (2019). Planetary health: The next frontier in nursing education. *Creative Nursing*, 25(3), pp.201–207. http://dx.doi.org/10.1891/1078-4535.25.3.201

Prescott, S. L. et al. (2018). The Canmore declaration: Statement of principles for planetary health. *Challenges*, 9(2), p.31. https://doi.org/10.3390/challe9020031

Raskin, P. (2006). *The great transition today: A report from the future* [online]. Available at: https://greattransition.org/archives/papers/The_Great_Transition_Today.pdf (Accessed 1 August 2021).

Redvers, N. (2021). The determinants of planetary health. *The Lancet Planetary Health*, 5(3), pp.e111–e112. https://doi.org/10.1016/S2542-5196(21)00008-5

Redvers, N., Poelina, A., Schultz, C., Kobei, D. M., Githaiga, C., Perdrisat, M., Prince, D., & Blondin, B. S. (2020). Indigenous natural and first law in planetary health. *Challenges*, 11(2), p.29. https://doi.org/10.3390/challe11020029

Salm, M., Ali, M., Minihane, M., & Conrad, P. (2021). Defining global health: Findings from a systematic review and thematic analysis of the literature. *BMJ Global Health*, 6(6), p.e005292. https://doi.org/10.1136/bmjgh-2021-005292

Schwab, K., & Malleret, T. (2020). *The great reset.* Geneva, Switzerland: Agentur Schweiz.

Snow, J. (1855). *On the mode of communication of cholera.* 2nd ed. London: John Churchill.

Sustainable Development Solutions Network. (2020). *Education for the SDGs in universities: A guide for universities, colleges, and tertiary and higher education institutions* [online]. Available at: https://resources.unsdsn.org/accelerating-education-for-the-sdgs-in-universities-a-guide-for-universities-colleges-and-tertiary-and-higher-education-institutions (Accessed 1 August 2021).

Tulchinsky, T. H. (2018). John Snow, cholera, the Broad Street pump; waterborne diseases then and now. *Case Studies in Public Health*, pp.77–99. https://doi.org/10.1016/B978-0-12-804571-8.00017-2

United Nations. (2019). *Only 11 years left to prevent irreversible damage from climate change, speakers warn during General Assembly high-level meeting* [online]. Available at: https://www.un.org/press/en/2019/ga12131.doc.htm (Accessed 1 August 2021).

United Nations. (2020). *The sustainable development goals report.* Available at https://unstats.un.org/sdgs/report/2020/ (Accessed 30 August 2021).

United Nations Department of Economic and Social Affairs. (n.d.). *Make the SDGs a reality.* Available at: https://sdgs.un.org/ (Accessed 1 August 2021).

United Nations Educational, Scientific and Cultural Organization (UNESCO). (2018). *Changing minds, not the climate.* Available at: https://en.unesco.org/news/act-now-act-boldly (Accessed 1 August 2021).

Velji, A., & Bryant, J. H. (2011). Global health: Evolving meanings. *Infectious Disease Clinics of North America*, 25(2), pp.299–309. https://doi.org/10.1016/j.idc.2011.02.004

Wallace-Wells, D. (2020). *The uninhabitable earth: Life after warming.* New York: Tim Duggan Books.

Watts, N. et al. (2019). The 2019 report of The Lancet Countdown on health and climate change: Ensuring that the health of a child born today is not defined by a changing climate. *The Lancet*, 394(10211), pp.1836–1878. https://doi.org/10.1016/S0140-6736(19)32596-6

Webb, K. (2018). Planetary health in the tropics: How community health-care doubles as a conservation tool. *The Lancet Global Health*, 6, p.S28. https://doi.org/10.1016/S2214-109X(18)30157-8

Whitmee, S. et al. (2015). Safeguarding human health in the Anthropocene epoch: Report of The Rockefeller Foundation–Lancet Commission on planetary health. *The Lancet*, 386(10007), pp.1973–2028. https://doi.org/10.1016/S0140-6736(15)60901-1

Winslow, C. (1920). The untilled fields of public health. *Science*, LI(1306), pp.23–33. https://doi.org/10.1126/science.51.1306.23

World Wildlife Fund (WWF). (2020). *Living planet report: Bending the curve of biodiversity loss: Summary* [online]. Available at: https://f.hubspotusercontent20.net/hubfs/4783129/LPR/PDFs/ENGLISH-SUMMARY.pdf (Accessed 1 August 2021).

Zylstra, M. J., Knight, A. T., Esler, K. J., & Le Grange, L. L. (2014). Connectedness as a core conservation concern: An interdisciplinary review of theory and a call for practice. *Springer Science Reviews*, 2(1), pp.119–143. https://doi.org/10.1007/s40362-014-0021-3

Chapter 2

Health Equity and Equal Access to Care for Better Health Globally

Rohana Basil Marasinghe and Ranige Maheshika Madhuwanthi

Contents

Introduction

Healthcare is defined as providing all the services related to the diagnosis and treatments of disease, or the promotion, maintenance and restoration of health including personal and non-personal services (WHO, 2016). The provision of better healthcare is a predominant goal in every healthcare sector. Governments and other regulatory authorities are taking considerable effort to establish better healthcare both locally and globally. Health systems around the globe are continuously focusing on providing accessible, equitable, good-quality, comprehensive and integrated care. To achieve the United Nations' 2030 Agenda for Sustainable Development Goals (United Nations, 2015), universal health coverage and health equity are seen as essential

DOI: 10.4324/9781003281047-2

requirements by the global health community. Many stakeholders are interested in planning and supporting to establish health equity and equal access to care worldwide (WHO, 2021). However, ensuring health equity and providing equal access to care are still a challenge for most developing nations due to insufficient resources, most notably technology infrastructure. For this reason, telenursing based on more affordable digital technologies is gaining popularity in Sri Lanka and has the potential to address health equity and equal access to care.

What Are Health Equity and Equal Access?

Health equity is an ethical concept of the absence of systematic disparities in healthcare provision or its social determinants of health between all kinds of social groups. That means everyone has a fair opportunity to achieve optimal health or to be as healthy as possible. As illustrated in Figure 2.1, there are two types of health equity, namely horizontal and vertical. When people who have equal needs require equal opportunities for equal access to healthcare, it is called 'horizontal equity.' Those who have unequal needs require unequal opportunities for access to healthcare and this is called 'vertical equity.' In practice, the main determinant is affordability. Ideally, those who cannot afford healthcare should receive it for free, similar to those who can afford to pay for the same care (Braveman et al., 2018).

Certain equity issues have arisen in almost all healthcare services. Out of many, major equity issues are healthcare quality, accessibility, health

Figure 2.1 Equality and equity.

financing system and resource allocation between urban (developed) and rural remote (less developed) areas in a country, and this mismatch is especially prominent in developing countries. Invariably, these issues would lead to certain health disparities in the society as well (Braveman et al., 2011).

Health disparities refer to variations in obtaining healthcare between different population groups. These disparities worsen when linked to disadvantaged determinants such as low income levels, rural areas, low educational status, unhealthy social connectedness, and food and housing insecurities, all of which affect health and well-being.

Health equity can be achieved by identifying such disparities and working towards alleviating them, for example, when individuals live in rural and remote areas with scarce medical personnel and/or facilities. In such instances, telemedicine solutions for consultations and treatment could be provided, and even remote screening for regular wellness would be useful as a preventive care service. Sometimes, there may be language barriers that also prevent people from seeking necessary care. In such circumstances, providing training for healthcare workers with necessary language skills would alleviate the problem. Being unable to provide such answers leads to poor health outcomes (Braveman, 2006).

Following is a list of social determinants of health (SDH) that influence health equities,

- Level of education
- Income and social protection
- Food insecurity
- Unemployment and job insecurity
- Working life conditions
- Housing, basic amenities and the environment
- Early childhood development
- Social inclusion and non-discrimination
- Structural conflict, war
- Access to affordable health services of decent quality (Williams, 2014)

Health equity is different from equality. Health equity acknowledges that different individuals have different needs and they each need different healthcare support to attain a similar outcome. Health equality is equal healthcare support being available for all individuals. The goal of equality is to promote fairness, but it can only work if everyone has the same needs. In brief, health equality ensures that everyone would receive the same standard, while health equity ensures that everyone would receive customized or individualized care to achieve the same level of health status (Culyer, 2019).

In short, to organize necessary resources to achieve an optimal level of healthcare, the multifactorial and interconnected nature of factors affecting equity and equality of healthcare provision is a challenge. However, every government and other authorities in healthcare provision are taking considerable effort to provide broad access to healthcare and to make it more equitable globally.

Healthcare System in Sri Lanka

The health system of Sri Lanka provides various preventive and curative healthcare services based on western medicine as well as indigenous medical services. The curative healthcare system has an extensive network from primary to tertiary levels throughout the country. There are hospitals, dispensaries and community care centres. Primary-level care institutions include central dispensaries, maternity homes, rural hospitals, peripheral units and divisional hospitals, which offer non-specialist, inpatient and outpatient care. As shown in Figure 2.2, nurse-led clinics are key for primary care in all areas. Secondary-level care institutions include base hospitals, district general hospitals and provincial hospitals that provide inpatient and outpatient care with certain special units. Tertiary care hospitals include teaching hospitals and other provincial hospitals, which have all facilities of secondary care institutions as well as other specialities and subspecialties, including specialist units such as neurology and cardiology. There are certain specific specialized hospitals such as for cancer and kidney diseases.

The core of preventive healthcare is managed by public health through divisional units known as Medical Officer of Health (MOH). MOH units provide public health services. These include comprehensive maternity care, including antenatal, natal and postnatal care, family planning, well women services, immunization and nutrition services clinics that are conducted systematically. Further, communicable disease prevention, school health and environmental and occupational preventive services are all provided through the MOH units.

When it comes to health administration, there are private and government healthcare services in Sri Lanka. All government health services are free to

Figure 2.2   Clinics run by Sri Lankan nurses.

all citizens. The private sector is available to those who carry health insurance or who can pay the fees and it provides care according to the market demand. Both the public and private facilities have outpatient and inpatient curative care, but these facilities are limited to urban and semi-urban areas of the country. Many health insurance schemes are available for those who can afford to purchase them.

Nurses play a key role in providing equitable healthcare and as resources that can make access to care possible for better health of clients. Until recently, the ministry of health produced nurses to be employed in the government sector. Now a considerable number of nurses have obtained their degrees from several of the universities that offer degree-level programmes through common university entrance. Nurses have a valued presence in caring for patients in hospitals, clinics and remote units for acute and preventive care services. Nurses also assist in the training of nurses, and thus are seen as contributing to advancing the health status of the country (Jayasekara & Schultz, 2007). Notably, nurses are in continuous contact with clients and, therefore, key to ensuring health equity and equal access through their care, advocacy, teaching and coordination with the other healthcare team members.

Status and Needs on Health Equity and Equal Access in Sri Lanka

Health equity and equal access to care are challenging areas in the Sri Lankan healthcare sector as in many other developing countries in South Asia. All of the population has access to free government healthcare at any time in the country through government healthcare institutions distributed within the whole country like a comprehensive network. Therefore, at a base level, all citizens have equal opportunities to access free healthcare in any area in the country. Although all citizens have access to free healthcare, there are certain issues in the distribution of health facilities within the country. General hospitals and teaching hospitals that have comprehensive healthcare facilities are centred in urban and semi-urban areas with higher population density, and thus are richer in infrastructure, technology and human facilities. The physical facilities and human resources are highly concentrated in these institutions. Therefore, a large number of people can easily access specialty care at one time and this is a success factor. Primary healthcare in the form of divisional hospitals and central dispensaries are distributed in rural areas of the country as the infrastructural facilities, human resources and population density are less in those areas. This distribution will lead to providing inequitable care in favour of populations in urban settings compared to the rural areas. Today, most people who need comprehensive, speciality care have to undergo the expense and time to travel to the urban facilities.

Because all citizens are free to visit any institute in the country, small institutions are underutilized in rural areas and some major institutions are overcrowded in urban areas. However, the service availability is at a satisfactory level even in remote areas of the country (Annual Health Bulletin, 2019).

Every individual has equal access to healthcare in the public sector. When a person comes to a hospital or a clinic, they are allowed to access any kind of care according to their need without any restriction. The healthcare is delivered through outpatient department (OPD) or as an inpatient. When clients come to the OPD and if they are fit to go after consultation, they can leave the hospital. If they need further treatment, they are admitted to a relevant unit and get further treatment. For follow-up care, patients are referred to a given clinic according to the need. For example, if a patient is diagnosed with diabetes, he/she is referred to the diabetic and endocrine clinic for further treatments and follow-up. If a client is diagnosed as pregnant, she is referred to the antenatal clinic for follow-up.

The nurses have a great responsibility to provide more equitable care for all clients in a hospital setting as they are the persons that have continual contact with the clients at all time. Providing health education is a vital part of nursing care. When providing such education sessions, nurses are considering the requirements of the client to provide more equitable care. For example; when providing health education in an obstetric clinic, all antenatal and postnatal mothers are allowed to participate in educational sessions providing equal access to care. Separate sessions are conducted for those antenatal and postnatal mothers who may have different needs, thereby providing more equitable care. Further, the client's educational level and socio-cultural status are also considered in their teaching approaches with the aim of explaining facts according to the level of understanding of the individual.

Sri Lanka is home to a number of ethnic groups and has a rich cultural heritage. The major groups are Sinhalese (74.9%), Sri Lankan Tamil (11.1%), Moors (9.3%) and Indian Tamil (4.1%) ethnicities. With regard to religion, the majority (70.2%) are Buddhists, while 12.6% are Hindus, 9.7% are Muslims and 7.4% are Christians (Annual Health Bulletin, 2019). Although the country has a written heritage of more than 2500 years old with a Sinhalese–Buddhist monarchy, there is a strong British colonial influence. English is spoken competently by about 23.8% of people and is commonly used in official and commercial work and more precisely referred to as the 'link language', while Sinhala and Tamil both are now national languages.

Nurses have an additional responsibility to pay considerable attention to the client's language and cultural values when providing care to ensure health equity. Most nurses are fluent in either Sinhala or Tamil language and some are fluent in English language as well. Nurses deliver care through these two national languages according to the client's ability to communicate and understand. This is important, especially when giving post-discharge instructions and health education for clients. Sometimes, the challenge comes when nurses are serving areas that are different from their mother tongue, but have compensated with the help of their colleagues. Thus, language differences have not usually been a major issue when delivering equitable care for people who are not fluent in either Sinhala or Tamil.

Further, nurses prioritize the care and needs of the clients and deliver the care according to priorities. As an example, if a client is critical and requires close monitoring, the nurses keep the client close to the nurses' station in the ward so that someone is always observing them as the nurses go about their business of caring for their other patients. The clients need specific care, and nurses are providing special care for them with the medical team.

As another example, in a medical ward, clients may need further referral rather than usual medical care in the ward. At this point, clients are referred to specific care referrals such as cardiology, oncology and physiotherapy, while other clients receive usual medical care in the ward.

Considering free services, most Sri Lankans opt for going to the public health sector and this leads to overcrowding and long waiting times. Therefore, people who can afford private healthcare do so and tend to seek healthcare from the private sector considering shorter waiting times and more facilities. The private sector provides certain healthcare facilities through hospitals, laboratories and clinics with charges. Most healthcare workers who are employed in the government sector also work part time in the private sector.

There are new developments, such as a few healthcare institutions functioning as semi-government, which combined the government and private sector. In this model, people have access to both free and paid healthcare services according to their abilities. The healthcare team is the same in both the free and paid healthcare services. The physicians and nurses work in the public health sector, and after their official hours, they then change to private care mode and provide healthcare services with charges in the same setting. For example, the physicians are consulting and nurses are caring for patients in obstetric and gynaecology clinics in their duty time. After the official clinic time, the physicians and nurses conduct private consultation services at the clinic. At this point, although any women who are registered to the clinic can participate in the clinic free of charge, they have to spend more time to receive care. Women who are registered or not registered to the clinic can participate in private consultation with charges but with shorter wait times. But the care-providing team and the setting are similar on these two occasions.

A network of MOH units is distributed across the urban, semi-urban and rural areas in Sri Lanka. This network facilitates the provision of more equitable care and equal access for every individual in any area of the country. Every individual belongs to one of the MOH units and they receive any kind of services provided by their MOH unit. For example, public health nurses and public health midwives are providing antenatal, postnatal, family planning, immunization and educational services through clinics and home visits for all people who have required these services within their responsible area. Public health inspectors (PHIs) visit schools, houses, workplaces, food handling places to inspect and provide services within their area. Therefore, everyone receives equitable care and equal access to preventive care.

Improving Health Equity and Equal Access through Digital Technology

The technological revolution, today, has tended to discover digital solutions for enhancing the quality of healthcare delivery. At present, most countries and certain stakeholders all around the world have been urged to direct their efforts towards creating a consistent digital health vision in line with the country's health priorities and resources. Activities such as developing action plans to deliver the proposed vision and creating frameworks for monitoring and evaluating digital health implementation and progress are important in health equity and equal access to care provision. Accordingly, certain industrialized countries are already delivering better healthcare through well-established, healthcare delivery systems empowered with digital technology, while other countries are still adopting technologies at different stages. These digital technologies have the potential to improve health equity and access to healthcare for better health in certain ways.

Nurses are playing an important and certain key role in the provision of better healthcare worldwide. The use of electronic health record (EHR) would facilitate nurses to access each client in a more comprehensive manner. Having an EHR would help nurses to more easily identify a patient's needs, capabilities and limitations for preparing a care plan that is shared with the doctors and other healthcare workers. Establishing a telemonitoring system would facilitate the reduction of movements of patients, thus saving time and resources in a busy ward or ICU setting to achieve health equity and equality. Proper alarming would facilitate better decision support which would reduce unnecessary interventions in the same manner. More importantly, for those areas outside the urban settings with limited resources, facilities or specialties, remote monitoring could make consultations, follow-up care and emergent care possible, thus alleviating health disparities. Patients who do not have sufficient money to visit better facilities could be provided tele-consultation remotely. Remote tele-consultation would minimize unnecessary transfers and long distance travel. When tele-consultation is coupled with tele-home care, it will ease patients at their homes while addressing equity issues. Tele-investigation would reduce costs and would expedite the diagnosis and management decision, thus addressing equity and equality alike. When combined with tele-pharmacy, comprehensive nursing care could be established. Telenursing is becoming a demanding area for nursing resources. For example, nurses could use EHR to register patients, involve in telemonitoring, assist in tele-investigations, link with tele-pharmacy and other referrals and even contribute to the discharge planning and follow-up care. In this way, the use of technologies has the potential to improve health equity and equal access, adopting technological advances. While facing the certain adverse effect of the digital divide, addressing health equity and equal access is one of the challenging yet important aspects for nurses in Sri Lanka.

Many capacity-development initiatives on digital health, digital health practices, are not yet commonly used in Sri Lanka (Marasinghe, 2010). Digital technology applications are found in the private health sector more than in the public health sector. Certain hospitals are functioning as semi government, telenursing facilities such as telephonic nursing. They have call centres empowered with telehealth. The healthcare team provides information for clients over the telephone regarding hospital admission, consultation specialities, channelling facilities, etc. Moreover, when clients come for private consultations through the call centre or e-channelling, they are allowed to enter for free healthcare services if they are unable to bear charges. People who live in rural or remote areas are allowed to access quality care through these telehealth services. Patients benefit from shorter waiting times and less travelling costs. In addition, nurses follow up with their clients over the telephone, such as in the COVID-19 pandemic, and maintain follow-up records after hospital discharge as needed. Recent developments with EHR integration to other systems would ensure the provision of equity and equal access to foreign nationals and through the provision of telehealth activities globally.

Although Sri Lanka has a well-established healthcare system providing health equity and equal access for all citizens and even foreigners, there is a high potential of inclusion of technology adopted practices such as telenursing that would strengthen the provision of equitable care and equal access to healthcare both locally and globally.

References

Annual Health Bulletin. (2019). *Medical statistics unit, ministry of health, nutrition and indigenous medicine, Sri Lanka.* Available at: http://www.health.gov.lk/moh_final/english/others.php?pid=110 (Accessed 12 September 2021).

Braveman, P. (2006). Health disparities and health equity: Concepts and measurement. *Annual Review of Public Health,* 27, pp.167–194. https://doi.org/10.1146/annurev.publhealth.27.021405.102103

Braveman, P. A., Kumanyika, S., Fielding, J., LaVeist, T., Borrell, L. N., Manderscheid, R., & Troutman, A. (2011). Health disparities and health equity: The issue is justice. *American Journal of Public Health*, 101(S1), pp.S149–S155.

Braveman, P., Arkin, E., Orleans, T., Proctor, D., Acker, J., & Plough, A. (2018). What is health equity? *Behavioral Science & Policy*, 4(1), pp.1–14.

Culyer, A. (2019). Efficiency, equity and equality in health and healthcare. *F1000Research*, 8(800), p.800.

Jayasekara, R. S., & Schultz, T. (2007). Health status, trends, and issues in Sri Lanka. *Nursing & Health Sciences*, 9(3), pp.228–233.

Marasinghe, R. B. (2010). Telehealth—Bringing healthcare to one's doorstep: How ready is Sri Lanka? *Sri Lanka Journal of Bio-Medical Informatics*, 1(3), p.125. https://doi.org/10.4038/sljbmi.v1i3.2056

United Nations. (2015). *The 17 goals: Sustainable development.* Department of Economic and Social Affairs, United Nations. Available at: https://sdgs.un.org/goals (Accessed 26 September 2021).

Williams, S. D., Hansen, K., Smithey, M., Burnley, J., Koplitz, M., Koyama, K., Young, J. & Bakos, A. (2014). Using social determinants of health to link health workforce diversity, care quality and access, and health disparities to achieve health equity in nursing. *Public Health Reports*, 129(1_suppl2), pp.32–36.

World Health Organization (WHO). (2016). *Health services.* Available at: http://www.who.int/topics/health_services/en/ (Accessed 1 June 2021).

WHO. *Global strategy on digital health 2020–2025.* Available at: https://www.who.int/docs/default-source/documents/gs4dhdaa2a9f352b0445bafbc79ca799dce4d.pdf (Accessed 1 June 2021).

Chapter 3

Social Determinants of Health: Trends and Issues in Three Developing Countries

Patrick Weber, Vivian Vimarlund, Ivana Ognjanović,
Oommen John, Ying Wu, Meihua Ji, B. Kavitha
and Suptendra Nath Sarbadhikari

Contents

DOI: 10.4324/9781003281047-3

Introduction

In general, the health status of an individual or population has been described as 'much a function of social support structures as the disease process itself' (Robichaux & Sauerlund, 2021). Creating healthy social and physical environments that promote good health for all is one of the major goals emphasized by the WHO (World Health Organization, 2008). Health starts in our homes and extends to our schools, workplaces and communities, with healthy attitudes in eating, activities and self-protection. Thus, the social determinants of health (SDoH) are influenced by the environments in which people are born, live, learn, work and earn their living. These determinants of health are an integral component of caring for patients and are inevitably influenced by the social interactions, the secure and safe conditions of individuals and access to the technologies in the era that we live.

Today, there is an increased focus on the social determinants of health with health promotion investments coming from cross-sector collaborations. With the importance of achieving economic efficiency, healthcare organizations worldwide are developing health plans, strategies and policies to expand the focus of their services to include the non-modifiable factors of age, gender, ethnicity/race and the modifiable ones of literacy, housing and standard of living in all programs to achieve better health outcomes.

Nurses are uniquely positioned to identify and address the issues that impact an individual's overall health. Basic to the 'nursing process,' is to assess, plan, implement and evaluate the care delivered to optimize health for a given patient. In caring for individuals, it is important to consider factors impacting patients' current health status and support, thus improving and maintaining health and wellness. Nurses are vital to ensuring that the full SDoH context of a person's life is included in delivering care that fits that unique individual's needs. The WHO's framework also emphasizes the need to integrate social concerns and principles of social justice into nursing and health policy (World Health Organization, 2020; Olson, 2016). At all times, even in the face of pandemics, nurses carry the responsibility for providing holistic care for every patient. WHO acknowledges the critical functions that nursing serves throughout our healthcare systems, and especially as advocates for their patients (World Health Organization, 2020).

In these pandemic times, nurses' roles in treating COVID-19 patients involve new dimensions of using digital technologies to communicate with the patient in isolation, to arrange family contact and virtual visits, as well as to do remote virtual visits with patients at home. An important difference in the COVID health scene has been the denial of family members to be able to accompany or to visit any patient. Frontline staff and informaticists responded to the needs of the patients and their family to be in contact and communicate with each other through innovative uses of mobile devices and newly created applications. Despite the additional time demands and emotional burdens placed on nurses to meet these crucial communication needs, nurses creatively taught each other how to use the mobile technologies available to them, such as smartphones, FaceTime or laptops, to enable that vital need for communication to happen: And even in the circumstance of a dying, nonresponsive patient, to make it possible for the family/loved ones to say goodbye.

Since the COVID pandemic, there has been an increased focus on the use of digital technologies for remote or virtual care and because of its potential contribution to decentralize care access (American Nurses Association, 2021) and as expressed as well in the Global Strategy on Digital Health 2020–2025 from the World Health Organization (World Health Organization, 2021).

Nurse informaticists play an essential role in designing and validating health information technology (IT) use in care delivery, including devices that enable clinicians to track data and deliver safe and efficient care. Borrowing from the American Nurses Association's definition, 'Nursing informatics is also seen as the specialty that integrates nursing science with multiple information and analytical sciences to identify, define, manage, and communicate data, information, knowledge, and wisdom in nursing practice' (HIMSS, 2021). Current research on the contribution of IT-based applications (systems and services) that involve nursing tend to focus on (1) sampling methods and reliable health data and (2) the use of eHealth platforms to allow citizens to access care or receive a service (Feeg & Rienzo, 2015). Research topics need to pay attention to understanding social determinant factors and nurses' role in obtaining this information for planning care, as well as the need for nurses' involvement in the increasing implementations of eHealth systems and services (McGonigle & Mustrian, 2021). Most electronic medical record systems today lack the ability to capture or process SDoH data elements. Thus, it's not surprising that studies focusing on nursing's perspectives for the need to integrate social determinants of health into care are almost totally lacking. Given the continued innovativeness of the healthcare area and the digitization processes that almost all countries have initiated to some degree, the nursing profession's challenge is to understand how all these factors impact nursing and how to navigate rapid change. Thus, there is a duality at play here: policy changes that emphasize inclusion of SDoH factors in healthcare delivery and rapid adoption of new technologies that nurses must learn to use. For nurse leaders and educators, therefore, it is imperative to determine how the social determinants of health can be realistically implemented into clinical practice. And to know that going forward, nurses will continually be called upon to use these new technologies in the full spectrum of healthcare settings across all geographies because of the rapid adoption of IT and digital tools by healthcare systems worldwide.

Three Case Studies

We offer examples from three different regions, the Balkan countries, India and China, to illustrate how the SDoH factors are embedded in the innovation processes that each country is doing. Issues such as the nurses' responsibilities to move research and developments in eHealth services for the deployment of services that influence social determinants of health are discussed. The description of Balkan countries, India and China demonstrates the challenges and hindrances that healthcare stakeholders should consider when renewing the nurses' role in the future and developing policies related to how to innovate with the help of IT-based innovations, described as eHealth innovations.

The Western Balkan Region

The Western Balkan region includes Montenegro, Serbia, Kosovo, Albania, Bosnia and Herzegovina, and Croatia. Economic and job opportunities in the Western Balkans are characterized by massive out migration of health professionals. Thousands of doctors, nurses, technical staff and medical caretakers leave annually. Over the past decade, the main destination for physicians and nurses is Germany followed by Austria and Scandinavian countries. The out migration trend of healthcare personnel has been continuously increasing since 2015 (World Bank, 2021). In addition to this, there is a widespread shortage of health personnel across the Balkan countries with the nursing shortage being the most acute. Almost 30% of staff positions in primary health center (PHC) are not occupied; this shortage is particularly problematic in rural areas, and there is a lack of national policies and/

or support from local municipalities to recruit candidates for training from rural areas.

Over the past three decades, the health systems in Western Balkan countries have undergone numerous transformations driven by geopolitical, legal, financial, demographic, scientific and technological progress. However, the evidence cited here on achieved changes is mostly related to Croatia, as an European Union (EU) country. These advancements have led to systemic changes in the structure, organization, financing and delivery of healthcare, including nursing care in Croatia.

The other Western Balkan countries (Bjegovic-Mikanovic et al., 2019; Vuković et al., 2019) are in the process to (1) adopt laws that regulate the nursing profession and recognize professional competence, (2) align with European Union (EU) standards and (3) integrate multidisciplinary approaches into existing curricula (Ivanišević et al., 2021). An issue identified as of key importance for the future is the need to improve the digital and computer literacy of nurses. Lack of skills, lack of institutionalized assistance by the government to the information communications technology (ICT) industry, limited e-government services and little export promotion assistance are identified as hindering progress and moving toward what we know as the 'digital economy' (International Telecommunication Union, 2020). The Organisation for Economic Co-operation and Development (OECD) offers the following definition:

> The Digital Economy incorporates all economic activity reliant on, or significantly enhanced by the use of digital inputs, including digital technologies, digital infrastructure, digital services and data. It refers to all producers and consumers, including government, that are utilising these digital inputs in their economic activities.
>
> **(Organisation for Economic Co-operation and Development, 2020)**

ICT Literacy and Access to Mass Media and Emerging Technologies

During the 2020–2021 COVID-19 pandemic period, several eHealth services have been developed and/or adopted to meet the unique needs of the COVID-19 situation and to be able to serve patients in real time. Some examples of services available today are:

- e-Pharmacy—provides all insured persons to receive information on the availability of medicines.
- e-Prescription—enables patients to see prescribed and realized prescriptions; chronologically monitor and search the results of biochemical analyses that they performed in the health center.
- e-Insurance—provides citizens with insight into the status of their health insurance as a basis for exercising the right to healthcare in healthcare institutions.
- e-Ordering—enables electronic ordering services, electronic prescriptions, reports for calculating salary compensation during temporary incapacity for work, certificates issued by selected doctors, and sick leave.
- e-Appointments—service for scheduling visits to selected doctors in health centers.

Telemedicine solutions were also developed to provide free psychological support to anyone in need and a call center for non-COVID patients with healthcare needs. The United Nations Development Programme (UNDP) supported the Ministry of Health Montenegro in the development of special software (web application) through which it will be possible to monitor individuals in real time and capture the condition of personal protective equipment (PPE), and in the development of medical equipment necessary for working during the COVID-19 pandemic, e.g., respirators, mobile ECG and such (United Nations Development Programme, Montenegro, 2017).

Nurses and technicians work in the areas of health promotion, disease prevention, treatment and rehabilitation. Nurses usually make the first contact with the patient and this is very important for establishing an appropriate relationship and gaining the person's trust. Nurses are included in observation and assessment of the physical and mental condition and behavior of their patients, and base their plans for care on this assessment. And importantly, the nurses' assessments provide important data to doctors for recognizing and monitoring the course of the disease, performing diagnostic procedures, continual observation (inspection of the disease) during treatment and evaluation over the course of care.

In general, due to Croatia's improvements to meet the EU standards and practices, our own legal frameworks and national strategic documents are well prepared and adopted. At the same time, there is a lack of practical implementation and achievements of our defined strategic goals.

The following paragraph presents policies and strategic documents in Montenegro related to the use of digital technologies in healthcare:

> It is important to note that the concept of interoperability and the introduction of e-Services potentially support the principle of integration in the process of providing healthcare and enable a timely and quality information exchange in healthcare at the national and international level.
>
> **(Smart Specialisation, n.d.)**

(See Strategy for the Development of Integral Health Information System and eHealth (2018–2023) with the Action Plan for the period 2018–2021.)

The use of digital technologies in the healthcare sector is fully supported by Integrated Health Information Systems (ISIS) and eHealth Development Strategy (2018–2023) in Montenegro's Master Plan. It is identified that strategic planning for the development of health information systems and eHealth services, in addition to direct national benefits, influences better regional cooperation, which shows the example of the EU countries and their efforts to improve eHealth for mutual benefit of both citizens and health systems. E-services need to be developed and made available to citizens and healthcare users, providing access to services within a single e-government system, following legislation and cooperating with competent authorities to increase access to health and health information through ICT.

The specific goals of the improvement and further development of ISIS and the strategic initiatives for the next few years target strengthening their IT platforms and infrastructure, with a special emphasis on delivering eHealth services within the EU's framework for privacy, consent and confidentiality. The Montenegro's Ministry of Health promotes the strategy for health reform and the necessary reforms to the health system in Montenegro, which shall provide better quality healthcare, improve health and improve the state of health of the population (Montenegro Ministry of Health, 2003).

India

In India, society is a place where a group of people live together and where an individual is born, grows up, works, lives and dies. During these human processes, there are circumstances, which strongly affect individual health outcomes. The circumstances such as poverty, improper housing, nutrition, pollution and poor access to primary healthcare play a major role in the health outcomes of the majority of Indians.

SDoH is a new area of growth to enable better population health management and data analytics in support of health. Interoperability of data is emphasized as well toward promoting the integration of SDoH data into the standard of digital care for all interventions in healthcare systems. Data management policy, standards and guidelines are a priority so that data can be shared across healthcare systems and government agencies with legal protections.

Nursing and Social Health Determinants

Nurses have an essential role in identifying and addressing issues influencing the overall health of individuals. Nurses assess, plan, implement and evaluate care to optimize health for patients. They also consider factors affecting patients' current health status and ensure that social determinants of health are included in the planning and delivery of patient care.

Nurses in India also focus on variables such as religion, education, income, poverty and housing during their initial assessment history collection of data. However, the nursing care plan is done only for assessed subjective and objective data related to clinical conditions, and social determinants are the least considered.

The health policies and framework in India emphasize practicing healthcare by integrating social determinants as the influencing factors in health outcomes. Nurses are expected (Olshansky, 2017) to lead in translating social determinants of health awareness into action by taking the following steps:

Teach SDoH content in all clinical courses, with students routinely assessing for SDoH in clinical settings and advocating for change to improve SDoH.

Develop an interprofessional practice to include social work representatives, public health, town planning, occupational health, police and firefighters, and many others who can address SDoH.

Prioritize nursing research on social and biomedical aspects of health to connect SDoH to health outcomes and develop nursing interventions that alleviate problematic SDoH (evidence-based practice).

Collaborate with social and community agencies and institutions to recommend that health policy can address harmful SDoH.

Similar to other countries, digital health interventions are revolutionizing the nursing profession. Nurses today use computers in the health delivery process at all levels of care, including daycare settings in India. Computer literacy for nurses has become a basic skill needed to practice.

The Government of India launched the health management information system (HMIS) in 2008 to convert local health data into useful, real-time information for clinical decisions and policy interventions. However, India still has a long way to go (Mukhopadhyay, 2011). There is scant attention on leveraging clinical and population-level data to address the direct determinants of health or, more broadly, social determinants of health.

The accrediting bodies and nursing councils have been forced to take steps to integrate technology and SDH into the nursing curriculum (Thornton & Persaud, 2018). Some examples are:

- Amplify clinical education experiences outside of the acute care setting.
- Develop interprofessional education initiatives that encourage social sectors collaboration.
- Focus on assessment skills such as motivational interviewing and empathetic inquiry.
- Increase curricular content related to social justice and advocacy.
- Create in-service learning programs to integrate social concern in clinical decision.
- Require faculty education programs related to SDoH and curricular content.
- Focus on improving workforce, student and faculty diversity.
- Encourage to acquire informatics literacy and competencies.
- Motivate practice by integrating informatics to address SDoH needs of the patient and community.

Many tools and strategies are emerging to address the social and digital determinants of health. The primary goal is to use assessments to review needed, proposed and existing social policies for their likely impact on health. There is a 'health in all policies' strategy, which introduces improved health for all and closing health gaps as goals to be shared across all areas of government.

China

Nursing was initiated in 1888 in China (Shen & Han, 2019). The nursing workforce in China has significantly improved over the years, especially after implementing the nursing regulation 'Nurse Ordinance' in 2008 (The State Council of People's Republic of China, 2008). Health human resource allocation is key to health equality for all. China had more doctors than nurses in the past (Anand et al., 2008), which has been reversed in the last few years. The nurse to population ratio has greatly improved from 1.52:1,000 in 2010 to 6.41:1,000 in 2019 (NHC-PRC, 2010, 2020). Although the overall trend in the number of registered nurses is increasing, the nurse density in the rural area remains about three times lower compared to that in the urban area. In addition, the equity of human health resources in eastern China is higher than that of the western and central China where economically underdeveloped regions are concentrated (Li et al., 2020). These economic conditions and scarcity of health professionals contribute to the limited accessibility of healthcare resources in these regions.

With the aging population in China, 66 million Chinese people with functional disabilities are expected by 2050 (World Health Organization, 2015). Chinese researchers have focused on social participation as a way to reduce the risks of functional disability in older Chinese adults.

The emerging burden of chronic disease and increasing health expenditures, the aging of the society, rapid urbanization and the lack of qualified health professionals in the poorly developed regions present marked challenges for the Chinese healthcare system. With uneven distribution of healthcare services and limited resources in China, health digitalization offers a great opportunity to minimize the gaps in health inequity. The internet penetration in China has reached 70.4%, and in 2020, there were more than 1.6 billion registered mobile phones (Statista Research Department, 2020). This extent of digital technology adoption provided a great channel for making healthcare access in remote areas possible. With the rapid development and evolution of information communication technology, China has adopted new models of healthcare services to overcome traditional barriers. Mobile healthcare has allowed health professionals to communicate and connect with patients remotely, greatly reducing costs, conserving time and making access easy. As a recent study has revealed (Lv et al., 2019), China's mobile medical market is growing rapidly with an annual growth rate of 116.4%. The driving force for leading the mobile health market included multiple platforms, such as digital medical platforms and Internet-based medical practice. Nurses also take initiatives in utilizing mobile health technologies to assist patients with the management of chronic diseases. For example, the Intelligent Individualized Cardiovascular Application for Risk Elimination (iCARE), developed by a research team at the School of Nursing Capital Medical

University, aimed to facilitate adherence to healthy behaviors and secondary preventive medications in patients with coronary diseases (Chen et al., 2019). Digitalization of health will surely shed light on the currently overwhelmed health system in China.

Case Studies Discussion

Many different steps have been taken in the regions included in these case studies to increase the engagement of nurses in the use of eHealth services that are intended to increase well-being or tackle relevant social challenges that influence social determinants. The data sampled in the case studies show that efforts to establish policies and regulations have been developed in all regions. However, the differences between countries remain large and are based on political, religious, sociocultural or socioeconomic issues. In general, the regions have adopted strategies to create technical infrastructures that support an increased digital presence and the deployment of personalized care services. However, as eHealth undergoes further digital transformation, it is important to examine empirical evidence about the expectations countries consider to be of key relevance for nurses.

Identifying Major Trends and Issues

Health systems in almost all countries are overloaded with managing the COVID-19 pandemic, mass vaccination campaigns against several diseases, development of health protection training and doing COVID-19 vaccination campaigns. As a consequence, nurses' work burden for doing basic, life-saving care has become more intense. However, nurses still involve themselves with the dissemination and provision of information. Especially during the periods of crisis, nurses work to make information available to all in understandable and accessible formats, with a special sensitivity to vulnerable populations, people with disabilities, migrants, the elderly or individuals that have difficulties in coping mentally, physically or financially with the pandemic (Pubra, 2020; The Lancet, 2020).

Health protection plans and strategies have acquired increasing importance during the last two years because of the COVID-19 pandemic. The epidemic of diseases and increasing chronic conditions are, nevertheless, demanding a shift in the types and locations of health services and a better collaboration of health professionals with other sectors. In parallel with this, healthcare providers are broadening the scope of health-influencing factors they address to include social determinants and how new technologies and digital tools play into this new ecosystem. Regions are therefore identifying how to prepare for future challenges and how to work with digital technology in healthcare and include social determinants of health. Some trends identified in the regions described above are:

Common Denominators in the Domain of Socio-technical Trends

- Increasing ICT literacy and availability to digital technologies.
- Update or development of policies and praxis.
- Looking at the future of nursing education.
- Improving practice.
- Codes of ethics.
- Provide a legal, ethical and normative framework that would be the basis for further development of ISIS and adequate implementation of eHealth services.

Common Denominators in the Domain of Digital Trends

- Increasing implementation and use of ICT-based services and systems in home-based care.
- Use of ICT to integrate and use of SDH data in clinical settings.
- Consumer engagement.
- Alternative sites and access to care (telehealth).
- Use of ICT to capture and use social data.
- Systems integrated with electronic health record systems (EHRs) to help patients avoid hospital visits by flagging social barriers that could be burdening their health.
- Software that screens patients for unaddressed social factors and refers them to resources that can improve outcomes.

As described in the case studies, the future of nursing seems to be associated with a broadening and redefinition of the task of nurses. A new division of work between physicians and nurses in some countries will be defined. Today nurses have some tasks that previously were reserved for physicians, for example, prescribing some medicines and how to use eHealth innovations. Integrating, analyzing and minimizing social determinants of health give a greater focus on community and preventive care and less focus on hospital-based care. Policies must be in place to support these changes, including payment and regulatory policies as well as the identification of services for specific nursing interventions and educational requirements, competency assessments and stakeholders' analysis to understand nurses' response to changes.

It is much more difficult to ignore the social, economic and physical conditions of health. The care begins to decentralize, returning to homes and communities, increasing telemedicine, telecare, homecare applications and collaborating with other sectors. In this context, nurses have a historic opportunity to reclaim and expand their original vision of nursing practice. Given the new landscape, with more and more employers and policymakers recognizing the importance of investing in the social determinants of health and health equity, the question that healthcare systems face is: what will it take to achieve a vision in which the nursing workforce is prepared and activated to play a leading role in addressing unmet needs in the 21st century?

Discussion

Rapid changes driven by new enabling technologies and paired with economic imperatives from a global pandemic are transforming care delivery worldwide. As our case studies detail, these transformation changes have required frontline nurses to work with new digital tools and the expectation to include sociodemographic factors in assessment and care delivery. In addition, nurses are called upon to provide digital education and guidance on caring for individuals to each other, family members and the patient. During this pandemic, we have seen efforts to improve mobile documentation for efficiencies and to give access to real-time patient information quicker. These changes are happening at the same time that nurses work under acute shortages in the face of very ill, vulnerable populations and their diverse healthcare needs. These challenges are not unique to any given country, rather they are a worldwide reality in these pandemic times. The case studies show that the realities of capacity and resource constraints are actual and of high relevance for moving into the global breadth and depth of the nursing profession in the near future.

Little is known in general about how healthcare systems are preparing for the new challenges of the millennium and how nurses will apply a holistic perspective when considering social determinants of health and the eHealth era. A fair question is exactly how do nurses integrate food inse-curity and housing factors to gain deeper insights into the root causes of illness, disability and poor quality of life? And furthermore, practically how are nurses to be given the resources and tools to address these complex issues that determine health or its absence? In response to these challenges, healthcare managers worldwide are developing strategies and policies that include issues such as: how to use eHealth applications to ensure access to services for patients, and to bypass independent socioeconomic and geo-graphical barriers.

However, these solutions are often centralized, produced by govern-ments, and often neglect the individuals and the contexts in which they live as well as their technological maturity. Today, large segments of our populations, for instance, work in one country but live in another. Further, individuals at all levels of society have become more technically literate and heavy users of social media, such as Twitter, email, online platforms, e-bank and e-commerce. As economies have become more global and country boundaries less visible, with digital technologies permeating every aspect of life, including healthcare, we can expect that the role of nurses will need to evolve to meet these trends. Similarly, we can expect these mega trends to significantly impact the planning and delivery of health services. The case studies included in this chapter show that these factors are consistent with the situation in the countries covered and that they, as other countries with the same socio-technical structure, are at various stages of responding to the new technologies and economic imperatives of these times.

These three case studies further show that it is necessary to acknowledge the role of the welfare model applied in the different countries and its effects on the possibility of transferring services to citizens and especially to disad-vantaged groups. There are large social inequalities in health within each of the countries as well as between them. (And these drastic inequities exist in developed countries also, even the wealthiest.) We see wide variations in the nurses' role descriptions between these countries, and all report an urban–rural imbalance in health personnel distribution. However, the case studies all report that regions expect, in general, to reduce social inequalities and increase the role of nurses in the accessibility and delivery of care.

The case studies describe an overall ambition to prevent diseases, specifi-cally those related to lifestyle issues. However, there are differences between the regions when it comes to policies and follow-up plans and measures. Some regions focus more on the constraints the profession (nurses) con-fronts today because of workplace constraints ICT and digital literacy, and others focus more on how eHealth applications can facilitate care delivery or services as well as facilitate interaction between nurses and citizens.

Several policies seem to be on development; nevertheless, there is an absence of follow-up measures or models to evaluate the impact of eHealth technologies in work performed by nurses or the changes and challenges technology will demand. Additionally, most policies focus on healthcare and health services delivered by physicians: We have been unable to find policies that explicitly include nurses, the role of nurses or the interaction of nurses with citizens and patients.

Thus, it is possible to conclude that the level of responsibility and the role of government are not clear. The healthcare sector is mentioned in all policies and strategies. However, there is no designated entity responsible for implementing the policies. The question remains: who owns the tasks for reducing inequalities, developing the structures to share responsibility and reallocating resources needed to accomplish these goals? The responsibility seems to be diffuse with no clarification of which authority is to do the work, which sectors are to collaborate at the national or regional level and where accountability will fall. Missing also is any mention of nurses' role in these initiatives and implementation of eHealth services.

To succeed, it is necessary to develop vertical collaboration and support and to clarify the degree of freedom, independence and capacity that the nurses, in general, will have to achieve the goals indicated by the WHO (World Health Organization, 2008). Although nurses recognize the importance of social determinants for the health of their patients, decision-makers need to develop policies with the needed resources and tools that enable nurses to put these new dimensions into the basic nursing process. At the community level, nurses can get involved in health planning and advocate for more supportive environments for health in which eHealth should be an important component but this needs to be coordinated and supported. Governments and healthcare organizations have to help nurses in addressing the social determinants in all their activities to achieve the goals stated by the 2008 WHO document.

To realize the goals of the WHO, it is necessary to move from theory to practice, and more concretely, to describe the objectives and tools used to reduce social inequalities. The goals are, unfortunately, vague today and do not include precise policies and measures. Social inequalities often follow the political agenda of governments and that may not include long-term healthcare plans or policies. Policies and funding often change with new political leadership, impacting the healthcare sector, technology investments, and education for the health professionals. For many countries, this uncertainty means that to go forward with these new role dimensions and technical competencies can be risky. In such a case, it will be necessary to renew the educational programs, offer professional development programs and develop collaboration with other professions. In addition, the responsibilities of nurses will need to be redefined and new technologies learned for eHealthcare delivery and services.

The need to embrace innovations that support the delivery of care that includes SDoH implies further changes in the role of nurses due to increasing demand for new knowledge and skills, different relationships between nurses (practice, education, research, leadership), and impacts interaction patterns with their actors (patients, physicians, technologies). It seems rational to argue that there is a need to put more attention on investigating how different regions work and plan for increasing the use of eHealth with a special focus on nurses so that they can renew and innovate the manner to offer and supply services that influence social determinants of health.

In parallel with this, eHealth research in developed countries has increased focus because of the potential contribution of technology to decentralize healthcare and enhance patient engagement. However, research on the contribution of eHealth to healthcare has often focused on access to sample populations and the use of reliable health data and the importance of clinical and health systems when citizens connect with an eHealth platform or service (eHAction, 2021). Less attention has been paid to understanding social determinant factors and how nurses impact an increasing implementation of eHealth systems as a professional group. This needs to change.

Although addressing the social determinants of health requires a broad range of actions that involve the collaboration of multiple sectors and local governments, nurses are important players and potential catalysts of change. Healthcare leaders, managers and decision-makers need to recognize the need for a social determinant of health approach to have healthier populations, reduce healthcare demand and contribute to effectiveness in the delivery of care.

References

American Nurses Association. (2021). *Empowering nurses to lead.* Available at: https://www.ana-events.org/PIAForum/?utm_campaign=264500%202021 %20ANA%20Policy%2C%20Innovation%20%26%20Advocacy%20VF&utm _source=NursingWorld&utm_medium=HeroBanner&utm_content=ANA%20PIA %20Forum

Anand, S., Fan, V. Y., Zhang, J., Zhang, L., Ke, Y., Dong, Z., & Chen, L. C. (2008). China's human resources for health: Quantity, quality, and distribution. *The Lancet*, 372(9651), pp.1774–1781. https://doi.org/10.1016/S0140-6736(08)61363-X

Bjegovic-Mikanovic, V., Vasic, M., Vukovic, D., Jankovic, J., Jovic-Vranes, A., Santric-Milicevic, M, Terzic-Supic, Z., & Hernandez-Quevedo, C. (2019, Oct). Serbia: Health system review. *Health Systems Transitions*, 21(3), pp.1–211. PMID: 32851979.

Chen, Y., Wu, F., Wu, Y., Li, J., Yue, P., Deng, Y., Lamb, K. V., Fong, S., Liu, Y., & Zhang, Y. (2019). Development of interventions for an intelligent and individualized mobile health care system to promote healthy diet and physical activity: Using an intervention mapping framework. *BMC Public Health*, 19, p.1311. https://doi.org/10.1186/s12889-019-7639-7

eHAction. (2021). D8.3 Post 2021 scenarios for eHealth policy cooperation. Co-funded by the *EU Health Programme, 2014-2020*. In 19th eHealth Network Meeting, June 2021. Available at: http://ehaction.eu/wp8-ehealth-national-policies-and-sustainability/ (Accessed 6 January 2022).

Feeg, V. D., & Rienzo, T. A. (2015). Computer use in nursing research. In V. K. Saba, & K. McCormick, eds., *Essentials of nursing informatics, 6th edition. nursing informatics and the foundation of knowledge*. New York: McGraw Hill Education. Chapter 47, pp.663–685.

Health Information Management Systems Society. (n.d.). *What is nursing informatics?* Available at: https://www.himss.org/resources/what-nursing-informatics (Accessed 16 September 2021).

ITU. (2020). *Digital innovation profile Montenegro*. ITU. Available at: https://www.itu.int/dms_pub/itu-d/opb/inno/D-INNO-PROFILE.MONTENEGRO-2020-PDF-E.pdf

Ivanišević, K., Kosić, R., Bošković, S., & Bukvić, M. (2021). *Implementation of the nurse professional competence scale in the Republic of Croatia*. PREPRINT (Version 1). https://doi.org/10.21203/rs.3.rs-475940/v1

Li, L., Zhao, Y., Zhou, X., & Lu, Z. (2020). Analysis on the current situation and equity of health human resource allocation in China. *Chinese Health Economics*, 39(11), pp.44–48.

Lv, Q., Jiang, Y., Qi, J., Zhang, Y., Zhang, X., Fang, L., … Lin, Z. (2019). Using mobile apps for health management: A new health care mode in China. *JMIR mHealth uHealth*, 7(6), p.e10299. https://doi.org/10.2196/10299

McGonigle, D., & Mastrian, K. (2021). *Nursing informatics and the foundation of knowledge, chapters 6–18*. World Headquarters: Jones and Bartlett Learning.

Montenegro Ministry of Health. (2003). Strategy for health care development in Montenegro. *Republic of Montenegro Government*. Ministry of Health, September. Available at: https://extranet.who.int/countryplanningcycles/sites/default/files/planning_cycle_repository/montenegro/montenegro.pdf (Accessed 16 September 2021).

Montenegro Ministry of Health. (2015). Master plan for healthcare development 2015–2020. *Montenegro Government*. October, Available at: https://www.gov.me/en/documents/fde2ae2d-2a46-44e2-bf7c-06fdf35f4998 (Accessed 6 January 2022).

Mukhopadhyay, A. (2011). *Effective social determinants of health approach in India through community mobilization*. Voluntary Health Association of India. https://www.who.int/sdhconference/resources/draft_background_paper9_india .pdf (Accessed 29 June 2021).

NHC_PRC National Health Commission of the People's Republic of China. (2010). *2010 China Health Statistics Yearbook*. Beijing: Publishing House of Peking Union Medical College.

NHC_PRC National Health Commission of the People's Republic of China. (2020). *2020 China Health Statistics Yearbook*. Beijing: Publishing House of Peking Union Medical College.

OECD. (2020). A roadmap toward a common framework for measuring the digital economy. https://www.oecd.org/digital/ieconomy/roadmap-toward-a-common -framework-for-measuring-the-digital-economy.pdf

Olshansky, E. F. (2017). Social determinants of health: The role of nursing. *American Journal of Nursing*, 117(12), p.11. https://doi.org/10.1097/01.NAJ .0000527463.16094.39

Olson, L. L., & Stokes, F. (2016). The ANA code of ethics for nurses with interpretive statements: Resource for nursing regulation. *Journal of Nursing Regulation*, 7, pp.9–20. https://doi.org/10.1016/S2155-8256(16)31073-0

Purba, A. K. (2020). How should the role of the nurse change in response to Covid-19? *Nursing Times*. Available at: https://www.nursingtimes.net/clinical-archive /public-health-clinical-archive/how-should-the-role-of-the-nurse-change-in -response-to-covid-19-26-05-2020/ (Accessed 8 March 2021).

Robichaux, C., & Sauerland, J. (n.d.). The social determinants of health, COVID-19, and structural competence. *OJIN: The Online Journal of Issues in Nursing*, 26(2). Available at: http://ojin.nursingworld.org/MainMenuCategories/ ANAMarketplace/ANAPeriodicals/OJIN/TableofContents/Vol-26-2021/No2-May -2021/Articles-Previous-Topics/The-Social-Determinants-of-Health-COVID-19 -and-Structural-Competence.html (Accessed 8 March 2021).

Shen, X., & Han, D. (2019). Review on the development of nursing discipline in China. *Continuing Medical Education*, 33(7), pp.28–29. https://doi.org/10.3969/j .issn.1004-6763.2019.07.017

Smart Specialisation for Montenegro Strategy. (2020). Digital Public Administration factsheet 2020 Montenegro. *European Commission*, April, pp 12–13. Available at: https://joinup.ec.europa.eu/sites/default/files/inline-files/Digital_Public_ Administration_Factsheets_Montenegro_vFINAL.pdf (Accessed 6 January 2022).

State Council of the People's Republic of China. (2008). Ordinance no 517. Nurse regulations. *LawInfoChina*. Available at: http://www.lawinfochina.com/display .aspx?lib=law&id=6664&CGid (Accessed 28 September 2021).

Statista Research Department. (2020). *Number of mobile cell phone subscriptions in China from December 2019 to December 2020*. Available at: https://www .statista.com/statistics/278204/china-mobile-users-by-month/

The Lancet. (2020). Redefining vulnerability in the era of COVID-19. *The Lancet* 395, p.1089. https://doi.org/10.1016/S0140-6736(20)30757-1 https://www.thelancet.com/ pdfs/journals/lancet/PIIS0140-6736(20)30757-1.pdf (Accessed 8 March 2021).

Thornton, M. & Persaud, S. (2018). Preparing today's nurses: Social determinants of health and nursing education. *OJIN: The Online Journal of Issues in Nursing*, 23(3), p.5. https://doi.org/10.3912/OJIN.Vol23No03Man05

United Nations Development Programme. (2017). *Montenegro, strengthening the health system*. https://www.me.undp.org/content/montenegro/en/home/projects/Health.html (Accessed 16 September 2021).

Vuković, I. T., Brdarević, M., Čukljek, S., & Babić, J. (2019). The attitudes of nurses towards internship in the Republic of Croatia. *Croatia Nursing Journal*, 3(1), pp.79–92.

World Bank. (2021). *Health workforce mobility from Croatia, Serbia and North Macedonia to Germany*. World Bank. https://documents.worldbank.org/pt/publication/documents-reports/documentdetail/489881614056529442/main-report (Accessed 16 September 2021).

World Health Organization. (2008). *Closing the gap in a generation: Health equity through action on the social determinants of health: Commission on Social Determinants of Health final report*. Geneva, Switzerland: World Health Organization, Commission on Social Determinants of Health. Available at: http://apps.who.int/iris/bitstream/handle/10665/43943/9789241563703_eng.pdf;jsessionid=FBC4105F22417A25D57922413164ADCE?sequence=1 (Accessed 30 July 2021).

World Health Organization. (2015). *China country assessment report on aging and health*. https://apps.who.int/iris/bitstream/handle/10665/194271/9789241509312_eng.pdf

World Health Organization. (2020). *WHO and partners call for urgent investment in nurses*. https://www.who.int/news/item/07-04-2020-who-and-partners-call-for-urgent-investment-in-nurses (Accessed 30 July 2021).

World Health Organization. (2021). *Global strategy on digital health 2020–2025*. Available at: https://www.who.int/docs/default-source/documents/gs4dhdaa2a9f352b0445bafbc79ca799dce4d.pdf (Accessed 6 January 2022).

Chapter 4

Leveraging a Unique Nurse Identifier to Improve Outcomes

Whende M. Carroll and Joyce Sensmeier

Contents

DOI: 10.4324/9781003281047-4

Introduction

Today, nursing's contribution to the health and care of individuals and populations is often invisible and difficult to measure. In part, the ability to demonstrate the value of nursing is compromised due to a gap in use of a unique identifier for nurses (Sensmeier et al., 2019). It is our position that national and global health systems need to uniquely identify nurses in electronic health record (EHR) and enterprise resource planning (ERP) systems and other technologies for documentation, education, research and training purposes. A unique nurse identifier is essential to the aggregation, synthesis and publication of data and research. These data capture nursing processes to enable scientific inquiry for researchers to measure and quantify the impact of nursing care on health outcomes. A unique identifier can offer visibility to demonstrate the value of nursing's role in contributing to safe, effective health practices. Coded data can be stored, aggregated and used in analyses and reports to link patient outcomes with nursing practice. A unique nurse identifier can serve as an important connection between ERP and EHR datasets to help measure the longitudinal performance of nurses. Nursing documentation can also be studied to measure nurses' impact on individual and population outcomes, patient safety, operational efficiency and clinical effectiveness (Figure 4.1).

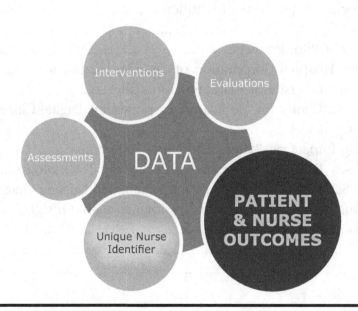

Figure 4.1   Unique nurse identifier data framework.

Nursing Knowledge: Big Data Science Policy and Advocacy Workgroup Efforts

The Nursing Knowledge: Big Data Science Initiative (2020) embraces a vision of better health outcomes resulting from the standardization and integration of the information nurses gather in EHRs and other information systems. The Initiative executes a national action plan through its workgroups to make nursing data sharable, comparable, timely and more relevant to improving health and health outcomes (Nursing Knowledge: Big Data Science Initiative, 2020). To further advance this vision, the Nursing Knowledge: Big Data Science Policy and Advocacy Workgroup identified the need for a unique nurse identifier to demonstrate the value and contributions of nursing care to improved patient outcomes.

In nursing, a unique nurse identifier is a defined code that represents the individual nurse and classifies an entity in health information technology (IT) systems, including repositories, registries, databases and knowledge bases. The nurse identifier code enables identifiable and actionable events in different health IT systems and technologies to be linked to nursing documentation. Associating a unique identifier with the nurse in multiple systems will allow for matching and capturing the nurse's activity in those systems, even if that activity is performed in disparate organizations (Sensmeier & Carroll, 2021).

The Nursing Knowledge Workgroup evaluated the available identifiers including the National Provider Identifier (NPI) and the National Council of State Boards of Nursing (NCSBN) Identifier (ID). The Centers for Medicare and Medicaid Services (CMS) require the NPI for healthcare workers to be paid by CMS as required by the Health Information Portability and Accountability Act (HIPAA) Administrative Simplification: Standard Unique Health Identifier for Health Care Providers; Final Rule from 2004 (Department of Health and Human Services Office of the Secretary, 2004). A unique, numeric identifier, such as the NPI, is of interest to researchers; Advance Practice Registered Nurses (APRNs) and MDs who bill Medicare/Medicaid; and registered nurses/professional nursing organizations who seek to obtain Medicare and Medicaid reimbursement for professional nursing services (e.g., care coordination) (Sensmeier et al., 2019). The identifier can also help demonstrate that each member of the care team is practicing to the full extent of their license and education.

NCSBN publishes a unique ID for each RN, LPN and APRN. The NCSBN ID is a free, publicly available identifier matched exclusively to an individual nurse and is automatically assigned to each nurse and nursing student upon registration for the National Council Licensure Examination (NCLEX)

(National Council of State Boards of Nursing, 2020). Each NCSBN ID is accessible via the Nursys database (Nursys, 2021) which comprises a suite of systems and databases containing nurse license and license discipline information. The Nursys nurse licensure database is the repository of the license and disciplinary data of the NCSBN member boards of nursing. The Nursys system allows nurses to track their own licenses and obtain up-to-date information on license status and notification when licenses are to be renewed. NCSBN assures data security of the system by maintaining proper data security policies, procedures and requirements.

Both the NPI and NCSBN ID are free, publicly accessible, unique identifiers that are available to all registered nurses. One advantage of the NPI is that its database is interprofessional and nurses are recognized, along with their interprofessional colleagues, as potential recipients of federal payment for services provided. There is no fee for application, nor is there any maintenance required, such as annual renewal (Office of the National Coordinator for Health Information Technology, 2017). However, a potential challenge to the widespread use of an NPI is that nurses must apply for it. Since most nurses do not provide care as sole proprietors, there is no clarity for how or when to apply for the NPI code. In addition, the application process is complex, and combined with the lack of a perceived need for each individual nurse to take action to obtain an NPI together represent important challenges.

After careful consideration of the benefits and challenges of the available identifiers, the Nursing Knowledge: Big Data Science Policy and Advocacy Workgroup recommends using the NCSBN ID as the unique nurse identifier for all nurses in the United States. The key factors in this decision include eliminating the need for each nurse to take action to complete the NPI application process, the automatic assigning of the NCSBN ID and the ease with which the NCSBN ID can be incorporated into technologies and systems via application program interface tools (APIs). Leveraging this identifier will be convenient for health systems to connect siloed systems, including the EHR, ERP and other technologies and systems. Importantly, feasibility and proof-of-concept (POC) pilots are currently in process, as described later in this chapter.

Advocating for a Unique Nurse Identifier

Widespread use of a unique nurse identifier will enable scientific inquiry whereby researchers can measure and quantify nursing care and its impact on health outcomes. This potential impact includes demonstrating each nurse's role in contributing to safe and effective health and care practices as well as enhancing enterprise resource planning. The appropriate use of nursing resources will also be informed through the use of a unique nurse identifier to examine the variability of direct nursing care time and cost per patient and the relationships between patient and nurse characteristics and nursing costs.

Policy Efforts

To realize the benefits of a unique nurse identifier, the Nursing Knowledge: Big Data Science Policy and Advocacy Workgroup began an advocacy campaign in 2020 to increase awareness and use of the unique nurse identifier. The workgroup developed the following policy statement which is foundational to this campaign:

> The NCSBN ID should be used by key stakeholders as a nurse identifier to help demonstrate the value of nursing through research and enhance individual care and health outcomes via more comprehensive documentation in the electronic health record (EHR), enterprise resource planning (ERP) systems and other technologies and systems.

The workgroup also created a call to action to further articulate the value and impact of the position statement and validate it through presentations, publications, research and proof-of-concept pilots.

Advocacy outreach to like-minded organizations began with the Alliance for Nursing Informatics (ANI), co-sponsored by AMIA (American Medical Informatics Association) and HIMSS (Health Information Management Systems Society). ANI is a collaboration of more than 25 distinct nursing informatics groups, globally representing more than 20,000 nurse informaticists and focusing on advancing nursing informatics leadership, practice, education, policy and research through a unified voice of nursing informatics organizations (Alliance for Nursing Informatics, 2021). ANI crosses academia, practice, industry and nursing specialty boundaries, working in collaboration with the nearly 5 million nurses in practice today (National Council of State Boards of Nursing, 2021). The ANI Policy Committee develops and submits public comments on topics relevant to its mission, which provides a vehicle for advancing the unique nurse identifier policy position.

The unique nurse identifier policy statement was approved by ANI on November 13, 2020 (Alliance for Nursing Informatics, 2020). Educational resources are available on the ANI website including the policy statement, frequently asked questions document, webinar recording, infographic and other reference materials (Alliance for Nursing Informatics, 2021). The ANI policy statement also informs public policy comments submitted by the organization. ANI member organizations disseminate the policy statement and related materials to each of their own individual members. The ANI member organizations can also link to the ANI policy statement and related materials from their own website and share the information via their social media platforms.

A groundswell of support for use of a unique nurse identifier is being realized. The American Academy of Nursing (Academy) Expert Panel on Informatics and Technology is developing a statement in support of adoption of a unique nurse identifier. This statement fosters the Academy's goal to *influence policy that achieves health equity, promotes wellness, eliminates racism and improves healthcare delivery.* The Academy disseminates, through collaborative partnerships with key policy stakeholders, nursing knowledge that informs sound and sustainable transformation addressing wellness, health promotion, behavioral health and serious illness.

The National Academy of Medicine (NAM) recently published a report, *The Future of Nursing 2020–2030: Charting a Path to Achieve Health Equity*, which outlines the nursing profession's role in advancing health equity and optimizing outcomes for diverse patients and communities (National Academy of Medicine, 2021). Importantly, this NAM report asserts the need for a national nurse identifier to facilitate recognition and measurement of the value of services provided by nurses. Further, it states that an identifier is important for performance metrics to incentivize nursing roles and functions that advance population health and health equity.

Proof-of-Concept Pilot Projects

Proof-of-concept (POC) pilot projects are being conducted internally at health systems, schools of nursing and innovation centers to verify that the proposed concept is achievable in the practical application of the NCSBN ID as a unique nurse identifier. This essential work begins a process to provide evidence to nurse leaders on the value of using the nurse identifier. Also, the piloting process is vital to defining the technical steps needed to determine how and if a nurse identifier functions as intended in multiple technologies.

POC pilots will help organizations implement and test the code's technical workflows to prove its feasibility, measure adoption and assess reporting capabilities on its benefits to patients and nurses. The following use cases and case study highlight the early stages of operationalizing a unique nurse identifier in clinical practice and nursing operations.

Use Case: *Hospital Corporation of America Healthcare*

Hospital Corporation of America (HCA) Healthcare believes that the process of matching nurses to their documentation assists in the assessment of the continuum of a nurse's expertise and career progression. Today, HCA links an NCSBN ID to each nurse in their health system to study nursing practice at the patient level and to aggregate nurse-specific data across their technology systems. HCA uses the unique nurse identifier in their EHR to assess policy-driven documentation of timely and patient-centric assessment based on years of nurse experience. One HCA facility examines the completion of nurses' pain assessment and pain management for orthopedic patients using the NCSBN ID. In this study, preliminary results indicate that approximately 70% of nurses complete the unit's required nurse documentation. In addition, they associate a nurse's career history of providing alternative therapies to patients (i.e., comfort measures, alternatives for narcotic pain management) and assess the timing of intervention documentation based on facility policy. These findings now enable tailored education and practice improvement for the new graduate's clinical experience.

HCA also uses the NCSBN ID to correlate nurse experience with competency assessment achievements for complex care. The health system hypothesizes that determining accelerated learning paths for nurses with less than one year of clinical experience who begin or transfer into a highly complex clinical setting can be successful. HCA's human resource data, coupled with competency assessment tools using the NCSBN ID, enable aggregation of these two datasets to measure the longitudinal performance of those nurses who want to start practicing in complex care environments earlier in their career. HCA will explore future POCs using the NCSBN ID to perform similar studies, which will measure clinical team contribution to health outcomes, such as those clinical teams that are providing highly effective care. They aim to pilot this effort to identify key characteristics of teams producing the best patient outcomes and replicate those attributes in simulations to test the possibility of more quickly developing positive team-based behaviors (Roberts, 2021, personal communication).

Use Case: University of Alabama-Huntsville

The University of Alabama-Huntsville is testing the NCSBN's eNotify system to acquire the unique nurse identifier for advanced-practice nursing students to obtain regular notifications of license status updates. In this POC pilot, the intention is to use the code in various internal IT systems to follow a nursing student's subsequent educational and career progression. This monitoring is vital for internal assessment of academic nursing programs. This systematic notification provides essential and accurate data about licensure and certification exam pass rates of their graduates, along with the geographic distribution of current licensure status. Also, through the NCSBN's Nursys database, the university receives timely updates of licensing status for nursing faculty and students' clinical preceptors which fills an additional need for educational programs (Alexander, 2021, personal communication). When graduates receive an advanced practice license from a board of nursing, the University of Alabama gets notice of license status changes via the Nursys eNotify system. Using the NCSBN ID, the university can then measure the time it takes master- and doctorate-level graduates to receive advanced practice licenses after completing the nursing program.

Case Study: Center for Medical Interoperability, Digital Citizen RN Model

The Center for Medical Interoperability (C4MI) is a cooperative research and development laboratory. This innovative center has piloted the use of the NCSBN ID in a simulated cardiopulmonary resuscitation (CPR) scenario. The C4MI POC studied the ability to link disparate healthcare data sources to evaluate caregiver performance during CPR events. This exercise aimed to assess the individual nurse, a *Digital Citizen RN*, identified by their NCSBN ID and a response team's interventions and performance during a CPR event. The C4MI simulation demonstrated how the known Digital Citizen RN caregiver could coordinate patient care within an emergency response care team by applying a nurse's credentials and CPR performance metrics. As a result of this pilot, researchers found they could analyze CPR event management and the response team's performance scoring using a unique nurse identifier. Further, the C4MI POC showed that nurses could harness data at the point of care for response teams to receive real-time clinical guidance and actionable insights into the effectiveness of interventions during CPR events using the NCSBN ID (Aldrich, 2021, personal communication).

Essential to the further adoption of a unique nurse identifier is additional testing in collaboration with healthcare technology stakeholders, such as technology systems developers and vendors. Additional POCs will effectively advance the effort to promote the unique identifier's use and further implement the code within clinical documentation and enterprise resource IT systems. Measuring the process and outcomes of using the unique nurse identifier in multiple technologies will also uncover additional challenges and opportunities. Further POCs will enable healthcare leaders to quantify the time, cost, and human and technical resources needed to operationalize a unique nurse identifier in practice to meet the goals of measuring the value and contribution of nursing care to individuals' health and nursing outcomes.

Demonstrating Impact on Patient and Nurse Outcomes

The characteristics of patient outcomes impacted by nursing care have been identified by Ying Liu and colleagues (2014). These characteristics are summarized into three categories—patient functional status, patient safety and patient satisfaction. Based on the authors' analysis (Liu et al., 2014), the concept of patient outcomes is defined more simply as the results of the nursing care that patients receive in hospital including maintenance of patient functional status, maintenance of patient safety and patient satisfaction. The unique nurse identifier can help evaluate the contribution of nursing practice to quality patient outcomes related to health promotion, injury and illness prevention, and alleviation of suffering. This correlation will help nurses continuously assess their clinical practice interventions in order to deliver safe, high-quality individual health, care and outcomes.

Evidence supports the imperative that nurses contribute to the prevention of adverse events in healthcare (Lucero et al., 2010), but there is lack of verification to show how nurses contribute to the prevention of negative or positive patient outcomes (Englebright & Jackson, 2017). A unique nurse identifier can lay the foundation for understanding the impact of nursing practice as it can associate nurse characteristics with patient characteristics from a larger dataset of health information within or across systems and organizations (Sensmeier et al., 2019).

Defining Nurses' Essential Value through Data and Technology

For several decades, nurse leaders have recognized the need for the use of a unique nurse identifier, without which the aggregation and use of data to improve nursing practice is not possible (Werley & Lang, 1988). Ingesting and manipulating the data points in technology systems associated with a unique nurse identifier enable the transparency of time, cost and the human resources needed to provide patient care. Different unique identifiers track and classify nursing services for billing, staffing and resource planning purposes. Robust nursing data analysis makes visible to health leaders and decision-makers the direct value of nurses' contributions in all care settings. The challenge of measuring nursing value is that intangible assets are generally unquantifiable. With the now-common use of EHRs, point-of-care documentation data make it possible to quantify clinical and administrative services. Also, other complementary technology systems used in patient care can capture the nurse's ID and feed it into their systems to measure nursing value. These systems may include intelligent IV pumps, single sign-in logins with the use of badges, bar code medication administration and point-of-care test devices that require unique user codes.

The tangible and intangible elements that institute nurse value are essential to capture for nurses to transform the clinical processes that impact value-based care (Welton & Harper, 2015). *Valuation* is an economic term used to determine the quantifiable worth and tactile usefulness of any venture. The valuation process involves financial valuing of a business or organization's resources and financial analyses, taking both quantitative and qualitative aspects of their worth, in dollars, through valuation studies (Rutherford, 2010). These inquiries provide a more precise depiction of the business's resources and expenditures, including determining the tangible assets of nursing knowledge, revenue efficiencies, patient health outcomes and enumerating intangible assets such as trust, caring and intuition (Rutherford, 2010). Proving valuation can give nurses their due acknowledgment as critical revenue drivers and cost savers in care delivery and operations. Valuation proven through testing the use of a unique nurse identifier can distinctly determine nurses' contribution to patient safety and quality of care, lower cost and in enhancing the patient experience and improving health outcomes.

Comprehending the accumulation cost of nursing documentation can encourage adoption and advocacy efforts for a unique nurse identifier. Valuation initiatives can build information that will substantiate the community's demand for adequate nursing investment (Rutherford, 2010). With large datasets derived from multiple healthcare systems and sources, nurses now have the means to show how they contribute to value-based care. Further, nurses can be at the forefront in defining value through the advanced use of information technology and big data along with and beyond the standard clinical documentation systems used today.

Research and Scholarly Inquiry—Studying Patient and Nursing Outcomes

Codified values are needed in all research as data points for the foundation of quantitative research that results in measurement of clinical-based phenomena to develop new care models, processes, policies and theories. The purpose of nursing research is to impart and enrich evidence that informs practice including nurses' actions and decisions in direct patient care and administration. Novel uses of data in scholarly inquiry, including a unique nurse identifier as a data source, will garner robust findings for nurse researchers to contribute to nursing science regarding the value and impact of nursing care on patient outcomes. Moving forward, nurses must use data in innovative ways to transform patient care and operations that lead to healthier outcomes.

A palpable hindrance to assessment and outcomes research today is the lack of data related to nursing processes and patient outcomes (Sensmeier et al., 2019). Insufficient data collection methodologies that yield reliable and valid measures of essential nursing care processes and patient outcomes result in inadequate evidence to demonstrate nursing's contribution to patient care (Lang, 2008). While today we develop measures that better capture nursing processes, the simultaneous widespread use of a unique nurse identifier will make the collection of relevant and comprehensive data more feasible (Sensmeier et al., 2019).

To that end, a unique nurse identifier used as secondary nursing data helps nurse researchers to aggregate, explore and synthesize findings of activities central to nursing practice. Studying nurses' clinical processes, such as clinical assessment, intervention and evaluation together with a unique nurse identifier, enables scientific inquiry for researchers to measure and quantify the impact of nursing care on health outcomes. Nursing research also enhances evidence-based practice, expands the nursing knowledge base and supports education based on nursing science. The dissemination of knowledge gained through research findings and socialized through publication, public speaking and scientific posters can drive nurses to change practice.

Measuring Quality and Nurse Outcomes for Actionable Insights

Currently, many technology systems do not provide a means to inform and support quality improvement (QI) initiatives that measure clinical safety and nursing care effectiveness. For instance, the current lack of integration of quality metrics data within EHR systems (Beale et al., 2021) is a missed opportunity for collective data sources to measure the outcomes of nursing activities that can improve clinical practice and transform care models. Clinical outcome metrics are becoming more transparent, mandated nationally and used to measure clinicians' impact on hospital and accountable care reimbursement (Centers for Medicare and Medicaid Services, 2021). Health outcomes and nurse-specific safety measures include those for patient falls and hospital-acquired conditions, such as pressure ulcers, IV infiltration rates and infections. Further, clinical interventions, assessments and reassessment metrics drive financial incentives and directly impact healthcare systems' costs and patient satisfaction (Lockhart, 2018). These metrics, which are precisely nurse-sensitive measures, can benefit nursing twofold. These measures can impart safety and quality improvement opportunities and create visibility into nurse performance at the aggregate, clinical setting and individual nurse level in the current value-based care landscape.

Structural, process and outcome quality measures are foundational for performance improvement. However, data manipulation between these three types of metrics is complex. The benefits of aggregating these metrics to identify essential correlations between nurse activities and observed nursing outcomes can help healthcare organizations improve health outcomes (Montalvo, 2007). Adding a unique nurse identifier as a healthcare data point to use in technology systems is a key enabler. Used in synergy with other metrics, the NCSBN identifier makes possible analytics that can mine robust and actionable insights for clinical effectiveness and identify transformation opportunities for quality and safety in patient care, thus quantifiably show-ing nursing's contribution to patient-centered care. Analyzing nursing data through this lens for quality and safety can demonstrate improved patient outcomes, increased patient satisfaction, and decreased complication and liability issues (Jones, 2016).

Nurses can easily track, trend and compare nursing care events through technology facilitated by using the unique nurse identifier. While quality metrics can measure nursing outcomes at the nursing aggregate and patient care setting levels, outcomes can also be assessed by the individual nurse's documentation. This new approach can quantify the value a nurse brings to the point of care to show the direct impact on an organization's cost, directly affecting value-based care scores, and associated reimbursement, highlighting a single nurse's return on investment. The addition of a unique nurse identifier can help discover nurse-specific contributions in the five steps of the nursing process—assessment, diagnosis, interventions, plan-ning and continuously evaluating the patient. Collectively, these insights will enable nurses to continuously improve processes to transform and deliver evidence-based practice, thus enhancing their visibility to healthcare lead-ership and decision-makers in a value-based model. Figure 4.2 presents a description of the data flow from generation of the NCSBN ID to actionable insights for patient and nurse outcomes.

As detailed in this chapter, nursing's contribution to the health of indi-viduals and communities is difficult to measure and often invisible, partly due to the absence of a unique identifier for nurses. A unique nurse identi-fier enables the examination of the variability of direct nursing care time and costs and the relationships between patient and nurse characteristics and costs. Benefits of a nurse identifier include quantifying nurse value, enhanc-ing research and scholarly inquiry and enabling the measurement of nursing outcomes though quality improvement projects and initiatives. All are imper-ative in today's value-based care environment and further advancement of nursing practice, science and the profession.

Looking to the Future

A unique nurse identifier used as a secondary data source in new technolo-gies can uncover nurse value and its association with improved patient and nursing outcomes. Healthcare is rich in data sources that pull from patient demographics, clinical environment data, medical claims, workforce data

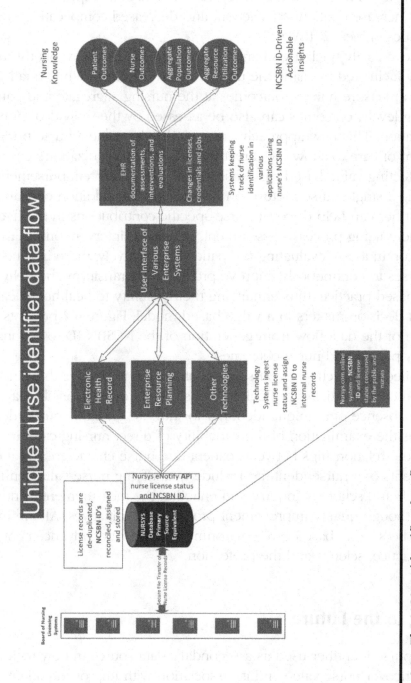

Figure 4.2 The NCSBN identifier data flow.

and digital health sources, such as wearables and personal safety device sources. Human resource files, education, professional certifications, staffing and wage information are all nursing workforce data examples. With a unique nurse identifier included in administrative healthcare technology systems, these data types can demonstrate nurse contribution in a value-based care landscape (Welton & Harper, 2015) through adding this data point into care processes in new technologies. As evidenced by recent pilot projects using a unique identifier to represent nurse distinctiveness in clinical practice, academia and through their career journey, there are emerging use cases for using a unique nurse identifier at the point of care and in operational processes within systems and technologies.

In the future, it will be nurses as data stewards who take charge to provide strong evidence for their contribution to value-based care using a unique nurse identifier. Intelligent and secure technologies that inform evidence-based care approaches, assist in clinical decision-making, safeguard data processes and protect and simplify data sharing can accelerate the act of proving nurse value in clinical quality and safety initiatives. Employing an emphasis on validating unique nurse identifier feasibility and testing using emerging technical specifications and workflows is essential. With the imperative to measure contribution to improving individuals' health and nurse outcomes, there is a significant need for increasing awareness, advocacy, research and education about how unique nurse identifiers serve as critical data points in EHR and ERP systems and other technologies. Nurses should consider forward-thinking use cases for the unique nurse identifier that solve challenging healthcare problems, such as reducing clinician documentation burden, furthering medical interoperability, fostering health equity and addressing health disparities. Nurse informaticists can lead transformational clinical and operational processes in partnership with data science teams and commercial healthcare technology vendors to embed the unique nurse identifier into new technology systems with their vital data management skills and innovative health IT perspectives.

With the evolution of telehealth and other forward-looking digital health technologies, it is imperative that nurses reach beyond the local and national workforce to harness the true power of global nursing care. To accomplish this, the NCSBN is working with its Canadian Nursing Regulatory Body membership to facilitate the exchange of nurse license and disciplinary data, using one NCSBN ID, between the US and Canadian nursing regulatory bodies. Upon successful completion of this transcontinental project, the

NCSBN will engage other international nursing regulatory body members to participate in the nurse matching process and the assignment of NCSBN IDs to its nursing workforce. The NCSBN envisions a future where, regardless of how many countries a nurse may hold a nursing license, they will have one NCSBN ID enabling the use of a unique nurse identifier to improve patient and nursing outcomes globally.

Conclusion

The time is now for demonstrating nursing's contribution to improving patient safety, quality care, operational efficiency and health outcomes. The documentation of clinical care ultimately resides with nurses requiring increased support from information technologies and systems to alleviate the burden. The use of a unique nurse identifier, such as the NCSBN ID, will detect identifiable and actionable events in disparate health IT systems and technologies. Adoption of a unique nurse identifier will distinguish the importance of nurses in continuously improving nursing care and systems, transforming and delivering evidence-based practice, and increasing nurse visibility to quantify value-based care. Moving forward, nurses can be data stewards who take the lead in providing strong evidence for their contribution to value-based care using a unique nurse identifier.

References

Alliance for Nursing Informatics. (2020). *Demonstrating the value of nursing care through use of a unique nurse identifier policy statement.* Available at: https://www.allianceni.org/sites/allianceni.org/files/ANI%20Unique%20Nurse %20Identifier%20Policy%20Statement%20FINAL4%20Approved%20071620.pdf (Accessed 6 June 2021).

Alliance for Nursing Informatics (2021). Available at: https://www.allianceni.org/ unique-nurse-identifier (Accessed: 26 May 2021).

Beale, N., Carroll, W., Aldrich, K., Alexander, S., Baernholdt, M., & Fields, W. (2021). The fingerprint of nursing: What a unique nurse identifier means for our future. *American Nurse*, 16(9), pp.21–24.

Centers for Medicare and Medicaid Services. (n.d.). *Hospital value-based purchasing program.* Available at: https://www.cms.gov/Medicare/Quality-Initiatives-Patient -Assessment-Instruments/HospitalQualityInits/Hospital-Value-Based-Purchasing (Accessed 27 March 2021).

Department of Health and Human Services Office of the Secretary. (2004). *45 CFR part 16 HIPAA administrative simplification: Standard unique health identifier for health care providers; final rule.* Available at: https://www.cms.gov /Regulations-and-Guidance/Administrative-Simplification/NationalProvIde ntStand/downloads/NPIfinalrule.pdf (Accessed 27 May 2021).

Englebright, J., & Jackson, E. (2017). Wrestling with Big Data: How nurse leaders can engage. In C. W. Delaney, C. A. Weaver, J. J. Warren, T. R. Clancy, & R. L. Simpson, eds., *Big data-enabled nursing. Education, research and practice.* Cham, Switzerland: Springer, pp.115–137.

Jones, T. (2016). Outcome measurement in nursing: Imperatives, ideals, history, and challenges. *OJIN: The Online Journal of Issues in Nursing*, 21(2). Available at: https://pubmed.ncbi.nlm.nih.gov/27854419/ (Accessed 27 May 2021).

Lang, N. M. (2008). The promise of simultaneous transformation of practice and research with the use of clinical information systems. *Nursing Outlook*, 56(5), pp.232–236. https://doi.org/10.1016/j.outlook.2008.06.011

Liu, Y., Avant, K. C., Aungsuroch, Y., Zhang, X. Y., & Jiang, P. (2014). Patient outcomes in the field of nursing: A concept analysis. *International Journal of Nursing Sciences*, 1(1), pp.69–74. https://doi.org/10.1016/j.ijnss.2014.02.006

Lockhart, L. (2018). Measuring nursing's impact. *Nursing Made Incredibly Easy!*, 16(2), p.55. https://doi.org/10.1097/01.NME.0000529956.73785.23

Lucero, R. J., Lake, E. T., and Aiken, L. H. (2010). Nursing care quality and adverse events in US hospitals. *Journal of Clinical Nursing*, 19(15–16), pp.2185–2195. https://doi.org/10.1111/j.1365-2702.2010.03250.x

Montalvo, I. (2007). The national database of nursing quality indicators™ (NDNQI®). *OJIN: The Online Journal of Issues in Nursing*, 12(3). Available at: http://ojin.nursingworld.org/MainMenuCategories/ANAMarketplace/ ANAPeriodicals/OJIN/TableofContents/Volume122007/No3Sept07/NursingQual ityIndicators.aspx (Accessed 27 May 2021).

National Academy of Medicine. (2021). Future of nursing 2020–2030: Charting a path to achieve health equity. Available at: https://nam.edu/publications/the -future-of-nursing-2020-2030/ (Accessed 26 May 2021).

National Council of State Boards of Nursing. (2020). *Promoting the role of the nurse with a unique nurse identifier.* Available at: https://www.ncsbn.org/L2L _Fall2019.pdf (Accessed 8 December 2020).

National Council of State Boards of Nursing. (2021). *The national nursing database.* Available at: https://www.ncsbn.org/national-nursing-database.htm (Accessed 29 July 2021).

Nursing Knowledge: Big Data Science Initiative. (2020). *Nursing knowledge: Big data science conference proceedings.* Available at: https://www.nursing.umn .edu/sites/nursing.umn.edu/files/nkbds_proceedings_2020.pdf (Accessed 26 May 2021).

Nursys. (2021). *About nursys.* Available at: https://www.nursys.com/About.aspx (Accessed 6 June 2021).

Office of the National Coordinator for Health Information Technology. (2017). *Standard nursing terminologies: A landscape analysis.* MBL Technologies,

Clinovations. Available at: https://www.healthit.gov/sites/default/files/snt_final _05302017.pdf (Accessed 27 May 2021).

Rutherford, M. (2010). The valuation of nursing begins with identifying value drivers. *Journal of Nursing Administration*, 40(3), pp.115–120. https://doi.org/10 .1097/NNA.0b013e3181d04297

Sensmeier, J., & Carroll, W. (2021). Improving patient outcomes through sharable, comparable nursing data through use of a unique nurse identifier. *CIN: Computers, Informatics, Nursing*, 39(2), pp.61–62.

Sensmeier, J., Androwich, I. M., Baernholdt, M., Carroll, W. M., Fields, W., Fong, V., Murphy, J., Omery, A., & Rajwany, N. (2019). Demonstrating the value of nursing care through use of a unique nurse identifier. *Online Journal of Nursing Informatics*, 23(2). Available at: https://www.himss.org/resources/demonstrating-value-nursing-care-through-use-unique-nurse-identifier (Accessed 27 May 2021).

Welton, J., & Harper, E. (2015). Nursing care value-based financial models. *Nursing Economics*, 33(1), 1, pp.14–19, 25.

Werley, H. (1988). Introduction to the nursing minimum data set and its development. In H. Werley, & N. Lang, eds., *Identification of the nursing minimum data set*. New York: Springer, pp.1–15.

Chapter 5

Impact of Social Media on Health: An Asian Perspective

Chiyoung Cha and Suhyun Park

Contents

DOI: 10.4324/9781003281047-5

Introduction

Social Media in Our Daily Life

With the rapid diffusion of Internet communication technologies, social media has penetrated our daily lives. However, there is no clear way to define what is 'social media.' This chapter considers social media to have the following common characteristics: (1) interactive Web 2.0 Internet-based applications; (2) user-generated content, i.e., text posts or comments, digital photos or videos, and data generated through all online interactions; (3) service-specific profiles that are designed and maintained by a social media organization and (4) online social networks that connect a user's profile with those of other individuals or groups (Obar & Wildman, 2015).

Social media platforms, such as *Facebook* and *Twitter*, mainly contain text and image files. With its evolution, various types of new platforms have emerged to serve different purposes. The newer social media applications have opted to change from the existing 'text/picture-oriented' forms to 'audio/video oriented' forms, which are easier to understand. Other notable trends of current social media could be categorized as asynchronized to synchronized—individual-produced to public-produced, permanent to temporal and non-filtered to filtered. These latest trends in social media are combined to form a variety of interaction types. For example, blogging or microblogging is a typical form of social media that allows people to interact with each other based on web based text, images and videos. In this asynchronous communication, a provider and a beneficiary of information can be clearly distinguished. In most cases, the subject of the text acts as a provider of information, while an unspecified majority will be the beneficiary. Recently, live-streaming, content creators connect with their audience in a synchronized way and gain immediate reactions. For example, *Twitter, Facebook, YouTube, Instagram* and *Tumblr* have recently added live-streaming services and, accordingly, have widened their users worldwide. *Clubhouse*, an auditory-based social media, is quickly gaining popularity worldwide as of 2021 (Strielkowski, 2021). The audio-only application hosts virtual rooms for live discussions, with opportunities for individuals to be the content creators and, at the same time, the consumers. Temporary videos or images, usually called 'stories,' are another distinguished trending feature. Stories in *Instagram* and *Snapchat* last for a certain period, after which they disappear by default. Filters with augmented reality (AR), which is an enhanced experience of the real world through digital elements (Investopedia, 2020) in social media, have also provided a fun aspect to smartphone users. For example, *Snapchat*, which proactively adopted AR, has gained more than 170 million daily users as of June 2020 (Matney, 2020). *TikTok* also delivers the ability to create AR videos using numerous filters and enhanced visual effects, where people can add a beard, change their gender or turn their face into a baby. It is now possible to make virtual works of art using this technology on reality-based images.

Social Media and Health Behaviors

Social media in its different forms has deeply amalgamated into the public's daily lives, determining the types of health information that people receive and influencing their health behaviors. This connection has deepened during the COVID-19 pandemic. When the unexpected pandemic hit, there was little reliable information. People turned to social media because it was the most easily accessible information outlet and provided the most up-to-date information. To some extent, social media exposure enhanced the public's COVID-19-related preventive behavior (Li & Liu, 2020; Liu et al., 2020) because people were able to get the latest information on infection control regulations.

Although the information people put on social media might not reflect their actual health behavior in real life (Roundtree, 2017), its influence on health and health behavior cannot be underestimated. The use of social media stands out in Asian countries, as Asia consumes social media to a high degree (Digital Marketing Institute, 2019). In South Korea, the monthly active users of *KakaoTalk*, a mobile messaging application, averaged 46 million in early 2021 (Kakao Corp, 2021). Similarly, in China, 73.7% of messaging users are on *WeChat* (Statista Research Department, 2020). *Line* is another popular mobile messaging application having 21 million users in Taiwan, 47 million in Thailand (Business.of Apps, 2020) and 84 million in Japan (Digital Marketing for Asia, 2020). These examples show how extensively social media is used throughout Asia, and thus, their importance to health information and health behavior.

Social Media and Health Information

Health Information on Social Media

A tremendous amount of health information is produced through social media by laypersons, health professionals and governmental bodies.

Additionally, artificial intelligence (AI) is a newly emerging source of health information on social media.

Prior to social media, health information from non-professionals used to be shared within the family and circle of friends. Nowadays, with the emergence of personal media such as *YouTube*, narratives on health and illness have become easy to find and retrieve. For numerous reasons ranging from care access to distrust of the health system, many people seek and rely on these personal postings as their primary source of information. Personal stories of health and illness experiences in easy-to-understand language provide useful real-life health information and the trial and errors in dealing with health issues. People empathize with these personal stories and those with similar health issues take consolation from them. One example of this is a *YouTube* content creator named Saebuk (Dawn in English), who has about 65,000 subscribers. Saebuk is a young woman who shared her experiences of fighting lymphoma, such as being hospitalized, getting chemotherapy, losing her hair and getting a wig, for more than a year until she passed away. Lymphoma is not a common disease in South Korea, especially for young women. For rare diseases or health conditions like Saebuk's, health information combined with real-life experiences can be valuable. In addition, stories of illness experiences by social media can reduce the stigma imposed on certain diseases.

Obtaining health information from non-professionals, however, often leads to credibility issues. A recent study on the analysis of *YouTube* content about spinal cord stimulation revealed that about three-quarters of the videos produced by laypersons were misleading (Langford et al., 2021). It could damage public health when the information is dealt with an unscientific approach or when the public tries to generalize their own health experiences.

Recently, health professionals and healthcare institutes have been actively delivering health information to the public through social media. As of April 2021, of the 44 certified tertiary hospitals in South Korea, 41 have at least one social media profile, in addition to their websites. The total number of social media channels handled by tertiary hospitals was less than four on average. *Naver* was the most frequently used social media platform and is a popular search engine in South Korea as well, with variations in social media channels as *Naver Café, Naver BAND, Naver Post, Naver TV,* and messenger *Line* (63 social media channels using *Naver* platform among 44 tertiary hospitals). *YouTube* (36 tertiary hospitals, average subscribers: 17,699) was the second most popular social media, followed by *Facebook*

(32 tertiary hospitals, average followers: 12,758), *Twitter* (12 tertiary hospitals), *Instagram* (11 tertiary hospitals) and *Kakao*, which includes *KakaoTalk Channel* and *KakaoTV* (8 tertiary hospitals). The contents of the social media run by health professionals focus on medical information such as causes of diseases, preventive methods, symptom management and treatment options. Health information shared by health providers through social media expands access to reliable health information to the public. However, most social media that produce health information are one-way communication channels, mostly asynchronized. Thus, there is a risk that laypersons might interpret given health information differently, which could lead to inappropriate health behaviors. Also, people cannot completely rely on this general health information as it is designed for the entire population, and what an individual often needs is tailored health information.

The use of social media by governmental bodies grew with the emergence of COVID-19. For April 2021, South Korea's Center for Disease and Control (CDC) uploaded slightly less than six *Facebook* posts daily, including holidays: from January to March 2021, the posts averaged 4.35, 5.96 and 6.03, respectively (see Table 5.1). From January to April 2021, health systems mostly posted COVID-19-related content exclusively (93.0–97.2%) on their social media site (https://www.facebook.com/koreadca). These COVID-19 postings covered live, daily briefings on statistics for new cases, deaths, test positive rates by locale, vaccination information, infection control guidelines and screening tests availability. With the beginning of vaccination drives in February 2021, vaccine-related posts increased from 6 in January to 42 in February and 34 in each March and April. It is interesting that although COVID-19 has prevailed for over a year and a half at the date of this writing,

Table 5.1   Contents of the Information Posted on the Korea CDC *Facebook* in 2021

Contents of posting	January	February	March	April
COVID-19 statistics	120	114	127	126
COVID-19 vaccination	6	42	34	34
COVID-19 screening test	1	0	0	1
COVID-19 infection control	0	5	12	10
Other COVID-19-related information	0	1	1	0
Microdust	6	5	13	5
Total number of postings	133	168	187	176

most of the content from Korea's CDC is still related to COVID-19. From January through April 2021, the number of people who clicked the 'Like' button for the posts was 52.85~67.70 on average per post, comments ranged from 4.08~13.65, and sharing of the posts was at 9.66~13.65 times per post. Korea's CDC worked hard to provide consistent information on COVID-19. The CDCs in Taiwan and China, as well as other Asian countries also use social media to provide up-to-date information on infection control. The CDC in Taiwan uses *Line* to update information on COVID-19 every day (Taiwan Centers for Disease Control, 2020), while the Thai CDC posts short updates via videos on *Facebook* (@thaihealth).

The accumulation of data on social media further provides materials for AI-based algorithms to produce health information, especially since people post detailed personal health information. For example, a study on a *Twitter* discourse about depression revealed that people detailed their depression experiences on social media, such as their daily feelings, changes in medication and visits to their doctors (Park et al., 2013). Additionally, the recent trends of open data sources from healthcare organizations or research centers (i.e., WHO, CDC and data.gov) make more data available for AI machine learning, and thus, more opportunities to produce accurate health information. Certain information can be searchable by topic, region and other factors.

Health Information Seeking and Sharing through Social Media

With increased health information being produced on social media, many people seek health information here. A recent study revealed that over half the people diagnosed with Crohn's disease in China utilized *Baidu* (65%) and *WeChat* (61%) when searching for disease-related information (Yu et al., 2019). People with Crohn's disease in China reported receiving not only informational support but also emotional and peer support from social media (Zhao et al., 2021). Sharing health-related information through social media may lead to changes in health behavior. For example, *WeChat*-based information sharing has increased the knowledge and awareness of edible oils in China (Zhu et al., 2018). Also, Cao and colleagues note that active engagement in social media among men who have sex with men has been associated with a recent increase in HIV testing (Cao et al., 2017).

When a social issue is raised, the entirety of social media sites is quickly flooded with information. With the COVID-19 pandemic, we witnessed a deluge of information, personal to professional, accurate as well as inaccurate, fact-based science to conspiracy theories pore into social media sites, creating what is being termed as an 'infodemic' (Depoux et al., 2020). An infodemic situation is critical because it can strongly influence people's behavior and further alter the effectiveness of the action plans deployed by public health organizations (Cinelli et al., 2020). Emotions such as anger combined with fake information are spread and accepted as facts by the public (Han et al., 2020). Some studies contend that fake news and misinformation may spread faster and wider than fact-based news (Cha et al., 2021; Vosoughi et al., 2018). At the same time, social media could serve as filtration in the flood of information to preemptively react to infodemics. To preemptively prevent an infodemic, social media surveillance is seen as the best method to track rumors in real time and to be able to counter false information timely (Islam et al., 2020). The Institute for Basic Science in South Korea initiated a campaign called 'Facts Before Rumors,' wherein they compiled over 200 rumors related to COVID-19 in the early phase of the pandemic and categorized them by 15 claims based on their similarities. Among these, only three were confirmed as fact-based news (IBS Data Science Group, 2020) (see Figure 5.1). While the COVID-19 pandemic made it clear that the real-time accumulation of social media data can serve as a starting point for effective communication systems planning, it appears that healthcare entities will continue to monitor public conversation through social media as a tool to inform their communication strategies (Park et al., 2020).

Role of Social Media on Health and Health Behavior

Response to Disaster and Crisis

Because social media can reach a massive population in an instant, it can also serve to monitor disease outbreaks and respond to community health crises. Social media can be used to provide timely information to an unspecified majority as well as to a targeted segment of the population. An example is the tracking of COVID-19 in South Korea. The tracking starts with an extensive, technology-based, contact tracing that identifies the recent movements of the confirmed patients. The data are anonymized, limited in duration and scope, and carefully disclosed to the public, which others can use to determine whether they may have had contact with any confirmed case. To explain, based on information on the location and time of the person who had a positive result, messages were provided to residents in

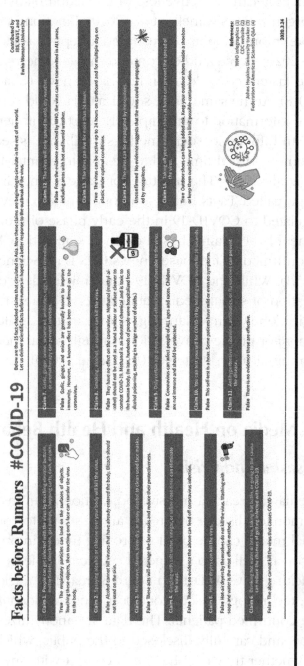

Figure 5.1   Facts Before Rumors project to preemptively respond to infodemic.

neighboring areas to disclose the route and to be inspected if the route over-laps. The identity of the person was kept private, minimizing the invasion of privacy. This tracking information is easily accessible through websites, smartphones or radio. In addition, it could track people who might have stayed in places where the COVID-19 patient stopped over to get *KakaoTalk* messages or to be tested for COVID-19.

With the analysis of social media content, specific health crises can be identified at a national level. South Korea has one of the highest suicide rates (Kim, 2020). A research team analyzed social media and identified patterns for search terms used by teenagers and adults. Teenagers tend to search for stress and move onto sports, drinking and suicide, while adults search for drinking before searching for suicide (Song et al., 2013). Based on the daily screening of frequent search terms from social media, preven-tive measures were designed to reach those at risk through public health advertisements and counseling services. Social media can also be helpful as a tool to encourage people to reach out to others during crises. Hanam City in South Korea uses *Instagram* to run crisis management programs target-ing COVID-19 pandemic response personnel. When people report anxiety, depression and burnout on a questionnaire via URL and QR code presented to the *Instagram* post, the city sends out burnout kits and lists of its 113 counseling institutes (@hajeongsen).

Support for Community Health

Social media has the advantage of quickly reaching out to wide audiences in a short time, and thus, can be used to advertise community health services and promote client engagement. Although public services provided through social media are hard to measure due to anonymity, evidence of its effective-ness is increasing and a valuable tool for specific population groups.

The Ministry of Health and Welfare in South Korea conducted various campaigns to improve physical activity and reduce alcohol consump-tion and cigarette smoking. During the COVID-19 pandemic in 2020, as people's physical activity decreased, Muju City ran a '10,000 steps per day for 60 days' project. Community members who joined the walking club posted their daily steps on the band. During the first term between June and August 2020, 151 community members participated; 23 com-munity members (15.23%) had completed the task and 88 (58.28%) had completed their tasks for 70.00% of the intervention period. For the sec-ond term between September and November, participating community members increased to 200; 40 community members (20.00%) completed the task and 108 (54.00%) had completed their task for over 70% of the time. Gunsan City runs an online community which enrolls 400 over-weight citizens annually to manage body weight. The program includes checks on body fat, diet menu plans, walking programs and exercise pre-scriptions. All these community-based health initiatives are done through social media platforms.

The Ministry of Health and Welfare held a contest on *Facebook* to mark the *World No Smoking Day* that encourages people to stop smoking by seeing the habit from children's perspectives. People were encouraged to film videos that contained children's answers to questions such as 'What are cigarettes?' or 'Why does your father smoke?'(Ministry of Health and Welfare of South Korea, 2016). A study from Hong Kong revealed that people use *WhatsApp* and *Facebook* social groups to assist in break-ing the smoking habit. These applications provide a valuable platform for cessation support and encouragement to report abstinence (Cheung et al., 2017).

Another example is the *Restart* campaign to reduce alcohol consumption. People who posted images or videos about doing group activities rather than drinking together on their social network services were randomly drawn and presented with rewards (Korea Health Promotion Institute, 2018). Another example is from the Pakistan Ministry of National Health Service who partnered with *Facebook* to address their citizen's misconceptions about the blood donation process. The result was an increase in voluntary blood donations and over 5 million registered blood donors as of June 2020 (Pakistan's Ministry of Health, 2020). These outcomes demonstrate the effi-cacy of using social media platforms as an outreach tool.

Enhance the Delivery of Care

Social media can also be used to promote client engagement in the pro-cess of disease management. By providing people with an easily accessible venue to participate in their healthcare virtually, social media applications such as *Microsoft Teams* and *Zoom* allow direct provider/patient communica-tion and facilitate access to care and treatment. In China, researchers inves-tigated whether patient education using social media increases the quality of bowel preparation before colonoscopy. In one study, *WeChat* was used along with standard education, and it turned out that patients who received social media instruction had better bowel preparation than the control group

(Kang et al., 2016). Wang and colleagues also assessed the effect of *WeChat* and short message service (SMS) on the bowel preparation for colonoscopy. Patients in intervention groups received education and reminder messages through *WeChat* and SMS before colonoscopy. The authors reported that adequate bowel preparation rates were the highest in the group who received messages through *WeChat*, followed by the group who received SMS, with the control group having the lowest rate (Wang et al., 2019).

Social media has also been used to manage mental health symptoms. Because face-to-face interactions were discouraged during the COVID-19 outbreak, social media was used as a useful channel to provide support. During the COVID-19 outbreak, many people were quarantined and experienced Corona blue (depressive feeling due to self-isolation and social distancing). In China, *WeChat* was used to provide support for individuals who stayed in quarantine wards in tertiary hospitals (Zhou et al., 2020). In this study, *WeChat*-based, interactive, individual counseling was provided for emotional and material support based on the patients' needs. Zhou and colleagues reported that patients in the study felt relieved and took COVID-19 more seriously after the intervention. In South Korea, UiWang city utilized *Instagram* (@sesimhan_uiwang) to communicate with those who were experiencing Corona blue. The city's posts received attention and in less than two months, residents posted more than 2,000 reviews sharing how they managed their health problems, such as their strategies to overcome insomnia and obesity.

Social media can also be an effective means to deliver care for the hard-to-reach population. Many people in Asian cultures miss the opportunities to receive appropriate care because they have difficulty disclosing their mental health issues due to cultural stigma. In Japan, online chat services for those who experienced depressive symptoms were used so that people who do not want to reveal their mental health issues could get help (Tokyo Mental Health Square, n.d.). In South Korea, social media was used to deliver counseling services to nurses, one of the hard-to-reach groups, as most nurses work 8-hour shifts. The researchers found that nurses who received cognitive behavioral therapy through *KakaoTalk* reported higher scores on sleep quality and quality of life than nurses who did not receive any intervention (Kim & Kim, 2017).

We are also beginning to see instances in which social media is used to aid the management of a specific disease. In China, *WeChat* was used for cardiac rehabilitation and controlling blood pressure compared to the usual care group (Chen et al., 2020). In South Korea, mobile instant messenger was reported to be effective in alleviating the anxiety of parents and compliance rate among children who underwent tonsillectomy (Yu & Kim, 2019).

Generation of Nursing Knowledge

Social media permeates our daily lives (i.e., *Facebook, Twitter, Instagram*). Although there are reports of nurses being hesitant to trust information on social media (Cha & Park, 2021), it has been reported that one out of five nurses in Israel acquired health information for personal needs on social media platforms (Zigdon et al., 2020). Another survey from Wang and colleagues reported that 84.5% of the registered nurses in China believe that social media had positively influenced their clinical practice. *WeChat* was the most frequently used social media platform, and it was used for receiving messages from work, networking, receiving news and relaxing. In addition, the researchers found that most nurses had reposted medical information on social media and shared the information retrieved from social media with their colleagues (Wang et al., 2019).

Alongside this trend, social media is increasingly finding a role in research. While traditional ways to recruit research participants can be geographically biased, pricey and time consuming, the use of social media in the recruitment stage supports effective, time- and resource-efficient research (McRobert et al., 2018). For example, the Korean Nurses' Health Study (Kim et al., 2017), a national cohort study to identify the determinants of women's health, has used social media to follow up with study participants since 2012. Use of social media in real time and recording individual and focus group interviews would be convenient and simultaneously prevent loss of data.

Social media can also serve as a delivery method for nursing interventions, and therefore monitor the target populations' health at the same time (Jackson et al., 2014). Using social media tools to connect with rare or hard-to-reach populations could also make it possible to offer them protected care services. For example, sexual violence survivors are still victimized and stigmatized in Asian societies: because no one speaks about their experiences, sexual violence survivors have little information on the healing process. The 'Sister, I will tell you!' program in South Korea includes storytelling of the survivors' healing experiences accompanied by mindful meditation designed for the purpose. The program's pilot study revealed that social media was effective in providing healing experiences to sexual assault survivors (Lee & Cha, 2021).

The Future

Need for Systemic Support for Utilizing Social Media for Care Delivery

The emergence of COVID-19 has explosively accelerated our dependence on social media, especially concerning health information. However, we learned that the speed and degree with which health information spread has little to do with the quality of that information. For example, uncensored misinformation surged in the mainstream, social media post-COVID-19. Little could be done to prevent the spread of health-related misinformation on social media. Thus, health professionals and health authorities proactively used strategies to share qualified health information. Hauer and Sood (2020) suggested seven strategies for using social media and curtailing misinformation: framing risk to promote preventive measures and reduce panic; engage online influencers; amplify the voices of experts; craft messages for lay audiences; create interactive forums where the public can access up-to-date information; be honest about what is known and unknown; have media and information literacy; and use recommended hashtags in posts for dissemination. In the post-COIVD-19 era, communicating with the public through social media has become an important role of health professionals, public health and government bodies.

For frontline nurses, it is crucial to have reliable information outlets to provide patients with appropriate care. However, there are few guidelines on how healthcare professionals should disseminate information on these platforms (Maben-Feaster et al., 2018). The American Nurses Association has established principles for using social media, as follows: (1) Nurses must not transmit or place individually identifiable patient information online. (2) Nurses must observe ethically prescribed professional patient–nurse boundaries. (3) Nurses should understand that patients, colleagues, organizations and employers may view posts. (4) Nurses should take advantage of privacy settings and seek to separate personal and professional information online. (5) Nurses should bring content that could harm a patient's privacy, rights or welfare to the attention of appropriate authorities. (6) Nurses should participate in developing organizational policies governing online conduct (American Nurses Association, n.d.). The National Council of State Boards of Nursing (2012) also provided similar guidelines with detailed explanations and examples for nurses. However, there is still a lack of official guidelines in many countries that are specific to nurses. Professional nursing organizations should take the lead in developing guidelines for disseminating nursing knowledge and utilizing social media in nursing work (Burton et al., 2016). As nurses account for the largest part of health professionals, their actions through social network services have significant power. Thus, clear and focused guidelines for nursing professionals are a key to enabling the dissemination of nursing knowledge and advanced education to a wide audience.

The World of the Metaverse in Healthcare

An increasing number of people engage in social interactions and extend themselves to social virtual reality (VR), a shared virtual environment. People in social VR have the perception of being and responding to each other in a realistic manner (Slater, 2009). In a virtual world, the way of interaction will expand and change dramatically, similar to what has happened with social media. The form of social media in the metaverse, which is a virtually shared space including objects, inhabitants and their relationships with a virtually defined time and largely synonymous, three-dimensional (3D) interactive environment (Web Archive of IEEE VW Standard Working Group, 2014) would be in a narrative story form rather than posting information in a text. For example, with the disappearance of time and space limitations, social interaction could occur on a large scale, through the broadcast of such social interaction itself. Traditionally, defined face-to-face interventions, such as cognitive-behavioral therapy, storytelling and mindfulness interventions, might be optimized in the metaverse, where illness experiences and medical treatment experiences can be shared in VR form. The role of social media on health will be more dominant as it evolves in a metaverse. VR in a metaverse form stands to expand the population who consumes health information beyond that of traditional social media because it diminishes language barriers and increases accessibility.

References

American Nurses Association. (n.d.). *Social media.* Available at: https://www.nursingworld.org/social/ (Accessed 22 May 2021).
Burton, C. W., McLemore, M. R., Perry, L., Carrick, J., & Shattell, M. (2016). Social media awareness and implications in nursing leadership: A pilot professional meeting campaign. *Policy, Politics, and Nursing Practice*, 17(4), pp.187–197. https://doi.org/10.1177/1527154417698143

Business of Apps. (2020). *Line revenue and usage statistics.* Available at: https://www.businessofapps.com/data/line-statistics/#4 (Accessed 28 May 2021).

Cao, B., Liu, C., Durvasula, M., Tang, W., Pan, S., Saffer, A. J., Wei, C., & Tucker, J. D. (2017). Social media engagement and HIV testing among men who have sex with men in China: A nationwide cross-sectional survey. *Journal of Medical Internet Research,* 19(7), pp.1–13. https://doi.org/10.2196/jmir.7251

Cha, C., & Park, S. (2021). Information flow and nursing care during the early phase of the COVID-19 pandemic. *Journal of Clinical Nursing,* in press, [published online ahead of print]. https://doi.org/10.1111/jocn.15898

Cha, M. et al. (2021). Prevalence of misinformation and fact checks on the COVID-19 pandemic in 35 countries: Observational infodemiology study. *JMIR Human Factors,* 8(1), pp.1–6. https://doi.org/10.2196/23279

Chen, S. et al. (2020). Characteristics and requirements of hypertensive patients willing to use digital health tools in the Chinese community: A multicentre cross-sectional survey. *BMC Public Health,* 20(1), pp.1–7. https://doi.org/10.1186/s12889-020-09462-2

Cheung, Y. T. D. et al. (2017). Online social support for the prevention of smoking relapse: A content analysis of the WhatsApp and Facebook social groups. *Telemedicine and e-Health,* 23(6), pp.507–516. https://doi.org/10.1089/tmj.2016.0176

Cinelli, M. et al. (2020). The COVID-19 social media infodemic. *Scientific Reports,* 10(1), pp.1–10. https://doi.org/10.1038/s41598-020-73510-5

Depoux, A. et al. (2020). The pandemic of social media panic travels faster than the COVID-19 outbreak. *Journal of Travel Medicine,* 27(3), pp.1–2. https://doi.org/10.1093/jtm/taaa031

Digital Marketing for Asia. (2020). *A complete guide to social media in Japan.* Available at: https://www.digitalmarketingforasia.com/a-complete-guide-to-social-media-in-japan/ (Accessed 28 May 2021).

Digital Marketing Institute. (2019). *Social media: What countries use it most & what are they using?* Available at: https://digitalmarketinginstitute.com/blog/social-media-what-countries-use-it-most-and-what-are-they-using (Accessed 16 June 2021).

Han, J., Cha, M. and Lee, W. (2020). Anger contributes to the spread of COVID-19 misinformation. *Harvard Kennedy School Misinformation Review,* 1(September), pp.1–14. https://doi.org/10.37016/mr-2020-39

Hauer, M. K., & Sood, S. (2020). Using social media to communicate sustainable preventive measures and curtail misinformation. *Frontiers in Psychology,* 11(October), pp.1–6. https://doi.org/10.3389/fpsyg.2020.568324

IBS Data Science Group. (2020). *Facts before rumors.* Available at: https://ds.ibs.re.kr/fbr/ (Accessed 22 May 2021).

Investopedia. (2020). *What is augmented reality?* Available at: https://www.investopedia.com/terms/a/augmented-reality.asp (Accessed 14 June 2021).

Islam, M. S. et al. (2020). COVID-19-related infodemic and its impact on public health: A global social media analysis. *American Journal of Tropical Medicine and Hygiene,* 103(4), pp.1621–1629. https://doi.org/10.4269/ajtmh.20-0812

Jackson, J., Fraser, R., & Ash, P. (2014). Social media and nurses: Insights for promoting health for individual and professional use. *The Online Journal of Issues in Nursing*, 19(3), p.Manuscript 2. https://doi.org/10.3912/OJIN .Vol19No03Man02

Kakao Corp. (2021). *2021 2nd Quarter earnings report*. Available at: https://www .kakaocorp.com/ir/referenceRoom/earningsAnnouncement?selectedYear=2021 (Accessed 12 Aug 2021).

Kang, X. et al. (2016). Delivery of instructions via mobile social media app increases quality of bowel preparation. *Clinical Gastroenterology and Hepatology*, 14(3), pp.429-435.e3. https://doi.org/10.1016/j.cgh.2015.09.038

Kim, A. M. (2020). Factors associated with the suicide rates in Korea. *Psychiatry Research*, 284(December 2019), p.112745. https://doi.org/10.1016/j.psychres.2020 .112745

Kim, J. E., & Kim, S. S. (2017). The effects of mobile social networking service-based cognitive behavior therapy on insomnia in nurses. *Journal of Korean Academy of Nursing*, 47(4), pp.476–487. https://doi.org/10.4040/jkan.2017.47.4.476

Kim, O. et al. (2017). The Korea nurses' health study: A prospective cohort study. *Journal of Women's Health*, 26(8), pp.892–899. https://doi.org/10.1089/jwh.2016 .6048

Korea Health Promotion Institute. (2018). *Restart*. Available at: https://www.khealth .or.kr/board/view?pageNum=1&rowCnt=10&no1=1&linkId=998611&menuId =MENU01178&schType=1&schText=절주 인증샷&boardStyle=&categoryId=&co ntinent=&country=&contents1= (Accessed 21 May 2021).

Langford, B. et al. (2021). YouTube as a source of medical information about spinal cord stimulation. *Neuromodulation*, 24(1), pp.156–161. https://doi.org/10.1111/ ner.13303

Lee, M. R., & Cha, C. (2021). A mobile healing program using virtual reality for sexual violence survivors: A randomized controlled pilot study. *Worldviews on Evidence-Based Nursing*, 18(1), pp.50–59. https://doi.org/10.1111/wvn.12478

Li, X., & Liu, Q. (2020). Social media use, eHealth literacy, disease knowledge, and preventive behaviors in the COVID-19 pandemic: Cross-sectional study on Chinese netizens. *Journal of Medical Internet Research*, 22(10), p.e19684. https://doi.org/10.2196/19684

Liu, L. et al. (2020). Exploring how media influence preventive behavior and excessive preventive intention during the COVID-19 pandemic in China. *International Journal of Environmental Research and Public Health*, 17(21), pp.1–27. https://doi.org/10.3390/ijerph17217990

Maben-Feaster, R. E. et al. (2018). Evaluating patient perspectives of provider professionalism on twitter in an academic obstetrics and gynecology clinic: Patient survey. *Journal of Medical Internet Research*, 20(3), pp.1–7. https://doi .org/10.2196/jmir.8056

Matney, L. (2020). *Snapchat boosts its AR platform with voice search, local lenses and SnapML*. Available at: https://techcrunch.com/2020/06/11/snapchat-boosts -its-ar-platform-with-voice-search-local-lenses-and-snapml/ (Accessed 21 May 2021).

McRobert, C. J. et al. (2018). A multi-modal recruitment strategy using social media and internet-mediated methods to recruit a multidisciplinary, international sample of clinicians to an online research study. *PLoS ONE*, 13(7), pp.1–17. https://doi.org/10.1371/journal.pone.0200184

Ministry of Health and Welfare of South Korea. (2016). *Nonsmoking campaign.* Available at: https://www.facebook.com/events/135267410213714/ (Accessed 22 May 2021).

The National Council of State Boards of Nursing. (2012). *Social media guidelines.* Available at: https://www.ncsbn.org/transcript_SocialMediaGuidelines.pdf (Accessed 22 May 2021).

Obar, J. A., & Wildman, S. (2015). Social media definition and the governance challenge: An introduction to the special issue. *Telecommunications Policy*, 39(9), pp.745–750. https://doi.org/10.1016/j.telpol.2015.07.014

Pakistan's Ministry of Health. (2020). *Pakistan's ministry of health boosts voluntary blood donations with facebook's blood donations feature.* Available at: https://socialimpact.facebook.com/success-stories/pakistans-ministry-of-health-boosts-voluntary-blood-donations-with-facebooks-blood-donations-feature/ (Accessed 22 May 2021).

Park, H. W., Park, S., & Chong, M. (2020). Conversations and medical news frames on twitter: Infodemiological study on COVID-19 in South Korea. *Journal of Medical Internet Research*, 22(5), p.e18897. https://doi.org/10.2196/18897

Park, M., Cha, C., & Cha, M. (2013). Depressive moods of users portrayed in Twitter. *Telecommunications Review*, 23, pp.304–316.

Roundtree, A. K. (2017). Social health content and activity on facebook: A survey study. *Journal of Technical Writing and Communication*, 47(3), pp.300–329. https://doi.org/10.1177/0047281616641925

Slater, M. (2009). Place illusion and plausibility can lead to realistic behaviour in immersive virtual environments. *Philosophical Transactions of the Royal Society B: Biological Sciences*, 364(1535), pp.3549–3557. https://doi.org/10.1098/rstb.2009.0138

Song, T. M. et al. (2013). Multivariate analysis of factors for search on suicide using social Big Data. *Korean Journal of Health Education Promotion*, 30(3), pp.59–73.

Statista Research Department. (2020). *China's mobile social media landscape 2019 published by Lai Lin Thomala, Aug 20, 2020 China's social media landscape is becoming more diversified. Tencent's WeChat still remains as the most popular mobile social media platform with 73.7 percent of respond.* Available at: https://www.statista.com/statistics/1069879/china-popular-social-media-platforms/ (Accessed 28 May 2021).

Strielkowski, W. (2021). *Clubhouse: Yet another social network?* Available at: SSRN 3832599 (Accessed 12 August 2021).

Taiwan Centers for Disease Control. (2020). *In response to the Wuhan pneumonia epidemic, line@疾管家 provides public interaction and consultation functions. people are welcome to use it.* Available at: https://www.cdc.gov.tw/Bulletin/Detail/0so3QVAZEqwADcevX04G9Q?typeid=9&fbclid=IwAR1s2PVnYY2447bVcsGuJrpesH79VZ6qXS3VwAKaF__cV4NJXHSUovoqyck (Accessed 16 June 2021).

Tokyo Mental Health Square. (n.d.) *Counseling and free trouble consultation.* Available at: https://www.npo-tms.or.jp/ (Accessed 22 May 2021).

Vosoughi, S., Roy, D., & Aral, S. (2018). The spread of true and false news online. *Science*, 359(6380), pp.1146–1151. https://doi.org/10.1126/science.aap9559

Wang, S. L. et al. (2019). Effect of WeChat and short message service on bowel preparation: An endoscopist-blinded, randomized controlled trial. *European Journal of Gastroenterology and Hepatology*, 31(2), pp.170–177. https://doi.org/10.1097/MEG.0000000000001303

Wang, Z. et al. (2019). Social media usage and online professionalism among registered nurses: A cross-sectional survey. *International Journal of Nursing Studies*, 98, pp.19–26. https://doi.org/10.1016/j.ijnurstu.2019.06.001

Web Archive of IEEE VW Standard Working Group. (2014). *Metaverse standards overview.* Available at: https://web.archive.org/web/20140608135859/http://www.metaversestandards.org/index.php?title=Main_Page#Category (Accessed 11 August 2021).

Yu, K. E., & Kim, J. S. (2019). Effects of a posttonsillectomy management program using a mobile instant messenger on parents' knowledge and anxiety, and their children's compliance, bleeding, and pain. *Journal for Specialists in Pediatric Nursing*, 24(4), p.e12270. https://doi.org/10.1111/jspn.12270

Yu, Q. et al. (2019). Internet and WeChat used by patients with Crohn's disease in China: A multi-center questionnaire survey. *BMC Gastroenterology*, 19(1), pp.1–8. https://doi.org/10.1186/s12876-019-1011-3

Zhao, J. et al. (2021). Health information on social media helps mitigate Crohn's disease symptoms and improves patients' clinical course. *Computers in Human Behavior*, 115(September 2020), p.106588. https://doi.org/10.1016/j.chb.2020.106588

Zhou, L. et al. (2020). Feasibility and preliminary results of effectiveness of social media-based intervention on the psychological well-being of suspected COVID-19 cases during quarantine. *Canadian Journal of Psychiatry*, 65(10), pp.736–738. https://doi.org/10.1177/0706743720932041

Zhu, R. et al. (2018). Decreasing the use of edible oils in China using WeChat and theories of behavior change: Study protocol for a randomized controlled trial. *Trials*, 19(1), pp.1–10. https://doi.org/10.1186/s13063-018-3015-7

Zigdon, A., Zigdon, T., & Moran, D. S. (2020). Attitudes of nurses towards searching online for medical information for personal health needs: Cross-sectional questionnaire study. *Journal of Medical Internet Research*, 22(3), pp.1–11. https://doi.org/10.2196/16133

Chapter 6

Consumer Access and Control of Data, Data Sharing, Consumer Participation

Lisa A. Moon

Contents

DOI: 10.4324/9781003281047-6

Introduction

The modern-day, digital health consumers find themselves at the center of the current data access, control and data sharing conversations through a set of national policies that are driving consumerism in healthcare and data exchange in the United States. The 21st Century Cures Act: Interoperability, Information Blocking, and the Office of the National Coordinator (ONC) Health Information Technology (HIT) Certification Program is a federal statute enacted in 2020 (45 CFR 170). The 21st Century Cures Act has several policies that are shaping consumerism in healthcare and information exchange. The effect of these policies is an emphasis on the individual's role in large, networked environments, as well as a mandate to develop the technologies and data standards needed to support these advanced access and data sharing capabilities. For example, the Trusted Exchange Framework and Common Agreement (TEFCA) (Federal Registry, 2020b) requires that a nationwide governance structure and legal data sharing agreements be designed to scale electronic health information exchange (21st Century Cures Act, Section 4003 (b)(c)). For the first time in history, the national policy framework recognizes the individual as a member of an information exchange ecosystem.

Previously, in the data sharing transaction, individuals were not named or recognized as active participants: they were simply the 'beneficiaries.' In contrast, the 21st Century Cures Act defines the consumer as a mediator of their health data through new technical requirements for patient access using APIs (application programming interfaces), Smart-on-FHIR (Fast Health Interoperability Resources): additionally, the Act includes an unconventional but progressive rule that bans healthcare information blocking from occurring in healthcare (Federal Registry 2020a). Previous statutes and policies encouraged health data to be shared for treatment, payment and operations (Health Information Portability and Accountability Act (HIPAA) and supported patients having access to view, download and transport a copy of their medical record (HIPAA, 1996). However, the HIPAA rules fell short of requiring specific information, data formats or common mechanisms to be used that would make it easy for a consumer to access, control or share their health data.

Technology trends are changing to meet new policies that create opportunities for consumers to access, control and share their health information. Increasingly in healthcare, emerging technologies are moving away from business to consumers (B2C) models and into consumer to business (C2B) models that aim to improve consumer health, engagement and empowerment. The B2C models exchange goods and services direct to consumers (Amazon, Walmart). In contrast, the C2B models allow consumers to be influencers; in some cases, a consumer can receive a commission for their insights and demand is driven by consumer requests for certain services or products. Through consumers answering basic sets of questions, healthcare organizations can tailor their interaction with patients and their caregivers. That means that healthcare C2B models are 'customized to me.' The needs of the individual end-user determine what the service looks like making innovation part of the goal. Healthcare is experiencing a shift into C2B through telemedicine, mobile, on-demand consumer health applications (apps) and behavior modification tools (NOOM; Livongo, 2021). The 21st Century Cures Act and related policies open up endless possibilities to a future where consumers and their input become key to future proofing new innovations and products. Ease of use of these new consumer-oriented apps will ensure consumer adoption with gains in self-directed, health promotion and participation in care-as-a-service (CaaS) platforms.

Regulatory Framework for Consumer Access and Control of Data

When technology intersects with consumers and their individually identifiable information, the first questions asked are: 'what about privacy?' and 'what are the "consent" requirements?' HIPAA information privacy, security and breach notification rules, and other regulations like *42 CFR Part 2* (sensitive data related to chemical dependency) form the legal basis of the health data sharing transaction. Information privacy refers to the ability of an individual to prevent certain disclosures of personal health information to any other person or entity (Markel Foundation, 2006; Markel Foundation, 2010). Data security addresses the protective measures (administrative, physical and technical safeguards) that limit or grant access to individually identifiable information based on authorization or permissions according to HIPAA (Rothstein, 2007; U.S. Department of Health & Human Services, 2013). The HIPAA breach notification rule links privacy and security controls to a duty to notify a consumer of the unauthorized access of their protected health information (PHI). Consent is expressed as an informed choice related to the individual's preference to share or withhold health information and specially protected data. Together, the three concepts of privacy, data security and consent are the contemporary underpinnings for trust in electronic health information exchange.

Information Sharing

Health Information Exchange (HIE) research findings have mostly focused on the attitudes, beliefs and perceptions of individuals when questioned about their health information being included in information exchange networks (Moon, 2017). More recent studies have focused on the factors that influence the health data sharing preferences of consumers. Preference is the ability to make a choice where there are alternatives. HIE has mostly operationalized binary consent expressions known as 'Opt-out' (choose to not participate) and 'Opt-in' (choose to participate) (ONC Patient Consent Models, 2020). Opt-out models applied to individually identifiable information mean that all health data belonging to an individual is not included in the network. Thus, when a provider looks for the individual's information, a message will be returned that "no information is found". The individual's information will either be suppressed, or it will not be accepted when message content reaches the HIE. Some have deemed the binary expression of opt-out and opt-in to be an informed choice. Research shows that consumers are influenced by a set of factors in these binary choices. Table 6.1 describes the statistically significant demographic attributes associated with affirmative and negative, health data sharing preferences derived from a critical review of the literature (Moon, 2017).

Cellphones and internet availability have made access to health data more attainable for consumers, though broadband issues do continue to impede some rural areas (Makri, 2019). In the near future, readily available healthcare technology APIs will enable individuals to be data mediators that direct the exchange of their electronic health information. Individuals already perceive that their providers have their health information for care. However, the Health Information National Trends Survey found that consumers also want to control access and determine who, when, for what purpose and for how long their health data are being used (NIH, n.d.; Moon, 2017). This movement toward more detailed or granular choice is also supported by the 21st Century Cures Act. However, the major obstacle to making access control a reality will be feasibility and readiness to support consumer choice and control.

Table 6.1 Statistically Significant Descriptive Characteristics Associated with Health Data Sharing Preferences of Consumers (Moon, 2017)

	Factors associated with affirmative consumer data sharing preferences	*Factors associated with negative consumer data sharing preferences*
Descriptive characteristics	• Age < 40 years • Age > 65 years • Children in household • Caregiver • Education • Employed • Income > 100,000 • Internet use • Male • White, non-Hispanic • Hispanic • Regular utilizers of healthcare	• Age 18–24 years — lack understanding • Age 40 to 65 — managing chronic illness or caregiver • Age > 65 years — managing chronic illness or digital divide • Education < high school • Female • Black and Asian • Non-White, Hispanic and Asian • Healthy individuals • Low Internet use

Access, Control and Choice

Consumers are demanding access, control and choice in sharing and withholding health data. The 21st Century Cures Act includes provisions for patient access to clinical, claims and provider information. There are more than 165,000 mobile health apps available (Kao & Leibovitz, 2017). Most consumer apps are focused on wellness and disease management; but increasingly, consumer applications that aggregate health records are becoming more available. The electronic health record (EHR) endpoints for most data retrievals do not often have data in a format that is interoperable or usable for patient API consumption. This results from immature and/or developing technology, standards and systems. This means that consumers may find that their desire to *access information* in a usable format through APIs, using standardized mechanisms may not be possible currently. This could be the case especially when you consider enabling functions like on-demand *control* of information that is mediated by the consumer to push, pull, query or withhold data. The goal has always been that an individual's health data would move with the consumer on the healthcare continuum with sharing and withholding based on personal *choice*. Consumer consent expression gives *voice* to informed choice, shared decision-making, and recognition of individual preference (Moon, 2017).

The consequence of increased control and choice is that patients begin to act more like consumers of a product, namely care and treatment. While technology is racing to meet the demand of healthcare consumers, funding has not been widely available for building the infrastructure needed. Previously in the Federal Meaningful Use (Promoting Interoperability) Program, funding was associated with new regulations that focused on the digitization of health data (US Department of Health & Human Services, 2014). And yet, funding for the new Patient API rule has not been made available as of this writing. When policy is linked with funding, we see widespread response that drives innovation, adoption and compliance. Without funding, the new Patient API rules may not advance or may require additional enforcement mechanisms to ensure compliance and movement that accomplish the work of clinical, claims and provider data aggregation and availability for consumers. As this transformation evolves, it is essential that we seize the opportunity to study the adoption patterns, end-user experience and widespread implications of consumer access and control of health data in the larger health system and information exchange network. This is essential because technology not used as intended is often abandoned or not adopted by a critical mass of individuals, thereby limiting the full impact of the technical enablement and augmentation of care processes and educational benefit.

With the most recent regulatory changes, individuals are being offered a more prominent role in the management of their health data. The digital health consumer of the future will own, control and produce their health data upon request because they will be the mediators of their protected information. With significant change in policy and legal regulation, consumers will note a shift in the power structures of long-held, health information management practices. The commonly known process of a "release of information" request may soon be outdated as the consumer takes on a more prominent role in data management. This change will signal that consumer mediated data management becomes the primary method consumers use to access their health data.

Data Sharing: Moving from Current to Future State

Safe, secure movement of e-health information ensures that healthcare providers and patients have access to protected health information at the point of care to support clinical decision-making, reduce error and improve health outcomes. Today, information mostly resides in separate databases that are part of EHRs and healthcare information systems (e.g., labs, pharmacy, public health). Interoperability relies on semantic, syntactic and physical interoperability. Semantic interoperability refers to the meaning of data represented in machine-computable logic, inferencing, knowledge discovery and data federation between information systems. Syntactic interoperability is about the message structure and standards needed for the message to be encoded. Physical interoperability, that is data exchange, is the technical mechanism or protocols used to interface and connect information systems so that electronic structured, encoded messages can be moved and shared.

The Office of the National Coordinator recognizes three types of information exchange:

1. Directed Exchange (or Direct Protocol) is a secure, encrypted (rest and transit) email that uses a private and public key and certificates that are identity validated for pushing healthcare data from one organization to another (Direct Project Wiki, 2019).
2. Connect or query-based exchange in healthcare is the open-source protocol used to search and discover accessible clinical sources of information on a patient (Connect Community Portal, 2018; Office of National Coordinator, 2021).
3. Consumer-mediated exchange is the ability of a consumer to manage their data including viewing, downloading and transmitting of their PHI based on their preferences (Williams et. al., 2012).

Directed Exchange is the most widely used form of physical interoperability (ONC, 2019). The sender pushes data to endpoints that are legally and technically connected in the network, and the messages are sent only when there is a provider–patient relationship on file in the reference data management system (Direct Project Wiki, 2019). This ensures that HIPAA relationships are maintained, and individually identifiable information used for treatment, payment and operations are available for providers and healthcare organizations. To accomplish this work, providers and healthcare organizations legally connect using data sharing agreements that include business associate agreements (BAA). Then the provider or healthcare organization will technically connect through a virtual private network (VPN), interface channel, or application programming interface (API) to send and receive health data. Information is mostly sent using Health-Level Seven International (HL7) feeds that include Consolidated Clinical Document

Architecture (C-CDA), Order Result (ORU), Medical Document Management (MDM), Vaccine Record Update (VXU), or Admission, Discharge or Transfer (ADT). Developing standards like Fast Healthcare Interoperability Resources use standardized data packets to move information between known end-points (ONC FHIR Fact Sheets, 2021).

Healthcare Technology Basics and Beyond

Data is transformed through cleansing and normalizing activities in large infrastructures that include an interface and integration engine, router and database at a minimum. For example, when an HL7 message is received into the interface engine, the message is surveyed for demographic data and message type and content. The integration engine receives and processes the message content based on rules that are on file in the rule's engine. The integration engine checks that consent to share is on file, and then runs business rules against the message content for use cases that are in the production environment. The router sends the data to other applications in the HIE that are needed for the use case and then the integration engine receives the data back (cleansed, normalized and transformed). The integration engine checks for the provider endpoint address for receiving data and the message router sends the information to the provider on record. The database keeps a copy of the message and an audit log of the data and transaction on file for a specified time period. The HIE does this same process repeatedly for millions of transactions, sending and receiving data that is critical for care delivery, treatment, quality and safety.

Data is applied to various scenarios known as use cases. The use cases vary depending on the end user and business case. The most popular use cases include admission, discharge and transfer notifications used to provide insights to providers on acute care utilization patterns of their patients. Likewise, the clinical data found in the C-CDA can be used to coordinate care. The C-CDA also contains information that in some cases can be used to meet some quality metrics and for analytics related to population health, cohort management and value-based care and alternative payment models. Individually identifiable information shared in an HIE may also be used to capture reference data on a given person to identify social needs like homelessness and food insecurity. For example, zip codes can be used to identify food deserts and the people who live in those areas affected by limited choices for food. The number and types of use cases that are in development vary by geographic region and are also dependent on the goals and objectives of collaborators and other stakeholders.

Data exchange innovations are focused on improving scalability, identity management and privacy. Graph databases are being tested to improve the management of care team relationships across expansive and diverse ecosystems. This approach is used to find patterns where conventional methods of analyses fail or are difficult due to large data files. Blockchain use cases are increasing as issues of fraud, waste and abuse increase and data privacy and security continue to be a significant issue. Because healthcare is data intensive, block chain as an immutable ledger-based system of transactions is a promising technology. The block chain transactions contain a cryptographic hash from the previous block, a timestamp and transaction data. Each block contains data about the previous block, thus creating a fully auditable chain with each block reinforcing the blocks before it. Block chain and smart contracts are poised to be the next-generation technology solving many problems that have plagued healthcare, business and finance.

Healthcare Information Networks

Today healthcare is reliant on electronic health records and health information technology and exchange vendors. EHRs capture and store health information when patients access the health system. EHRs continue to evolve but remain siloed, disparate systems unless they are technically connected to a large health information exchange or health information network or local integration engine. Large EHR vendors are members of national networks that are developing, such as the eHealth Exchange (eHX), CommonWell, CareEquality, and CARIN Alliance. These national networks form a policy fabric of business rules and practices to ensure that healthcare compliance standards are applied across the distributed network. Some national networks like Sequoia have implemented interoperable platforms to enhance national information exchange (Sequoia Project, 2021). A use case for a primary healthcare exchange is based on the sharing of HL7 CCD messages using a query-based exchange model. Integration platforms are becoming increasingly popular because of their tremendous electronic message and data processing power. Integration platform vendors include technologies like InterSystems and Orion Rhapsody. At the same time, *edge computing* is gaining ground as available computers in healthcare organizations are networked to join processing power making it equivalent to supercomputers

(Gartner, 2021; ONC, 2018). Importantly, edge computing technologies can harness available microprocessors and apply machine learning and artificial intelligence (AI) to adapt new data without human interference (Hamilton, 2018; Gartner, 2021). In combination with other technologies, such as APIs that allow on-demand query and response back from large, available data-sets, rapid advancements are being made in proactive predictive analytics. Healthcare is also exploring the use of APIs to move interoperability into a future proof space where persistent interfaces that are costly to maintain become obsolete, and data on demand allows spontaneous, proactive meth-ods of data exchange to take their place.

As technology advances and large infrastructures become a part of the networked ecosystem of healthcare, there is an innate risk that the con-sumer role may be underappreciated. In the current model of information exchange, consumers have little knowledge of their health data location, the sharing of that information or the various secondary uses of data that are in play (treatment, payment, operations, quality, improvement, incen-tives). This creates a situation where the healthcare consumer has little if any control, choice or voice over their health data and its movement or use. With the assistance of policy initiatives and legal regulation, like the 21st Century Cures Act, the consumer moves from a place of dependence to one of prominence and impact. This shift signals that the consumer in future data exchange will be the primary actor, initiator and main beneficiary.

Role of the Nurse Informaticist

The role of the nurse informaticist (NI) is critical in supporting consumers to become active, member participants of data sharing. In the applied version of the nurse informaticist role, the nurse will act as an expert business ana-lyst knowing the clinical workflows, use cases and the end-user roles neces-sary for referral and information exchange to be fully implemented. As an advocate for the consumer role, nurses across the board will need to have sufficient knowledge to encourage individuals to access, control and share their health data for care and treatment. To be effective in this consumer space, the nurse informaticist must stay up to date on policy, regulation and operational impacts of proposed rules and the changes that are forecasted in the domain of consumer-mediated data management. Having current knowl-edge of policy and regulatory changes is essential for the NI nurse's ability to design the use cases and scenarios that can move a patient from a passive to an active participant in their data exchange.

Health information technology includes activities that can be led by nurse informaticists in support of technical design, application development, system configuration and implementation. Working with stakeholders including consumers/patients to gather business requirements is the first step. Then the business needs are translated into technical requirements. This work is typically done in tandem with the identification of data sources, data flow diagramming, data model development and creation of technical specifications. If the concept design moves into development, then programming and coding are completed, the system is tested and then moved into production. If the use case can be accomplished with an off-the-shelf software solution or application, then the configuration of the system must be considered. To demonstrate this critical work the following case study is provided.

CASE STUDY

SOCIAL DETERMINANTS OF HEALTH (SDOH) DATA CAPTURE, USE AND INTEROPERABILITY

Opportunity

The local hospital and their accountable care organization (ACO) recognize a national trend to proactively identify patient social welfare needs as a strategy to deliver more comprehensive person-centered healthcare. In particular, the accountable care organization is aware that they need to collect information on housing insecurity from patients to meet additional criteria for a new program that targets homelessness. The ACO creates a task force that is asked to consider ways to proactively engage patients during their clinic visits to identify additional needs related to social determinants of health (SDoH). The primary beneficiaries of this project are individuals, patients and their families. The ACO knows that the work will most likely include not only the identification of specific patient needs but may also require that the clinic connect patients with a resource that can address the identified problem. This means that patients must be an active part of the planning, design and implementation of a system that captures data about them and uses it for identification of resources based on their unique needs. Proactive patient engagement, empowerment and the individual consumer voice are essential to meeting the grants requirements.

Resources to Consider

- 360X and Social Determinants of Health (SDoH) Referral Implementation Guide (360X Confluence, 2021)
- Social Interventions Research & Evaluation Network (SIREN), Gravity Project (USCF, 2021)
- HL7 Release 2 Primary Standards & Clinical Document Architecture (CDA) (HL7 International, 2020)
- HL7 Release 5 Draft Ballot FHIR Resource Consent (HL7 International, 2021)
- PRAPARE Assessment Tool (NACHC, 2021) and accompanying EHR implementation guide
- DirectTrust Accreditation and Direct Project Wiki

High-Level Description Objectives

The ACO must identify the specific use case(s) that support the work described in their project charter. A use case is a specific situation in which a product or service or technology can be used to solve a particular problem. The ACO project team has determined that the primary project use case is the collection of information during patient clinic visits needed to identify social welfare needs. The secondary use case is to enable closed-loop referrals between clinic staff and a subset of community-based organizations. The ACO also considers the technical requirements necessary to enable both use cases and identify ways to empower patients to choose their preferred community organization. Technical requirements take into consideration the EHR, SDoH screening and electronic referral technology including any interoperability capabilities. Figure 6.1 shows a closed-loop referral.

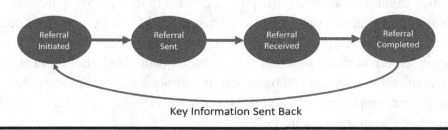

Figure 6.1   Electronic closed-loop referral.

Approach

The project takes place within the context of healthcare so certain requirements must be met to establish trust with a patient who is the primary
project beneficiary. Trust is important because healthcare generally involves
uncertainty and risk. To improve trust the project team establishes a consumer advisory group to obtain feedback on the project outcomes. The
project team finds that information privacy and consent to share data are
foundational components of the project demonstration. This is because
protected health information collected on social welfare needs is considered
confidential. Keeping information private and data secure is foundational
to building trust. The project team also finds that they must address data
sharing legal agreements between their clinic and community-based organization, and they must identify a validated SDoH assessment tool that is
consumer focused.

Through an environmental scan and consumer-based focus groups, the
task force identifies a set of basic functions that the information system must
have to support the project objectives.

1. Establish relationships between individual patients and their care team.
2. Capture consent preferences for data sharing and program participation.
3. Enable electronic data capture for screening of social welfare needs.
4. Enable electronic community-based referral.
5. Enable electronic data sharing between trusted data sharing
   organizations.

During the project discovery phase, conversations with clinic staff, administration and HIT staff show the current EHR does not include a validated
assessment tool needed to collect SDoH data. The project team recommends
to leadership that an SDoH assessment tool be identified that can be built
into the current system. In addition, the ACO needs to identify a method to
capture patient consent. A system external to the EHR may also be used to
send referrals to community-based systems that meet the patient's unique
social welfare needs. Since the referral must be secure, the project team recommends an encrypted, direct secure message enabled, closed-loop referral
system that ensures safe and secure electronic communication. Closed-loop
referral software is usually based on bidirectional message capabilities that
allow both the clinic staff and the community-based organization to electronically communicate using HIPAA compliant technology. The ACO also

notes that referral information must be posted in the patients' chart. The project team considers the use of structured, codified data capture so that information collected can be used to measure success of the program and progress of the patient.

Project Plan

To complete the project the ACO develops a work plan with the main objectives, activities, deliverables, budget and estimated timeline. The project is led by the nurse informaticist who is supported by the clinic grant manager and HIT director. A series of meetings are scheduled. Key project team members are recruited including a patient(s), provider, case manager, program staff, the operations manager, HIT/EHR specialist and the quality improvement staff. The group works through the plan to understand the current and desired future state. A patient journey map is completed to describe the various touchpoints in the screening and care process related to SDoH identification and referral management. The project team identifies capabilities that are available in their information systems and list the technical gaps that need to be considered in a procurement process. The project team works through the approval of new technology, budget and a critical path for implementation.

Structured Data and Interoperability Standards

The nurse informaticist and HIT analyst identify data types, formats and code sets needed. They review clinical document architecture (CDA) technical specs to understand whether relevant data needed for the project is available. A review of the ONC 360X confluence page and the implementation guide is completed to better understand the technical requirements needed to send and receive a closed-loop referral (Direct Trust Standards, 2021). This includes identification of currently available transport methods in their environment (direct, VPN, etc.). The nurse informaticist performs a short review of the most widely used and validated SDoH assessment tool, PRAPARE, to determine fit. This includes examination of the implementation guide for EHRs. A full cross-walk is completed between the PRAPARE assessment tool and data needed to satisfy the data requirements of the project. The team identifies referral platforms available in the market and does a cursory review of available documents that outline the technical capabilities for data exchange including

HL7 International relevant implementation guides. This information provides the foundation for the design, development and implementation work.

Design, Development and Implementation

The nurse informaticist leads the design of workflows that support the new work, identification of a validated tool for capturing SDoH data, confirms that current consent processes will be adequate and identifies new patient engagement and education materials that need to be available. This includes provider education and staff training on new tools and processes. The technology is chosen, implemented and tested. The technology is moved to production and post implementation observations are completed to identify enhancements or defects in the current tools and process. The nurse informaticist tests both sides of the bidirectional exchange capabilities with staff and deems it ready for deployment. System integration is verified, and data validation is completed. This final stage fully initiates the referral platform so that community-based organizations can receive referrals electronically and the referrals can be tracked, monitored and scheduled timely.

The project team debriefs, collects lessons learned and completes a report considering any additional recommendations that need to be delivered to the ACO leadership. The nurse informaticist initiates an ongoing monitoring process to determine program success and uses metrics, key performance indicators or other measures of success deemed appropriate. Monitoring includes patient interviews and measures based on patient outcomes to determine whether the program meets the person-centered objective. Monitoring also includes measuring patient levels of confidence that their health information is used with their consent, for the specific purpose, under the permitted use and with safeguards necessary to provide choice, control and voice.

Scenarios like the one depicted in this case study are taking shape every day in healthcare. Millions of dollars of funding are flooding the healthcare market to enable SDoH screening and the link of a patient to appropriate community-based organizations. It is critical that the nurse informaticist and project teams architect include consumers into the planning, development and demonstration of these emerging systems. Likewise, it is important that nurses' voices are at the table where data exchange is being designed so that common workflows and developing use cases take into consideration the work of end-users, namely healthcare staff, patients and families.

Consumer Participation

The number of digital health consumers continues to increase creating demand for new governance models where individuals have access and control. The 21st Century Cures Act recognizes the strong link between consumers and data ownership. Trusted Exchange Framework and Common Agreement (TEFCA) identifies an individual as a member of information exchange networks for the first time. This recognition brings opportunities for healthcare consumers to become part of the larger distributed network as mediators of directed exchange. Technology continues to advance as new healthcare applications are developed that allow individuals to aggregate and share their health data with whom they want, and when they want to share for the purposes that they deem necessary. Implications of the healthcare consumer mediating their personal health data and sharing activities create new challenges. Healthcare organizations and providers need to develop policies and practices that recognize the power of the consumer voice in making data sharing choices.

Nurse informaticists must also consider any associated or developing ethical obligations that may arise from more progressive consumer data sharing scenarios. Ethical considerations may broadly include sharing health data for the common or public good. Public good in data sharing requires that one think about use, purpose, risk of harm and outcome. Ethics emphasize the moral responsibility of the individual, known as moral agency. Individual moral agency is determined by knowledge and informed choice. Individual moral agency (free will and individualism) is challenged in networked ecosystems (Moon, 2017). If an individual does not have knowledge about, or has not made an informed choice, then they may not be able to exercise moral agency. The issue is that as the network(s) increases, the free will of the individual is proportionally diminished. This means that individual preference as a part of choice may not be applied because data needed for larger, health system activities like quality, population health, cohort management, value-based, care management are a secondary use of data that was captured during care and treatment activities used without consumer consent. This is not to say that these initiatives are not important or necessary. It is meant to make nurse informaticists sensitive to an individual's self-determination and autonomy related to data management in healthcare and the consumer's ability to control their personal asset, namely their health data. At a time when healthcare networks and data exchange are advancing, nurses and other healthcare providers must pay close attention to the preferences of consumers (data sharing or otherwise) and apply strong ethical principles to ensure that justice (equal distribution of resources based on benefits and burdens), beneficence (desire to do good) and autonomy (self-determination and individual preference) are preserved.

References

360X Confluence. (2021). Office of the National Coordinator. *HealthIT.gov*. Available at: 360X and Social Determinants of Health (SDoH) Referrals—360X—Confluence (healthit.gov) (Accessed 6 May 2021).

Connect Protocol. (2018). *Connect community portal*. Available at: https://connecto-pensource.org/ (Accessed 14 October 2019).

Direct Trust Standards. (2021). *Direct Trust accreditation for direct message protocol*. Available at: https://directtrust.org/?s=Direct+Trust+accreditation+for+direct+message+protocol (Accessed December 31, 2021).

Federal Drug Administration. (2016). *21st Century cures act*. Available at: https://www.fda.gov/regulatory-information/selected-amendments-fdc-act/21st-century-cures-act H.R.34 - 21st Century Cures Act 114th Congress (2015-2016) (Accessed 31 December 2021).

Federal Register. (2020a). *Standardized API for patient and population services*. Available at: https://www.federalregister.gov/d/2020-07419/p-121 (Accessed 6 May 2021).

Federal Register. (2020b). *Trusted exchange framework and the common agreement*. Available at: https://www.federalregister.gov/d/2020-07419/p-113 (Accessed 6 May 2021).

Gartner. (2021). *2021 strategic roadmap for edge computing*. Available at: www.gartner.com (Accessed 21 July 2021).

Hamilton, E. (2018). *What is edge computing: The network edge explained*. Available at: https://www.cloudwards.net/what-is-edge-computing/ble (Accessed 31 December 2021).

HIPAA. (1996). *Health Insurance Portability and Accountabily Act, 1996*. Available at: https://www.cdc.gov/phlp/publications/topic/hipaa.html (Accessed 31 December 2021).

HL7 International. (2020). *CDA release 2. HL7 Standards Product Brief - CDA® Release 2 | HL7 International*. Available at: http://www.hl7.org/implement/standards/product_brief.cfm?product_id=7 (Accessed 31 December 2021).

HL7 International. (2021). *Release 5 draft ballot FHIR consent resource*. Available at: http://hl7.org/fhir/2020Sep/codesystem.html Consent - FHIR v4.6.0 (Accessed 31 December 2021).

Kao, C. K., & Liebovitz, D. M. (2017). Consumer mobile health apps: Current state, barriers, and future directions. *PM&R*, 9(5), pp.S106–S115.

Livongo. (2021). *Product of Teledoc*. Available at: https://www.livongo.com/ (Accessed 7 September 2021).

Makri, A. (2019). Bridging the digital divide in health care. *The Lancet Digital Health*, 1(5), pp.e204–e205.

Markel Foundation. (2006). *Connecting for health common framework*. Available at: MARKLE COMMON FRAMEWORK: CONNECTING PROFESSIONALS | Markle | Advancing America's Future (Accessed 14 April 2014).

Markel Foundation. (2010). *Building a strong privacy and security policy framework for personal health records*. The Center for Democracy & Technology. Available at: CDT—Building a Strong Privacy and Security Policy Framework for PHRs (Accessed 14 April 2014).

Moon, L. A. (2017). Factors influencing health data sharing preferences of consumers: A critical review. *Health Policy and Technology*, 6(2), pp.169–187.

National Association of Community Health Centers (NACHC). (2021). *Protocol for responding to and assessing patients' assets, risks and experiences (PRAPARE)*. Available at: About the PRAPARE Assessment Tool—NACHC (Accessed 3 May 2021).

National Institute of Health. (n.d.). *Health information national trends survey (HINTS)*. Available at: https://health.gov/healthypeople/objectives-and-data /data-sources-and-methods/data-sources/health-information-national-trends -survey-hints (Accessed 8 September 2021).

NOOM. (2021). Available at: https://www.noom.com/ (Accessed 7 September 2021).

Office of the National Coordinator. (2018). *170.315(h)(2) direct project, edge protocol, and XDR/XDM*. Available at: https://www.healthit.gov/test-method/direct -project-edge-protocol-and-xdrxdm (Accessed 15 October 2019).

Office of the National Coordinator. (2019a). *Direct exchange: Q & A for providers*. Available at: Directed Exchange: Q&A for Providers (healthit.gov) (Accessed 21 June 2021).

Office of the National Coordinator. (2019b). *What is HIE?* Available at: https://www .healthit.gov/topic/health-it-and-health-information-exchange-basics/what-hie (Accessed 14 October 2019).

Office of the National Coordinator. (2020). *Patient consent for electronic health information exchange*. Available at: Patient Consent for Electronic Health Information Exchange | HealthIT.gov (Accessed 10 June 2021).

Office of the National Coordinator. (2021). *FHIR fact sheet*. Available at: FHIR Fact Sheets | HealthIT.gov (Accessed 22 June 2021).

Rothstein, M. A. (2007). Health privacy in the electronic age. *Journal of Legal Medicine*, 28(4), pp.487–501.

Sequoia Project. (2021). *What's the difference between eHealth exchange, care quality, and The Sequoia Project? —The Sequoia project*. Available at: https:// sequoiaproject.org/about-us/whats-difference-ehealth-exchange-carequality -sequoia-project/ (Accessed 7 September 2021).

The Direct Project. (2019). Wiki Page Implementation Group. Available at: http:// wiki.directproject.org/Main_Page (Accessed 2 December 2019).

University of San Francisco California (USFC). Social Interventions Research & Evaluation Network (SIREN). (2021). Available at: The Gravity Project | SIREN (ucsf.edu) (Accessed 3 June 2021).

U.S. Department of Health & Human Services. (2013). *Health information privacy.* Available at: https://www.hhs.gov/hipaa/for-professionals/privacy/index.html (Accessed 7 September 2021).

U.S. Department of Health & Human Services. (2014). *Better care, smarter spending, healthier people: Improving our health care delivery system with an engaged and empowered consumer at the center.* Available at: CMS (Accessed 6 May 2021).

Williams, C., Mostashari, F., Mertz, K., Hogin, E., & Atwal, P. (2012). Office of the National Coordinator: The strategy for advancing the exchange of health information. *Health Affairs*, 31(3), pp.527–536.

Chapter 7

Data Security Implications in Digital Health: A Cautionary Tale

Elaine Zacharakis Loumbas and Marisol Peters

Contents

DOI: 10.4324/9781003281047-7

Introduction

A culture of security in the healthcare continuum starts top-down. It must be embraced and promoted by board members, senior executives and top company leadership and incorporated into the daily activities of employees. A key example of a perfectly preventable breach based on organizational cultural practices regarding security is that of the *WannaCry* virus's impact on the UK National Health Services (NHS). On May 12, 2017, a crypto ransomware called *WannaCry* was unleashed to the public impacting over 230,000 systems throughout more than 100 countries (National Accounting Office, 2017). Among the impacted was the UK's NHS health system and several of its trusts. Approximately 34% of the 236 trust sites were impacted to some degree by the virus. Extent of impact included approximately 6,900 canceled appointments, redirected ambulances and emergency patients to other healthcare systems, delayed test results and more.

The UK's National Audit Office reported the breach stemming from several factors that had they been addressed in their maintenance security practices would have prevented the breach. First, the trusts failed to adhere to the Department of Health and Cabinet Office 2014's recommendation to migrate away from Windows XP systems by April 2015. And secondly, trusts failed to heed the warning alerts sent out by NHS Digital informing all sites to update Windows 7 systems with the latest Microsoft release against WannaCry (BBC, 2017). Microsoft had released a patch to prevent against infection in March 2017—two months before the May ransomware attack. A culture of adhering to best practices such as migrating away from unsupported systems and proper patch management would have prevented this massive attack from the impact it had on the NHS.

The Growing Pandemic of Healthcare Data Breaches

In 2020, healthcare data breaches of 500 or more records were reported at a rate of more than 1.76 per day (HIPAA Journal, 2021). As shown in Figure 7.1, 2020 saw 642 large data breaches reported by healthcare providers, health plans, healthcare clearinghouses and business associates of those entities—25% more than in 2019, which was also a record-breaking year (HIPAA Journal, 2021 reference for figure).

The rapid expansion of technology in healthcare has ushered in an era of security risk that rivals that of the financial industry. Breaches in

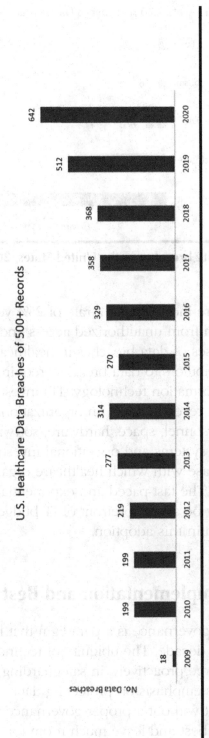

Figure 7.1 Cybersecurity attacked in healthcare, 2020.

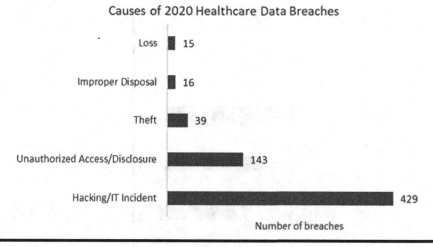

Figure 7.2 shows Causes of 2020 Healthcare Data Breaches:
- Loss: 15
- Improper Disposal: 16
- Theft: 39
- Unauthorized Access/Disclosure: 143
- Hacking/IT Incident: 429

Number of breaches

Figure 7.2   Causes of security breaches in the United States, 2020 (HIPPA Journal, 2021).

the healthcare industry are increasing at a rate of 25% year after year. The majority of incidents stem from unauthorized access and IT-related breaches. Figure 7.2 shows the causes of data breaches in healthcare.

The two leading contributors to data breaches require a cultural shift for healthcare industries. Information technology (IT) investments have historically been perceived as a revenue drain on organizations with huge overhead expenditures in personnel, space, hardware, software and devices. This outdated view of IT systems and operational investments has been a huge contributor to the ease with which healthcare organization systems can be accessed and hacked. The fast-paced and exponential growth of technology requires that security be at the forefront of IT budgeting. The following outlines steps to be taken in this adoption.

Security Controls Implementation and Best Practices

Information security (IS) governance is a paradigm that has exponentially taken shape over the last decade. The ubiquity of technology has driven organizations to take charge proactively, in safeguarding their data. However, the drive primarily places emphasis on protecting data at rest and in transit while the reality is that without a proper governance framework, these attempts are parochial at best and leave much room for vulnerability and risk. The following highlights the control framework selection and implementation processes.

Developing a Security Strategy for Healthcare

Security strategy development must be performed with two primary focuses: (1) all assets have been fully identified, classified, qualified and quantified based on business impact analysis; (2) a threat analysis has been completed per asset. These two focuses provide the foundation on which to start identifying which control frameworks align best with the organizational goals. Examples of assets in the healthcare industry include lab and radiology results stored in an electronic medical or health record (EMR/EHR), insurance payer information stored in revenue cycle systems, patient demographics, and more. The value of these assets is directly commensurate to the risk of exposure to the asset. A comprehensive asset valuation allows for the organization to fully assess the cost of assets in the event of a successful breach.

Once assets have been fully evaluated, next comes the development of a strategy for security. A security strategy must be driven off the objectives that organizations wish to achieve for each of its assets. Using the example of insurance payer information, an objective might read, 'Ensuring data redundancy in case of accidental loss.' Such an objective can be easily planned for with nightly backups, off-site storage, etc. Before any organization can pursue addressing all its objectives by asset type and valuation, adoption of frameworks must be established to serve as the guideline to this endeavor.

The control framework selection process should be based on alignment with industry type. Commonly adopted control frameworks in healthcare include but are not limited to:

- **HIPAA**—The Health Insurance Portability and Accountability Act of 1996 is a federal law which drove the creation of standards aimed at protecting patient health information (Gregory, 2018). While the law highlights the objectives as per HIPAA Security Rule, it does not, however, outline specific practices to achieve the goal of data protection. (HIPAA is discussed in further detail below.)
- **ISO/IEC 27001**—An international standard aiming to assist organizations on how to best manage information security. It is divided into two sections comprising 7 requirements and 14 controls.
- **NIST SP 800-53**—National Institute for Standards and Technology (NIST) Special Publication (SP) 800-53—'Security and Privacy Controls for Federal Information Systems and Organizations' (Gregory, 2018).

Primarily adopted by US government entities the context of healthcare applies to Veterans Affairs (VA) healthcare systems. NIST controls are made up of 18 categories. Although originally created for US federal information systems, NIST controls have been adopted by many industries in great part due to its detailed implementation guidelines.

- **PCI-DSS**—The Payment Card Industry Data Security Standard control framework targets the protection of, specifically, credit card information. PCI-DSS consists of 12 control objectives. Healthcare organizations that accept co-pays and deductibles in the form of credit card payments must adopt this specific framework in conjunction with others.

These and other control frameworks can be adopted in combination depending on the objectives and practices of the organization. Most are not mandatory but exist to provide sets of guidelines to follow as best practice. Adopters should not treat this as a 'one size fits all,' but instead choose the controls within selected frameworks that meet the needs of the business. To successfully develop a security strategy, healthcare organizations should perform a thorough health check of the current state. This allows for a complete gap analysis between the current and the future goals determined by asset.

Creating a Culture of Security

Organizational culture spans far beyond that of the collective beliefs, values and business philosophies; it includes the embedded practices and accountability in everyday interactions and functional practices. Organizational cultures must be closely tied to the business policies and practices. It is for these reasons that security must be a central component of the culture. The following outlines the risks and vulnerabilities by functional groups and how best to remediate.

End-User Awareness and Accountability

A user's regard for information security can be attributed to three key factors: (1) extent of education and training provided regarding best practices, (2) understanding of organizational impact in case of a breach and (3) awareness of consequences to an individual, if their actions lead to a breach.

Social engineering is the umbrella term used to describe manipulation techniques used to breach information through direct human interaction of some sort. Some of the most common social engineering techniques include phishing and whaling attempts, scareware where users receive false alerts regarding malware on their systems, and smishing or SMS phishing where text messages are used to direct victims to malicious sites. The 2017 Verizon Data Breach Investigations Report identified that 43% of all breaches involve some form of social engineering effort and that of those 93% were in the form of phishing attempts. There are many practices organizations can adopt to safeguard themselves against social engineering practices. Such practices include:

- **Background Checks and Personality Assessments**—Human resource (HR) can be a security administrator's best friend. Background checks provide in-depth insight into a person's past professional and workplace behaviors, while personality assessments provide insight into the behavioral aspects of a candidate, such as motivators and team performance. Employee personality and characteristics paint a picture of whether they take precautions in their actions or if they are more maverick in nature. Precautionary employees are less prone to risky practices with regard to information security.
- **Job Descriptions**—Traditionally, job descriptions primarily focus on functional activities, key performance measures for job performance, roles and responsibilities and such. However, job descriptions should incorporate security verbiage as it applies to the position. Take for example the role of a director of risk and compliance: this position is both a highly targeted position due to its hierarchy within the organization and has the added risk of access to many levels of personal health information (PHI) and personal identifiable information (PII). The job description for this role should include verbiage on managing their personal passwords in forms like 'User shall not use any easily identifiable passwords that include personal information' and/or 'User shall not share nor right down passwords where easily accessible.' To take responsibility and accountability one step further, organizations should also include verbiage regarding logging off systems such as, 'User shall ensure application and desktop are completely logged off when stepping away and at the end of workday.' This practice is extremely important and applies heavily toward public facing roles such as those of nurses and doctors as they log into systems which have the most sensitive of information and are often pulled away to differing areas. Ensuring logging off as common practice in any employee's role is essential.

■ **Training and Education**—The ubiquitous nature of technology has created an environment where cybercriminals have grown cleverer in their attempts. Victims, however, have not increased their awareness and understanding of the threat landscape. It is for this reason that organizations must make security awareness and training part of their core curriculum and daily practice.

  – **Onboarding**—All employees should be trained on the organization's security policies and procedures and be made aware of repercussions stemming from failure to adhere.

  – **Security Agreements**—Employees should all sign a contractual agreement with the organization promising to adhere to all security related policies and procedures.

  – **Annual Training**—Most organizations have yearly compliance training. Security re-training should be incorporated and adjusted as needed based on changing market needs.

  – **Periodic Reminders**—Organizations' information technology (IT) or information systems (IS) leadership should promote an environment of security awareness by communicating monthly on best practices, what to look out for, how to escalate and what proper incident response steps are. Desktop logon warning banners are another great deterrent control as they serve to discourage poor judgment and behavior.

  – **Phishing Simulation Campaigns**—Social engineering vulnerabilities are primarily the personnel themselves, whereas the external threat vectors are cybercriminals targeting them. As phishing attempts account for the greatest threat with personnel, efforts in reducing this specific vulnerability should be prioritized. Phishing simulations allow organizations to test employee response to phishing attempts by replicating a potential attack and tracking and trending responses. Simulations log how far an employee went through the steps of the phishing attempt, e.g., did the employee just click on the link or did they go as far as entering their credentials and so on. This information can then be shared with both stakeholders and department leadership. Moreover, these simulations lend themselves to yearly reviews, whereas those that fail the simulations repeatedly can be addressed more formally as part of their review.

Senior Leadership and Support

Although the concept of security in any industry is one that is given credence to, this is often an unspoken truth. It stands to reason that all executive and board members support the concept of security, but support must be made public to highlight the value that the organization places on security. Executive leadership should promote security during periodic town hall sessions and other company-wide forums. Human resource leadership should highlight the importance of security during interviews and onboarding. Departmental and functional leadership should both embody and promote daily adherence to security within every function and process.

Security is not a by-product of IT or IS functions but instead a core function that should be ingrained into the values and beliefs of the organization. The information utilized daily in operations should be perceived as valuable assets, and as such, those protective and deterrent measures surrounding its protection should be valued also. Organizational culture in today's environment must include information security.

Prevention against Common Threats in Healthcare

The Health Information Technology for Economic and Clinical Health Act (HITECH) of 2009 advanced technological adoption in healthcare with the inception of Meaningful Use (OCR, 2013; CMS, 2015, 2021). This incentivizing model created a massive adoption of electronic medical record systems for both private practices and hospital organizations. As part of the staged adoption approach, data capture evolved into data utilization for surveillance, quality outcomes and creation of diagnosis-specific interventions. This stage fully evolved into data sharing for syndromic surveillance, care coordination and patient engagement. In today's arena, scheduled appointments, registrations, procedure results and documentation, and claims processing are all performed electronically. This electronic phenomenon comes with a whole new set of vulnerabilities, risks and threat vectors.

Some of the more common threats come in the form of social engineering efforts which can have a high degree of manageability with proper control efforts. These require minimal technical intervention and are more human centric in nature. Other threat vectors, however, target weak or poor security control practices surrounding networks, servers, access control, among others. The following are some of the technical targets for organizations to focus on:

■ **Network Infrastructure**—Network vulnerabilities lend themselves to the greatest degree of risk from external threat vectors. Network security should be treated as the highest priority when designing control measures. An organization's network architecture spans every department as well as providing access to every system and database. It is for these reasons that organizations should seek experienced network administrators and engineers with a strong acumen in security. A network vulnerability assessment should be conducted annually. The following are network focused technologies and best practices:

– Vendor-Supported Devices—In the healthcare industry, it is common practice to have laboratory instruments, radiology modalities and other biomedical devices be operated and maintained by the supplier vendors themselves. These devices should always reside on a segmented, virtual local area network (VLAN) disallowing potential spread in the case of an infection. Often, these devices are not consistently updated with software patches and thus provide a high degree of risk.

– Intrusion Detection Systems (IDSs)—IDSs are intended to collect information on normal traffic flow to create a volume baseline. IDSs then, periodically, review network traffic to measure against established baselines to identify anomalies. Any anomalies detected are then reported to the network team.

– Intrusion Prevention Systems (IPSs)—IPS technologies aim to review network traffic flows and prevent any potential exploits. To fully take advantage of IPS features, it is a best practice to ensure that all inbound traffic is first decrypted before being viewed by the IPS.

■ Firewall Management—Network firewalls are one of the greatest defenses against external vector attacks when properly configured and deployed. Firewalls are security-specific network devices used to prevent unauthorized access to private networks that are connected to the Internet. Private networks are referred to as local area networks (LANs). External traffic is managed through configuration of policies where anything falling outside of the policy configuration is blocked. Organizations use 'demilitarized zones' (DMZs) to serve as an Internet-facing perimeter network to protect the internal-facing LAN from untrusted traffic (Rouse, 2019). Best practice dictates that organizations employ a dual-firewall schema where one firewall sits directly in front of the enterprise LAN and the second protects routers, mail servers, web servers and any other Internet-facing servers by residing directly in front of the web-facing systems. Figure 7.3 depicts this dual-firewall architecture.

■ **Access Control**

– Segregation of Duties (SoD)—Primarily used to prevent fraudulent activities (Gregory, 2018). Best practice dictates that security privileges be

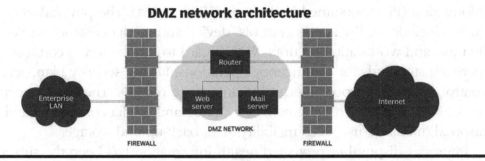

Figure 7.3   Illustration of the dual-firewall architecture (Lutkevich, 2019).

given to differing security team members where no one individual has complete security access across multiple platforms and technologies.

- – Role-Based Access—Access by roles should be revisited once a year by department leadership to ensure that it aligns with current threat identification performed by information security (IS). Access should be based on both role and departmental functional needs.
- – Two-Factor Authentication (2FA)—Provides excellent security for both in-house staff and remote personnel. 2FA can be in the form of a pin number sent to a mobile device stored within the system or in the form of a smartcard.
- ■ Security Patch Management—Refers simply to the practice of deploying system patches to fix vulnerabilities or errors across an enterprises' systems. Essentially, patches are lines of code intended to fill in a gap in an application, operating system or server where risk has the highest degree of realization.

HIPAA Security

The HIPAA Administrative Simplification defines the regulatory framework for standardized electronic transactions in healthcare for the United States (Center for Disease Control, 2018). Under this framework, there are several implementing regulations, including privacy and security regulations. The HIPAA privacy regulations fall into three categories of safeguards: (1) physical, (2) technical and (3) administrative.

Physical Safeguards in HIPAA Regulations

The HIPAA security regulations contain several recommended and required safeguards for physically securing a workplace to protect personal health information (PHI) contained in the area (HHS, 1996a). The physical safe-guards include facility access controls, device and media controls, workstation use and workstation security. With regard to facility access controls, there are standards for contingency operations, facility security plan, access control, validation procedures and maintenance records. The HIPAA security regulations also have requirements for device and media controls related to disposal, media re-use, accountability, data back-up and storage.

Improper disposal of protected health information has been the subject of a number of notable enforcement actions. Some of these scenarios might not have been so obvious to the employees at the time, but the actions described below now serve as a compliance checklist for companies.

Shredding paper with protected health information is a standard practice for healthcare entities to comply with HIPAA. Many healthcare entities have locked confidential bins for the shredding of paper PHI, but compliance measures are not just needed for paper. For example, PHI that may be on labeling for pill bottles needs to be properly removed as part of the disposal process. A number of the large pharmacy chains were the subject of a television expose story where investigational reporters went through dumpsters at pharmacies finding a treasure trove of PHI. The Department of Health & Human Services entered into a settlement agreement with CVS for US$ 2.25 million and with Rite Aid for US$ 1 million (Department of Health & Human Services, 2017).

Furthermore, hard drives, storage devices and other devices must be erased or destroyed when they are no longer necessary to ensure complete deletion of PHI. Affinity Health Plan ("AHP") settled with the Department of Health & Human Services for $1,215,780 for impermissibly disclosing ePHI of up to 344,579 individuals when photocopier hard drives were not properly erased prior to returning the photocopiers to a leasing company. AHP failed to assess and identify the potential security risks and vulnerabilities of ePHI stored in the photocopier hard drives. So, lesson learned, from a compliance perspective, make sure all printers and scanners that store data are scrubbed prior to disposal or transfer.

Ensuring physical spaces are secure is part of implementing proper physical safeguards under HIPAA; combined with technical safeguards of encrypting data also avoids potential liabilities. Lahey Clinic Hospital, Inc. paid a US$ 850,000 settlement to the Department of Health and Human Services for a cybersecurity breach (Healthcare Finance, 2015). In 2011, one of Lahey's unencrypted laptops containing the ePHI of around 600 people was stolen from the hospital's radiology center. Lahey failed to encrypt their laptops, and the stolen one was kept in an unlocked, unmonitored room, thus failing even the most basic of technical and physical safeguards of PHI information.

Technical Safeguards

The HIPAA security regulations contain several recommended and required technical safeguards (HHS, 1996b). These legal requirements become the framework for cybersecurity procedures, and they start with 'access control.' Access controls are the set of mechanisms, policies and procedures an organization uses to ensure that **only** those who have a right to know are given access to protected health information. This function extends to the technical policies and procedures for electronic information systems that maintain the electronic protected health information. For these system operations, access is given to those third-party entities or software programs that have been granted access rights for functions such as, billing, analytics or decision support.

Secondly, supporting access are audit controls that capture and report on who accesses what information with a time and date stamp. Taken together, this tracking and inspection function consists of the supporting hardware, software and/or procedural mechanisms that record and examine activity in information systems that contain or use electronic PHI (ePHI). The third set of requirements relates to technical safeguards taken along with an organization's policies and procedures that protect electronic PHI from improper alteration or destruction. The fourth area covers the systems and procedures used for person or entity authentication and to verify that a person or entity seeking access to ePHI is the one claimed. Finally, there are technical safeguards regarding transmission security to guard against unauthorized access to ePHI that is being transmitted over an electronic communications network.

Ensuring that proper access controls are in place is an important compliance objective that carries severe legal risk and financial costs for a healthcare system or provider. As an example, a software update of WellPoint Health's database diminished the security of their ePHI, as the company did not fully evaluate the update's effect (Ouellette, 2013). The third-party vendor that implemented the update also failed to note that their actions resulted in a temporary security lapse. This security lapse allowed unauthorized personnel to have access to the ePHI of individuals within WellPoint's database; and consequently, those seeking to access the database's ePHI were able to do so without identify verification. The company's lack of safeguards to ensure that only authorized persons were able to access the application's database resulted in WellPoint settling with the Department of Health & Human Services for $1,700,000 (Ouellette, 2013). For over a year and a half, WellPoint disclosed the ePHI of over 610,000 people before the breach was identified (Kolbasuk, 2013).

Another example captures the risk for Home Health and Hospice organizations where clinicians commonly carry laptops to deliver care in the patient's home. The clinicians may forget and keep that laptop in their car or put it in their car's trunk thinking it secure, resulting in frequent thefts of these laptops. In the instance of the Hospice of North Idaho (HONI), a laptop containing the ePHI of nearly 500 people was stolen; HONI was deemed to have failed to appropriately secure their ePHI by allowing it to be stored, unencrypted on a portable electronic device (Office of Civil Rights, 2012). HONI paid a settlement of $50,000 to the Department of Health and Human Services for this ePHI breach. The lack of both proper security measures and risk analysis lead to this settlement.

There are several examples of enforcement actions where there were technology breaches causing the improper disclosure of PHI. For example, New York Presbyterian Hospital and Columbia Medical Center settled with the Department of Human Services for US$ 3.3 million and US$ 1.5 million when there was an impermissible disclosure of ePHI impacting 6,800 patients to Google and other Internet search engines when a server was not properly configured (HHS, 2014a). In this instance, a physician connected a personal server to a larger network and created a security issue that was undetected by the IT staff until it was too late.

As part of the settlement, New York Presbyterian Hospital and Columbia Medical Center (NYP/CU) agreed to implement a Corrective Action Plan where: (i) NYP/CU would conduct a thorough risk analysis that incorporates all electronic equipment, data systems and applications controlled, administered or owned by NYP/CU and (ii) NYP/CU will develop new policies and procedures to address and mitigate any security risks regarding information access management, and device and media controls which must be approved by the Department of Health & Human Services, Office of Civil Rights (which is the branch of the government agency responsible for HIPAA) (HHS, 2014b).

As was described above, one of the most common ways that the security of data becomes compromised by employees is with phishing events as described in the social engineering section above. Most often, phishing occurs when a hacker sends an email to an unsuspecting user who clicks on a link in the email, thereby allowing the hacker to penetrate a company's computer systems. In 2020, Premera Blue Cross paid $6.85 million in a settlement with the Department of Health & Human Services over a 2015 incident involving phishing (Landi, 2020). Essentially, a hacker sent an email to a Premera employee while posing as an individual from Premera IT. This email contained a link that the Premera employee clicked on, resulting in malware installation that allowed for the hacker to obtain the ePHI of individuals within Premera's database (Bernstein, 2021). This cyberattack went undetected, resulting in the release of over 10 million people's PHI (Miliard, 2020). Premera failed to comply with HIPAA by not implementing risk analysis and management procedures that would have prevented phishing from occurring.

One of the most significant HIPAA security breaches happened to Anthem Blue Cross Blue Shield. A cyberattack at the insurance company exposed data of 79 million people, which resulted in a $16 million settlement (Morse, 2018). Anthem was found guilty of failing to identify and respond to security incidents, in addition to their lack of conducting risk analyses and implementing access controls. The magnitude of this data breach is very concerning because it exposed the medical, financial and personal information of over a third of the US adult population: this case exemplifies the overall concerns of cybersecurity challenges. In 2017, there was a system-wide Equifax data breach that exposed most of the financial information of the United States' adult population (Morse, 2018). Hackers were able to access Equifax's vulnerable systems through a web portal that was linked to Equifax's servers; upon investigation, it was found that Equifax failed to properly secure their online systems on multiple levels (Fruhlinger, 2020). Both Anthem and Equifax breaches were believed to have been committed by a foreign government actor which introduces a whole new threat level to the cybersecurity for a country and its citizens. Nonetheless, the government will still look to see from a compliance perspective what was missing from the security compliance infrastructure that allowed this system penetration to happen.

Administrative Safeguards (HIPAA Reg)

Implementing policies and procedures for the HIPAA security regulations is the basic requirement for the administrative safeguards for a *covered entity* to govern how PHI should be handled throughout the organization. A covered entity (and business associate) must implement policies and procedures to prevent, detect, contain and correct security violations. A security official should be assigned to be responsible for the development and implementation of the policies and procedures related to the use of PHI. There should be policies and procedures to ensure that all members of its workforce have appropriate access to PHI and to prevent those workforce members who do not have access to PHI. Additionally, there should be policies and procedures for authorizing access to electronic PHI.

Training is a key aspect of compliance. Entities need to implement a security awareness and training program for all members of its workforce (including management). Responding to security incidents is also very important. Entities should implement policies and procedures to address security incidents. In the event of an emergency or other occurrence (such as a fire, system failure or natural disaster), there should be a contingency plan to respond. Entities should also perform a periodic technical and non-technical evaluation in response to environmental or operational changes affecting the security of PHI.

Many security officials will say that the best encryption will not solve a lot of the cybersecurity incidents, because many of the issues that occur are caused by human error. This is why training is so important for organizations so that employees are aware of the risks and the proper compliance measures. Eliminating cyber risks completely is hard to do; rather, it becomes a risk management exercise. Training, training and more training is a key compliance function for organizations.

A covered entity may permit a business associate to create, receive, maintain or transmit electronic PHI on the covered entity's behalf only if the covered entity obtains satisfactory assurances that the business associate has put in place the appropriate infrastructure, procedures and commits to safeguarding the information. There are many instances where a healthcare entity delegates function to a business associate, and the business associate ends up causing the cybersecurity issue. Business associates are part of the 'chain of trust' and also need to aggressively comply with the HIPAA security standards.

There are numerous instances where business associates can create cybersecurity incidents for their covered entity customers. Understanding the potential vulnerabilities and knowing not just about the operations of your business associate, but who they might have as third-party vendors and subcontractors that will have access to PHI is important from a 'due diligence' perspective in today's environment. The Solar Winds security breach is an example of where a business associate can get hacked and in turn cause their customers to be compromised. Solar Winds is a software company which provides system management tools for network and infrastructure monitoring and other technical services to thousands of organizations globally. The hack infiltrated their systems and created backdoors to their customers' systems and the data in their systems. As businesses utilize cloud-based computing, the interconnectivity of these systems needs to be considered from a security perspective as part of the overall compliance plan.

Other Legal Implications for Digital Health—Other Federal and State Laws

HIPAA establishes 'a floor' for privacy and security protection, but there are other federal and state laws that supplement HIPAA. At both the federal and the state levels, there are specific laws that address sensitive health conditions. There are also both federal and state laws addressing security breaches.

Laws Related to Sensitive Health Conditions

There are several federal and state laws protecting sensitive health information. Two of the most significant federal privacy laws related to sensitive health conditions are GINA and 42 CFR Part 2 (CMS, 2010). GINA stands for the Genetic Information Nondisclosure Act (Gregory, 2018). It is a federal law that protects genetic information. CFR means "Code of Federal Regulations". The HITECH Act promulgated the HIPAA omnibus rules which incorporate provisions of GINA into the HIPAA privacy scheme. Forty-two CFR Part 2 establishes privacy protections for alcohol and substance abuse information (HHS, 1996a). Additionally, there are both federal and state laws regarding AIDS. All 50 states have specific laws regarding mental health information as well as other sensitive health conditions. Many states have genetic privacy laws that have more protections than GINA. There are also state laws related to sexually transmitted diseases and other sensitive health conditions.

From a cybersecurity perspective, security breaches of sensitive health information could potentially be even more serious than breaches of other types of health information. Many of these laws have restrictions on the use and disclosure of such information with specific consent forms needed to transmit this information. HIPAA has a specific provision that an authorization is required for the disclosure of psychotherapy notes. Systems that contain these types of health information need to have extra privacy and security procedures in place for safeguarding this highly sensitive information. Often, data bases utilizing protected health information for healthcare operations and data analytics need to consider these laws prior to utilizing this information, and any transmissions of such information should be encrypted and otherwise compliant with applicable security rules. Thinking about the improper disclosure of patients who have highly sensitive health conditions not only raises legal issues, but significant ethical issues in how this sensitive information is safeguarded.

Closing Statement

There are new and evolving cybersecurity risks happening every day, and consequently, new laws and regulations are constantly developing in this area in an effort to address the new threats. Most states have data breach statutes as well as cybersecurity officer requirements. There are remedies available through State Attorneys General and Consumer Protection Organizations. Often, in large national cybersecurity breaches, such as the Equifax breach, the States' Attorneys Generals will act together in joint enforcement activities. Healthcare entities need to be proactive in this area, not just to avoid enforcement but to protect important business assets and to secure healthcare information of their patients.

References

Bernstein, M. (2021). Premera blue cross to pay $74M over data breach. *GovTech*. Available at: https://www.govtech.com/security/premera-blue-cross-to-pay-74m -over-data-breach.html (Accessed 15 June 2021).

British Broadcasting Company. (2017). NHS could have prevented WannaCry ransomware attack. *BBC News*. October 27. Available at: https://www.bbc.com/ news/technology-41753022 (Accessed 30 March 2021).

Centers for Disease Control. (2018). Health Insurance Portability and Accountability Act. *CDC.gov*. Available at: https://www.cdc.gov/phlp/publications/topic/hipaa .html (Accessed 19 September 2021).

Centers for Medicare and Medicaid. (2010). Federal substance abuse regulations, 42 CFR part 2. CMS and ONC final regulations define meaningful use and set standards for electronic health record incentive program. *CMS.gov*. July 13. Available at: https://www.cms.gov/newsroom/fact-sheets/cms-and-onc-final -regulations-define-meaningful-use-and-set-standards-electronic-health-record (Accessed 17 September 2021).

Centers for Medicare and Medicaid. (2015). Meaningful use regulations, 42 CFR part 495. *CMS.gov.* April 15. Available at: https://www.cms.gov/Regulations-and -Guidance/Legislation/EHRIncentivePrograms/Downloads/Modifications_MU _Rule.pdf (Accessed 19 September 2021).

Centers for Medicare and Medicaid. (2021). *Prospective payment system final rule: Program requirements 2021.* Available at: https://www.cms.gov/regulations -guidance/promoting-interoperability/2021-program-requirements (Accessed 2 January 2022).

Department of Health & Human Services. (1996a). *Health Insurance Portability and Accountability Act, the privacy rule is located at 45 CFR Part 160 and subparts A and E of part 164.* Available at: https://www.hhs.gov/hipaa/for-professionals/ privacy/index.html (Accessed 19 September 2021).

Department of Health & Human Services. (1996b). *Health Insurance Portability & Accountability Act of 1996, Pub L. 104–191, 110 Stat. 1936, HIPAA Stat.* Available at: https://www.hhs.gov/hipaa/for-professionals/index.html (Accessed 2 January 2022).

Department of Health & Human Services. (2014a). Data breach results in $4.8 mil- lion HIPAA settlements. *HHS.gov.* May 7, 2014. Available at: https://www.hhs .gov/hipaa/for-professionals/compliance-enforcement/examples/new-york-and -presbyterian-hospital/index.html (Accessed 23 May 2021).

Department of Health & Human Services, OCR. (2014b). *NYP resolution agreement and CAP clean for OCR 4.20.14.* Available at: https://www.hhs.gov/sites/default /files/ocr/privacy/hipaa/enforcement/examples/ny-and-presbyterian-hospital -settlement-agreement.pdf (Accessed 2 January 2022).

Department of Health & Human Services. (2015a). HIPAA settlement reinforces lessons for users of medical devices. *HHS.gov.* Available at: https://www.hhs .gov/hipaa/for-professionals/compliance-enforcement/agreements/lahey.html (Accessed 23 May 2021).

Department of Health & Human Services. (2015b). NYP resolution agreement. *HHS .gov.* June 18, Available at: http://www.hhs.gov/ocr/privacy/hipaa/enforcement/ examples/ny-and-presbyterian-hospital-settlement -agreement.pdf (Accessed 19 September 2021).

Department of Health & Human Services. (2017). CVS resolution agreement. *HHS .gov.* Available at: https://www.hhs.gov/hipaa/for-professionals/compliance -enforcement/examples/cvs/index.html (Accessed 22 May 2021).

Fruhlinger, J. (2020). Equifax data breach FAQ: What happened, who was affected, what was the impact? *CSO Online.* Available at: https://www.csoonline.com /article/3444488/equifax-data-breach-faq-what-happened-who-was-affected -what-was-the-impact.html (Accessed 15 June 2021).

Gregory, P.H. (2018). GINA. Genetic information nondisclosure act of 2008, Pub. L. 110–233, 122 Stat 88. In *CISM®: Certified information security manager exam guide.* New York: McGraw Hill Education.

Healthcare Finance. (2015). Available at: https://www.healthcarefinancenews.com /news/lahey-pays-850k-widespread-hipaa-non-compliance (Accessed 28 July 2021).

HIPAA Journal. (2021). 2020 healthcare data breach report: 25% increase in breaches in 2020. *HIPAA Journal*, January 19. Available at: https://www.hipaa-journal.com/2020-healthcare-data-breach-report-us/ (Accessed 10 September 2021).

HITECH Act of 2009, 42 USC §139.

Kolbasuk, M. (2013). WellPoint to pay $1.7 million settlement. *Data Breach Today.* Available at: https://www.databreachtoday.com/wellpoint-to-pay-17-million-settlement-a-5904 (Accessed 15 June 2021).

Landi, H. (2020). Premera blue cross to pay 6.9 million to HHS for 2014 data breach. *Fierce Healthcare*, September 2020. Available at: https://www.fierce-healthcare.com/tech/premera-blue-cross-to-pay-6-9m-to-hhs-for-2014-data-breach (Accessed 19 September 2021).

Lutkevich, B. (2019). DMZ in networking. *TechTarget*. Available at: https://searchsecurity.techtarget.com/definition/DMZ (Accessed 10 September 2021).

Miliard, M. (2020). Premera blue cross to pay $6.85M to settle 2015 breach. *Healthcare IT News*. Available at: https://www.healthcareitnews.com/news/premera-blue-cross-pay-685m-settle-massive-2015-breach#:~:text=The%20breach%20at%20the%20Washington,data%20of%2010.4%20million%20people (Accessed 23 May 2021).

Morse, S. (2018). Anthem pays $16 million in record HIPAA settlement for data breach. *Healthcare Finance News*. Available at: https://www.healthcarefinancenews.com/news/anthem-pays-16-million-record-hipaa-settlement-data-breach (Accessed 15 June 2021).

National Audit Office. (2017). *Investigation: WannaCry cyber attack and the NHS - National Audit Office (NAO) report*. Available at: https://www.nao.org.uk/report/investigation-wannacry-cyber-attack-and-the-nhs/ (Accessed 30 March 2021).

Office of Civil Rights. (2012). Department of Health & Human Services. 2017, HHS HIPAA breach settlement involving less than 500 patients. *HHS.gov*. Available at: https://www.hhs.gov/sites/default/files/ocr/privacy/hipaa/enforcement/examples/honi-agreement.pdf (Accessed 19 September 2021).

Office of Civil Rights. (2013). *Department of health & human services, final rule: HIPAA 45 Parts 160 and 164*. Available at: https://www.govinfo.gov/content/pkg/FR-2013-01-25/pdf/2013-01073.pdf (Accessed 19 September 2021).

Ouellette, P. (2013). Wellpoint and HHS agree to data breach resolution. *Health IT Security*, July 12. Available at: https://healthitsecurity.com/news/wellpoint-and-hhs-agree-to-health-data-breach-resolution (Accessed 19 September 19, 2021).

Rouse, M. (2019). What is DMZ (networking)?: Definition from WhatIs.com. *SearchSecurity*. Available at: https://searchsecurity.techtarget.com/definition/DMZ (Accessed 10 September 2021).

Chapter 8

Data Security, Cybersecurity, Legal and Ethical Implications for Digital Health: A European Perspective

Christoph Ellßel and Daniel Flemming

Contents

DOI: 10.4324/9781003281047-8

Data in Digital Health and Nursing

Due to their central role in healthcare, nurses have always been an information hub for patients, other clinicians and within their own profession. Nurses often use and produce or collect data, information and knowledge within nursing, its management or research—in both analog and digital modes. Digitalization in healthcare is commonly referred to as 'eHealth.' The World Health Organization (WHO) defines eHealth as 'the cost-effective and safe use of information and communication technologies to support health and health-related areas, including health services, health surveillance, health literature, and health education, knowledge and research' (WHO, 2021). This WHO definition outlines a wide range of use cases for data, information and knowledge in healthcare that encompasses the individual, professional and institutional levels. Thus, eHealth is not an end in itself, but must serve different concepts of healthcare, in which nurses often play a prominent role (Hübner, 2006). Regardless of setting or level, the core of digital health is valid, current, legal and ethical data (Gerlach et al., 2021). Implementing adequate safeguards against theft or loss, dealing with regulatory imperatives as well as addressing essential ethical concerns is crucial for the success of digital health solutions.

Primary Use

Certainly, the bulk of digital applications are designed for and used in clinical settings. As shown in Figure 8.1, data generation and primary use of data happen in hospitals/clinics, in residential and long-term care and in domiciliary home care by patient/family and healthcare professionals.

A variety of front-end, mobile or digital solutions may be used in direct patient care delivery; however, the core is still the capturing and storage of the various data and information in the electronic patient record. There are both semi-structured elements, for example, progress notes, and structured entries, such as diagnoses, medications,

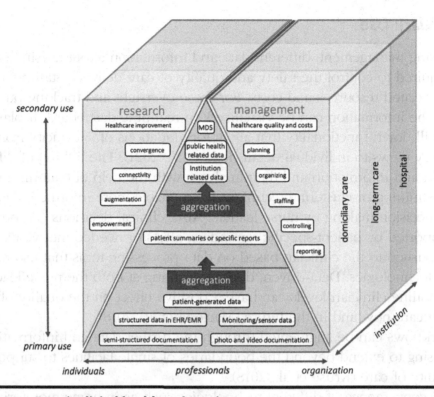

Figure 8.1   Data in digital health and nursing.

interventions and outcomes (Häyrinen et al., 2008). Patient-generated data may also be included in the person's electronic patient record (Marceglia et al., 2017). The data can be collected using wearables or monitoring devices for measuring cardiac functioning and blood sugar levels or for capturing vital signs and physical activity (Rodriguez-León et al., 2021; DeVore et al., 2019). Alternatively, information can be obtained through diary entries (Rodriguez et al., 2019) or questionnaires or surveys (Tiase et al., 2020). Depending on the application, further information can be provided via images (e.g., in the context of wound care (Dong et al., 2019)) or via telehealth tools (Rygg et al., 2018).

If patients are transferred between departments or facilities, it is important to ensure continuity of care with a seamless flow of information between those involved. Information from the point of care will be aggregated to a discharge summary (Huebner et al., 2010) or special reports (Roberts et al., 2018). Further aggregation of data and information results in the form of the minimum datasets (Ranegger et al., 2015; Mack et al., 2020) that can be used for quality assurance at the level of institution or for statistical purposes in the context of public health.

Secondary Use

In nursing management, different data and information about nursing care are required to control the safety and quality of care delivery, staffing and the associated resources and costs. For these oversight and tracking purposes, the information can be visualized on real-time dashboard displays with drill down functionality that allow for gradations of specificity from summary views to individual detail (Role et al., 2021). The linking of different data and information and their analyses with the help of data mining, process mining or clustering techniques can enable more informed, data-based decision-making by nurse leaders. Also, clinical decisions can be better supported by patient-specific reminders, alerts or needed interventions being pushed to the clinician based on data processing tools that use new digital technologies. Data-driven, decision-making at both the nurse leader and frontline clinician levels can have a positive effect on the quality of nursing care now and in the future (Macieria et al., 2018).

Workflows can be augmented through the further data and information processing to extend beyond the boundaries of single facilities to support continuity of care (Kruse et al., 2018).

The convergence of different technologies such as in-home-monitoring, smart technologies and robotic systems will lead to a convergence of the different knowledge domains (Sapci et al., 2019). Additionally, the development and easier dissemination of new knowledge by using information and communication technologies like artificial intelligence (AI) will empower patients (Power et al., 2020) but also nursing by expanding and shaping their professional roles.

These new digital applications and technologies open up new areas for health and nursing research, and greatly increase the knowledge and skills complexity facing nursing and nurses in the informatics field.

Data Security and Cybersecurity

Securing data from unauthorized access, change, theft or loss usually relies on technical and operational standards of data security or cybersecurity (EU Cybersecurity, 2020). In general, these standards are established and maintained by international as well as European and national institutions, in terms of both political and technical issues. In the following section, we review these standards and show how the European and national frameworks interact.

European Frameworks

As of 2021, cybersecurity is not mentioned in treaties of the European Union (EU) as an area of European legislation. Rather, European frameworks address cybersecurity issues through policy guidelines, e.g., the 2013 Cybersecurity Strategy—last updated 2020 (EU Cybersecurity, 2020). The EU Cybersecurity policy targets providing cyber and physical 'resilience' against security threats and aims for technological sovereignty. Through a revised *Critical Entities Resilience* (CER) directive (EU Critical Entities Resilience, 2020), it also addresses issues of strengthening the protection of critical infrastructure and explicitly mentions issues of health and health providers. However, its influence is limited to political aims and providing funding for academic and industrial research and development (R&D) as well as industry investment. A common European technological standard for implementing cybersecurity measures or referencing industry standards is currently not available.

National Data Security Frameworks

Apart from the rather small *European Union Agency for Cybersecurity*, the European Union lacks a common institution for data security, even though a variety of institutions exist on national levels that establish national solutions for the cybersecurity or the protection of critical infrastructure. The *Bundesamt für Sicherheit in der Informationstechnik* (BSI) in Germany or the *Agence Nationale de la Sécurité des Systèmes d'information* (ANSSI) in France are two examples. These two organizations among others provide advice to governments, providers of critical infrastructure and industries, and also maintain public standards of (enterprise level) security guidelines, and provide up-to-date sets of basics for certification (e.g., the IT Baseline Protection Catalog of the BSI, 'IT Grundschutz'; (Schildt, 2021)). Those guidelines implement risk- or threat-based approaches based on classifications of designated data uses as well as the consequences of loss or disruption. The national developed guidelines draw on global industry standards like (e.g., ISO 27001/27002) for documentation and provides a comprehensive approach on how to set up and maintain a secure environment for storing and processing different classes of data, providing hands-on best practices for health data environments. Furthermore, national self-regulatory industry standards regarding technological impact assessment like the *VDI Technikbewertung 3780*, by the *Association of German Engineers* (VDI) also influence national data security implementations (VDI, 2000).

Threat Assessment

The goal of the guidelines within the European Economic Area (EEA), such as the *IT Baseline Protection Catalog*, is to assess risks for any IT system in order to establish an acceptable level of protection, security and safety. This risk-based approach does not aim to providing an absolute safe environment. The goal is to systematically address threats for the integrity, availability, security and system safety; and to do so proactively to ensure a level of protection adequate to the demands and level of data stored/processed. By focusing on threat assessment, in most cases a high degree of individualized protection can even be achieved without detailed regulations. Guidelines like the *Baseline Protection Catalog* are the basis for voluntary self-certifications, as it also includes a detailed threat assessment that would suggest technical, infrastructural, organizational and personal measures needed for protection.

Security in Cloud Computing

In cloud computing, the actual place of data storage (e.g., a specific, known hard drive) is not relevant, as long as data is available online. Usually, cloud computing includes contracts on terms and conditions for service availability. Customers are not aware of where their data are being stored or mirrored for redundancy. From a technological or economical view, using cloud computing methods is advisable under certain circumstances; however, further aspects affecting security (e.g., the financial stability of the hosting provider or the trustworthiness) currently have to be monitored, as well as information regulations observed.

Within the member states of the European Union, technological standards of services may differ due to various national agencies, so in most cases, international industry standards are agreed upon. In addition, from a legal point of view, storing or processing data in the cloud anywhere within the legal jurisdiction of the EEA is usually not a problem as it refers to similar rules. However, cloud computing possibilities are limited, especially in transferring, storing or processing health data in countries with lower protection standards. In such instances, a case-by-case review is considered necessary (see also major discussions regarding 'Safe Harbour,' 'Schrems I' and 'Schrems II' (Spies, 2020) on the comparability of data protection standards in the United States and the EEA).

Big Data

Big data is in many cases linked to questions of cloud computing, but not necessarily addressing the same issues. A growing number of European countries, as well as the EU itself, are building open health databases, which make it mandatory for public-funded research programs to contribute in open standard formats (e.g., Yale Open Data Access/YODA). In most cases, big data relies on anonymous data, meaning that there is no link to an individual. The secondary use of anonymous data enables a much broader scope of processing and does not require explicit consent. From a security point of view, aspects of re-identification have to be considered. It is obvious that securing files enabling a reconnection of personal with health data has to be accounted for by the very strong standards as outlined above, but makes the handling of the anonymous data and opening it up much easier, also for collaborative works.

The growing number of open databases within the EU (like the European Data Portal/EDP) sheds light on the growing significance of big data within the EU (Figure 8.2).

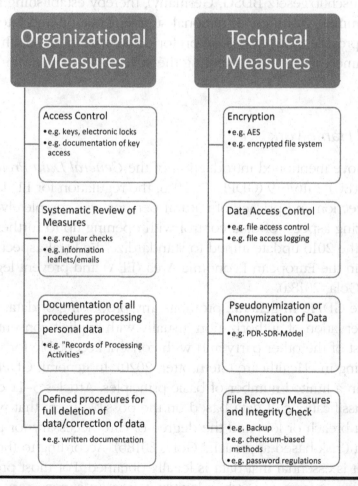

Figure 8.2   Technical and organizational measures Art. 32 GDPR—examples and relations. Source: diagram by authors.

Legal

The term 'privacy' in the United States' history of ideas has a much broader understanding compared to Europe: it is understood here that privacy refers to a European concept of private in reference to 'the public' (van den Hoven et al., 2020). From a systematic point of view, privacy protection in European law is essentially based on two principles. These principles are rooted in measures that aim to secure human privacy, and common personal law that focuses on individual's rights in relation to society and principles of liberty or individual freedom to act (Charta of Fundamental Rights of the EU, 2012; Gola, 2018b). Within the EU, privacy rights are established through the *General Data Protection Regulation* on a common EU level (GDPR, 2016), as well as through a number of nation-based privacy laws (e.g., Bundesdatenschutzgesetz BDSG, Germany), thereby establishing a complementary common ground with national supplementation and interpretation. The GDPR provides special protection for data concerning health and sets the legal framework for implementing the state-of-the-art data protection measures.

GDPR–EU Framework

With the above mentioned introduction of the *General Data Protection Regulation* (EU) 2016/679 (GDPR) in 2016, the regulation for EU law in terms of data protection and privacy of natural persons was completely revised. By centralizing aspects of data control with opening up to further national regulation, the 2016 update aimed to standardize the legal aspects of data processing in the European Economic Area (EEA) and prevent legal 'forum shopping' (Gola, 2018a).

While the GDPR, in general, prohibits any processing of data, it allows it under a reservation of authorization, usually with explicit consent or legitimate interest of the other party and with consent acceptable for wide-ranging processing in eHealthcare (Steinrötter, 2020). In general, GDPR rulings are rooted in a limited number of basic principles. Articles 5–11 categorize different classifications of data based on the possible harm that would be caused by a breach or loss and the degree of care necessary for processing the data ('risk-based approach,' Gola, 2018b). According to these basic principles, it is essential that data is legally obtained. For most processing and storage apart from research, a legitimate reason is necessary and any processing is bound by it. Furthermore, it is essential to implement measures to delete data after usage and provide periods of data retention. Apart from these legal requirements, the processing or storage of data generally is not allowed in the EEA. Within the GDPR, health data is seen as a subcategory of data and is legally defined as 'data concerning health, i.e. data related to the physical or mental health of a natural person, including the provision of healthcare services, which reveal information about that person's health status' (Article 4 GDPR). Health data is part of the special categories of data associated with elevated requirements of processing in Article 9 GDPR (Schulz, 2018). As such, health data requires *explicit*, usually written consent of the party affected, even in cases where the treatment services are provided on a contractual basis (e.g., a contract governing medical treatment).

Paradigms

In general, the GDPR relies on the principles of 'privacy by design,' 'data protection by design' and a 'risk-based approach.' This approach comes in accordance with the above mentioned technical classification of data by its designated use, where health data usually is protected in strict limitations of processing (Gola, 2018b):

- 'Privacy by design' focuses on a need-to-know basis in collecting data, minimizing (personal) information collected without clear assessment of the potential usage.
- 'Data protection by design' relies on the proper use of technology in processing data and minimizing the risk of loss through appropriate technical and organizational measures, also connected with a limited principle of 'data protection by default', therefore using privacy ground rules as a default.
- 'Risk-based approach' analyses data collected and processed especially focusing on the social impact of data lost and/or published, i.e., associating data protection measures furthermore by the severity of its content (e.g., data affecting patients' sexual orientation in comparison to names or telephone numbers).

To implement these paradigms, in a number of cases, a Data Protection Impact Assessment (DPIA) must be done (Art 35 GDPR) before collecting data. This holds especially in cases where 'risky' data, or data with the potential to cause serious harm if published (e.g., cases mentioned in Article 9, health data) is to be collected. Once more, this approach refers back to the classification of data by its (designated) use, not by its source. Usually, DIPA means analyzing the classes of data collected and providing adequate protection measures on a risk-based model in written form. In adhering to the classification of the designated use, the use of management data (without data affecting health), therefore, is much easier than, e.g., research data (possibly without potential usage limitations). As such, the origin of data (e.g., sensors, ePrescription (eP))—is only of limited importance in the assessment of the data collected, as the prospective use is of much higher relevance to categorize the data.

Technical and Organizational Measures

Connecting these legal requirements and paradigms with actual implementations (e.g., in health providing institution) subsequently relies on technical and organizational measures, which, if set up in accordance and are well maintained, can limit liability in case of breaches (Art 32 GDPR). As the fines stipulated by law are comparably harsh and may seriously affect the organization's financial well-being, the proper implementation and documentation of technical and organizational measures are highly advisable.

Taking the needed safeguards usually means that the measures have to be appropriate for the categories of data stored and processed. In general, the risk assessment would take on the following correspondence— the higher the risk, the more careful the proper measures, planning and project documentation needs to be. Usually, data concerning health are attached to high risks for impacting the personal rights of the subject: These projects demand a high standard of data protection measures, both technologically and organizational. 'Appropriate' measures do not have to be completely risk-free. But, following the principles outlined above, a serious assessment of the likelihood of the loss or theft of data is necessary. Therefore, a broad variety of measures is possible, as long as they are considered to be 'adequate.'

Unfortunately for the field, the GDPR itself makes no current requirements on how to implement such measures, but delivers a set of standards for examining the adequacy of measures with the case's individual circumstances. These include, among others as outlined in Article 32 GDPR: state of the art; implementation costs; nature, scope, context and purposes; and the risk of varying likelihood and severity for the rights and freedoms of natural persons in case of loss or publication. Taken together, these categories deliver the basis for a framework for collecting and processing digital health data. In general, 'state of the art' means implementing well-established, industry standards for health data like the *Baseline Protection Catalog* by the BSI (BSI, 2007) and maintaining current documentation of re-evaluation for standard health data. This usually means that core processes of data collection, storage, processing, deletion and rectification are well documented, and standards are kept current. Aspects of physical access control, documentation of access of records, etc., usually are part of those standards and are essential for managing associated risks.

National Regulations

The stipulations in Article 9 GDPR for 'health by design data' intentionally leave room for national laws ('opening clause'). Therefore, most member states have chosen to implement further regulations and a variety of detail regulations are in coexistence (like the *Bundesdatenschutzgesetz* BDSG-neu) among the EEA. In the field of health data, those mainly are addressing the issues of research, insurance or infectious diseases data, sometimes even leaving room for regional regulations, linking to questions of administering health (Schreiber and Gottwald, 2020). However, the basic set of standards draws on the standards defined by the GDPR, so in most cases apart from, e.g., public health, the influence from national law in general is rather limited.

Anonymization and Pseudonymization

As the GDPR's regulations are limited to cases of *personal* data, anonymizing data provides a reliable method of using data without the 'legal strings attached.' Anonymizing means successfully and irrevocably deleting any personal references. Pseudonymization means that all personal references are replaced by a placeholder. The data is still attributable, but only for someone in possession of a file linking the placeholder to the real identity ('Personal Data Record—Scientific Data Record'; PDR-SDR). However, the limitations are as such, that in reality, re-connecting personal data to the health data in question has to be highly impractical though not impossible (Münch, 2017). This requirement limits its application in the field of, e.g., rare diseases or personalized treatment, as by just blanking or replacing a real name someone familiar with the process or the field could be able to re-identify the individual in question by the circumstances described. Applying correct measures of anonymization therefore is crucial, with methods ranging from obfuscating/masking (partial) data to explicitly shuffling data or using data hashes. As long as the methods to ensure data anonymity are considered appropriate, the regulations of the GDPR, as well as the national laws, are met, therefore enabling a huge range of data processing options. This usually is the case for entering data into public (national) health databases used for research or 'big data' analyses.

Ethical Implications

While the collection of large scopes of data is, as mentioned, at the core of digital health, it also raises serious ethical concerns, which need to be addressed. Historically speaking, the concept of privacy is comparably new, but refers to established philosophical concepts of individual liberty and freedom of action: This often conflicts with government and social order aspects. Here we provide a limited overview of the various aspects of ethical approaches with a special focus on current European practices in the field, as issues at stake are usually complex and under pressure by economic changes (Weber, 2019).

Data sovereignty and data ownership are conflicting theories. Both provide the philosophical–ethical background of the legal requirements stipulated in the GDPR underlying the concept of 'informed consent.' This context is crucial for understanding current ethical approaches toward digital health. However, philosophical and ethical approaches reach out far beyond the issues of the GDRP, discussing aspects of intrusion and acceptance as well as of fear and skepticism. Therefore, while the GDPR gives us a general framework for legal implementations, the broader discussions address the key aspects of interaction between humans and technology (Weber, 2019; Lühmann and Raspe, 2008). Other than in the United States, privacy in the European tradition is more seen as a question of control within private settings or thoughts (e.g., home, places where one is staying, letters), and rather less as an individual's general 'right of being left alone' (Warren & Brandeis, 1890).

Data Sovereignty

Data sovereignty results from the notion that humans produce and provide data all the time. It is rooted in an understanding of personal philosophy. Data sovereignty focuses on the implications and risks associated with data used and potential hazards for the individual's future freedom of action by controlling the degree to which one is aware of providing data. For example, just by observing someone talking about being very tired, looking pale, collecting the mail and immediately afterward with an expression of horror using a mobile phone, a keen observer would be able to analyze a behavioral pattern and presume a possible chain of events. The question, therefore, is not so much *that* data is provided *at all*, but whether this happens intentionally or at least with the expectation that the data is stored or used. By enabling the individual to control this, freedom of action is secured and establishes a right to be informed about (and to deny) the usage of any kind of personal data, may it be in written form or by actions (e.g., CCTV, sensor data). Therefore, to ensure that data collected is acceptable, informing the individual in an adequate way is crucial: They must be aware of the consequences, and the higher the risk, the more detailed the information to the individual has to be. In addition, it is essential that the understanding has to be seen from the individual's perspective, presented in plain language and simple concepts. When it comes to digital, eHealth data, information toward the provider of data has to be as simple as possible but must cover the complexity involved.

Data Ownership

In contrast to the idea of data sovereignty, theories of data ownership are strongly linked to concepts of transactional or contractual philosophy. Using personal data as a legitimate trade item (e.g., trading personal information against free or discounted web portal access like Facebook or WhatsApp), control is limited to frameworks for the economic sphere only (Schulz, 2018). As popular as such ideas are in 'non-essential' domains like entertainment or shopping, its influence is limited when it comes to healthcare or public administration. The ethical unavailability of certain data for purposes of trade or marketing comes from concepts of natural law (e.g., human rights). This restriction means less frequent aspects of market ideas in healthcare and narrower influence. Ethical assumptions based on data ownership and/ or 'data against treatment' are usually less frequent in the sphere of institutional health, but are under discussion in the fields of personal apps (e.g., for a healthier lifestyle) or individual fitness tracking.

Informed Consent

Drawing on current models of ethical interaction and discourse ethics, the key to having the legal and ethical permission to do data collection relies on an individual being able to give meaningful consent. Therefore, aspects of vulnerability (e.g., in misleading patients with the possibility of a cure, misusing trust in health providers or patients being under the influence of drugs affecting decision-making) are essential to address, as well as options to change or alter one's decision.

Informed consent also relies on the idea that all necessary information that can be understood by the persons affected regarding potential dangers and potential benefits be given. That usually means refraining from extensive medical or legal jargon, limiting the scope of information provided to an amount that can be interpreted and providing answers to further questions.

Current debates in ethics and (data) philosophy include aspects of data concerning the core of individual liberties and if it is acceptable to demand a consent as the consequences are impossible to foresee. This discussion focuses on mass data ('big data'), tracking individuals' behavior 24/7 for years and weighting the (massive) loss of privacy against the possible enormous gains from research. In addition, questions of a limited understanding have to be considered when it comes to patients with restrictions of free will due to impaired mental states due to injury or diseases involving dementia/neurological issues.

Ensuring the individual's free decision in (not) consenting can be complicated in reality, and influenced by economic and busy work environments, especially in healthcare settings. From an ethical perspective, relying on established standards and trying to prevent surprising clauses or deceptive information help minimize possible infractions by respecting the individual's free will, decision-making.

Further Concepts

In addition to these theories, so-called 'utilitarian philosophy' ideas have been discussed in the field of digital health as well. Utilitarian theories generally represent the idea that the better for most, the more acceptable something is. This common good concept is having a major impact, especially on questions of participation in research studies with limited or no influence on the participating individual's well-being. Even minor in its influence, this utilitarian debate is happening in European institutional healthcare philosophy and is affecting current debates on public health and big data.

Applied Frameworks

Based on these theories discussed above, several frameworks regarding practical implementations of technological innovations in nursing or healthcare have been developed. Mainly, those refer to theories of discourse ethics, including aspects of viability in daily routines, privacy issues or specific problems in patients with limited ability to understand the complex problems. Frameworks like *MEESTAR* (Weber, 2016) or *Value Sensitive Design* (Friedman, 1996) provide helpful assessment tools for addressing ethical issues in health or nursing settings.

Summary

Data is at the core of digital health. To address the connecting fields of industry standards, legal requirements and ethical considerations, it is necessary to maintain coherent planning and understand the borders and interactions of technology, law and ethics. As all fields mentioned above interrelate on various levels, a broad understanding of the limits and subsequent rules is essential—not only to generate usable data but also to address more significant concerns in society toward digital health.

Usable data in digital health has to be obtained and processed in legal ways within the EEA, which means following the regulations of the GDPR. Embedded are the philosophical concepts of non-ownership of data and free will, as illustrated in Figure 8.3. In this framework, 'informed' consent is the basis for individual decisions and maintaining autonomy. As the GDPR itself is open to changing technological standards, no reference implementation is provided, but various current standards suit the needs. National guidelines like the *IT Baseline Protection Catalog* (BSI, 2007) can be considered sufficient to address those regulatory requirements by providing risk- and threat-based assessments. Implementing technical, infrastructural, organizational and personal measures in accordance with the Catalog's guidelines provide a framework for storing and processing health data in an acceptable way. The common ground for all of these requirements is their focus on designated uses and a risk-based approach regarding threats and possible harm caused by loss or publication of data.

To successfully implement innovative digital health solutions as well as to transition established routines or techniques toward the digital age, it is crucial to understand the chain of references from ethics-to law-to industry standards for a reasonable implementation, as presented in this chapter. Working with interprofessional teams usually means collaborating with specialists from various fields: A collective understanding of the process is essential for success. As such, for ensuring public acceptance for innovative

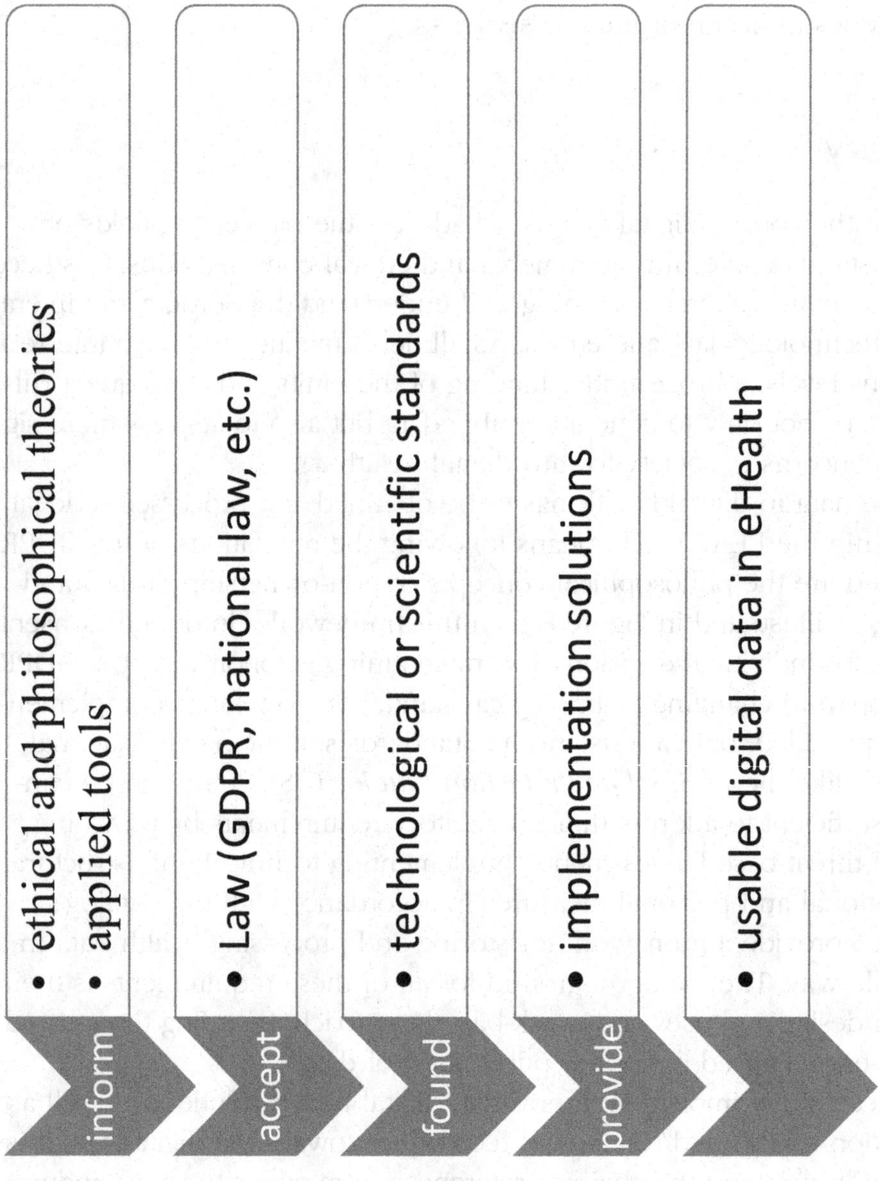

Figure 8.3 How to obtain valid, current, legal and ethical data. Source: diagram by authors.

developments in the field of digital health, understanding the 'bigger picture' should be considered indispensable.

References

Association of German Engineers (VDI), eds. (2000). *Technology assessment 3780: Concepts and foundations*. 9th ed. Dusseldorf: VDI-Verlag.

BSI Federal Office for Information Security. (2007). *BSI: Baseline protection catalogue*. Available at: http://www.bsi.bund.de/gshb/deutsch/download/it-grund-schutz-kataloge_2006_de.pdf (Accessed 30 August 2021).

DeVore, A. D., Wosik, J., & Hernandez, A. F. (2019). The future of wearables in heart failure patients. *JACC: Heart Failure*, 7(11), pp.922–932. https://doi.org/10.1016/j.jchf.2019.08.008

Dong, W., Nie, L.-J., Wu, M.-J., Xie, T., Liu, Y.-K., Tang, J.-J., Dong, J.-Y., Qing, C., & Lu, S.-L. (2019). WoundCareLog APP: A new application to record wound diagnosis and healing. *Chinese Journal of Traumatology = Zhonghua Chuang Shang Za Zhi*, 22(5), pp.296–299. https://doi.org/10.1016/j.cjtee.2019.07.003

Friedman, B. (1996). Value-sensitive design. *Interactions*, 3, pp.16–23.

Gerlach, F. et al. (2021). *Digitalisierung für Gesundheit. Ziele und Rahmenbedingungen eines dynamisch lernen Gesundheitssystems. Report of the German Council of Health System Experts*. Berlin: Sachverständigenrat zur Begutachtung der Entwicklung im Gesundheitswesen. Available at: https://www.svr-gesundheit.de/fileadmin/Gutachten/Gutachten_2021/SVR_Gutachten_2021_online.pdf (Accessed 25 May 2021).

Gola, P. ed. (2018a). *Datenschutzgrundverordnung VO (EU) 2016/679. Kommentar*. 2nd ed. Munich: Beck.

Gola, P. (2018b). Introduction. In P. Gola, ed., *Datenschutzgrundverordnung VO (EU) 2016/679. Kommentar*. 2nd ed. Munich: Beck, pp.123–146.

Häyrinen, K., Saranto, K., & Nykänen, P. (2008). Definition, structure, content, use and impacts of electronic health records: A review of the research literature. *International Journal of Medical Informatics*, 77(5), pp.291–304. https://doi.org/10.1016/j.ijmedinf.2007.09.001

Hübner, U. (2006). Telematics and nursing does the German electronic health card improve patient care for persons with nursing needs? *GMS Medizinische Informatik, Biometrie und Epidemiologie*, 2(1). http://www.egms.de/en/journals/zma/2006-2/mibe000020.shtml

Hübner, U., Flemming, D., Heitmann, K. U., Oemig, F., Thun, S., Dickerson, A., & Veenstra, M. (2010). The need for standardised documents in continuity of care: Results of standardising the eNursing summary. *Studies in Health Technology and Informatics*, 160(Pt 2), pp.1169–1173.

Kruse, C. S., Marquez, G., Nelson, D., & Palomares, O. (2018). The use of health information exchange to augment patient handoff in long-term care: A systematic review. *Applied Clinical Informatics*, 9(4), pp.752–771. https://doi.org/10.1055/s-0038-1670651

Lühmann, D., & Raspe, H. (2008). Ethik im health technology assessment: Anspruch und Umsetzung. *Zeitschrift für Evidenz, Fortbildung und Qualität im Gesundheitswesen*, 102(2), pp.69–76.

Macieira, T. G. R., Smith, M. B., Davis, N., Yao, Y., Wilkie, D. J., Lopez, K. D., & Keenan, G. (2018). Evidence of progress in making nursing practice visible using standardized nursing data: A systematic review. *AMIA Annual Symposium Proceedings*, 2017, pp.1205–1214.

Mack, D. S., Jesdale, B. M., Ulbricht, C. M., Forrester, S. N., Michener, P. S., & Lapane, K. L. (2020). Racial segregation across U.S. nursing homes: A systematic review of measurement and outcomes. *The Gerontologist*, 60(3), pp.e218–e231. https://doi.org/10.1093/geront/gnz056

Marceglia, S., D'Antrassi, P., Prenassi, M., Rossi, L., & Barbieri, S. (2017). Point of care research: Integrating patient-generated data into electronic health records for clinical trials. *AMIA Annual Symposium Proceedings*, 2017, pp.1262–1271.

Münch, F. (2017). *Autonome Systeme im Krankenhaus. Datenschutzrechtlicher Rahmen und strafrechtliche Grenzen*. Baden-Baden: Nomos.

Power, K., McCrea, Z., White, M., Breen, A., Dunleavy, B., O'Donoghue, S., Jacquemard, T., Lambert, V., El-Naggar, H., Delanty, N., Doherty, C., & Fitzsimons, M. (2020). The development of an epilepsy electronic patient portal: Facilitating both patient empowerment and remote clinician-patient interaction in a post-COVID-19 world. *Epilepsia*, 61(9), pp.1894–1905. https://doi.org/10.1111/epi.16627

Ranegger, R., Hackl, W. O., & Ammenwerth, E. (2015). Implementation of the Austrian nursing minimum data set (NMDS-AT): A feasibility study. *BMC Medical Informatics and Decision Making*, 15, p.75. https://doi.org/10.1186/s12911-015-0198-7

Roberts, J. C., Johnston-Walker, L., Parker, K., Townend, K., & Bickley, J. (2018). Improving communication of patient issues on transfer out of intensive care. *BMJ Open Quality*, 7(4), p.e000385. https://doi.org/10.1136/bmjoq-2018-000385

Rodriguez, S., Hwang, K., & Wang, J. (2019). Connecting home-based self-monitoring of blood pressure data into electronic health records for hypertension care: A qualitative inquiry with primary care providers. *JMIR Formative Research*, 3(2), p.e10388. https://doi.org/10.2196/10388

Rodriguez-León, C., Villalonga, C., Munoz-Torres, M., Ruiz, J. R., & Banos, O. (2021). Mobile and wearable technology for the monitoring of diabetes-related parameters: Systematic review. *JMIR mHealth and uHealth*, 9(6), p.e25138. https://doi.org/10.2196/25138

Role, J., Chao, H., Rosario, C., Ho, P., & Hodgkins, M. (2021). Inpatient staffing dashboard: A nursing-information technology collaborative project. *Computers, Informatics, Nursing: CIN*. https://doi.org/10.1097/CIN.0000000000000778

Rygg, L. O., Brataas, H. V., & Nordtug, B. (2018). Introducing videoconferencing on tablet computers in nurse-patient communication: Technical and training challenges. *International Journal of Telemedicine and Applications*, 2018, p.8943960. https://doi.org/10.1155/2018/8943960

Sapci, A. H., & Sapci, H. A. (2019). Innovative assisted living tools, remote monitoring technologies, artificial intelligence-driven solutions, and robotic systems for aging societies: Systematic review. *JMIR Aging*, 2(2), p.e15429. https://doi.org/10.2196/15429

Schildt, H., ed. (2021). *IT-Grundschutz-Kompendium*. Berlin: Bundesamt für Sicherheit in der Informationstechnik.

Schreiber, K., & Gottwald, B. (2020). Gesundheits-App auf Rezept. Die neue Datenschutzprüfung im Digitale-Versorgung-Gesetz. *Zeitschrift für Datenschutz*, 2020(8), pp.385–390.

Schulz, S. (2018). Artikel 7. In P. Gola, ed., *Datenschutzgrundverordnung VO (EU) 2016/679. Kommentar*. 2nd ed. Munich: Beck, pp.328–350.

Spies, A. (2020). Schrems-II-Urteil des EuGH und die USA: Mehr Licht! *Zeitschrift für Datenschutz*, 2020(10), pp.549–550.

Steinrötter, B. (2020). Datenschutzrechtliche Implikationen beim Einsatz von Pflegerobotern. Frühzeitig eingeholte Einwilligungen als Schlüssel für zulässige Geriatronik-Anwendungen. *Zeitschrift für Datenschutz*, 2020(7), pp.336–341.

The European Union. (2016). *Regulation (EU) 2016/679 of the European Parliament and of the Council of 27 April 2016 on the protection of natural persons with regard to the processing of personal data and on the free movement of such data, and repealing Directive 95/46/EC (General Data Protection Regulation)*. Brussel: European Commission. Available at: https://eur-lex.europa.eu/eli/reg/2016/679/oj (Accessed 25 May 2021).

The European Union. (2020a). *Directive on the on the resilience of critical entities*. Brussels: European Commission. Available at: https://ec.europa.eu/home-affairs/sites/default/files/pdf/15122020_proposal_directive_resilience_critical_entities_com-2020-829_en.pdf (Accessed 1 September 2021).

The European Union. (2020b). *EU cybersecurity strategy. The EU's cybersecurity strategy in the digital decade*. Brussels: European Commission. Available at: https://digital-strategy.ec.europa.eu/en/library/eus-cybersecurity-strategy-digital-decade (Accessed 25 May 2021).

Tiase, V. L., Hull, W., McFarland, M. M., Sward, K. A., Del Fiol, G., Staes, C., Weir, C., & Cummins, M. R. (2020). Patient-generated health data and electronic health record integration: A scoping review. *JAMIA Open*, 3(4), pp.619–627. https://doi.org/10.1093/jamiaopen/ooaa052

van den Hoven, J. et al. (2020). Privacy and information technology. *The Stanford Encyclopedia of Philosophy* (Summer 2020 Edition) (online). Available at: https://plato.stanford.edu/archives/sum2020/entries/it-privacy/ (Accessed 25 May 2021).

Warren, S., & Brandeis, L. (1890). The right to privacy. *Harvard Law Review*, 193(IV). Available at: http://faculty.uml.edu/sgallagher/Brandeisprivacy.htm (Accessed 25 May 2021).

Weber, K. (2016). MEESTAR²—Ein erweitertes Modell zur ethischen Evaluierung sozio-technischer arrangements. In R. Weidner, ed., *Technische Unterstützungssysteme, die die Menschen wirklich wollen*. Hamburg: Helmut-Schmidt-Universität, pp.317–326.

Weber, K. (2019). Methoden der ethischen Evaluation von IT. In C. Draude et al., eds., *INFORMATIK 2019 workshops lecture notes in informatics (LNI).* Bonn: Gesellschaft für Informatik, pp.431–444. https://doi.org/10.18420/inf2019_ws47

WHO EMRO | eHealth. (2021). *Health topics.* (o. J.). Abgerufen 22. Juni 2021, von. Available at: https://www.emro.who.int/health-topics/ehealth/

Chapter 9

The Impact of Digital Technologies, Data Analytics and AI on Nursing Informatics: The New Skills and Knowledge Nurses Need for the 21st Century

Charlene H. Chu, Aaron Conway, Lindsay Jibb and Charlene E. Ronquillo

Contents

DOI: 10.4324/9781003281047-9

Introduction

In Part 1, we briefly highlight a few key areas of nursing practice impacted by digital technologies, artificial intelligence (AI), machine learning (ML) and data analytics. This description will provide the snapshot of the practice context and the technological/digital ecosystem within which nurses work, as well as the risks and benefits related to current technologies. In Part 2, we highlight the skills and knowledge that nurses need to navigate the digital world in a safe, ethical and equitable way. Inherent in the latter half of the chapter is the reconceptualization of 'traditional' nursing roles and the meaningful evolution of nursing to advance the profession.

Part 1: The New Digital Age of Nursing and Technologies

Digital Technologies and Its Impact on Nursing

Digital technologies impact clinical decision-making, workflows, provision of compassionate care and care modalities (virtual or in-person) impacting nursing practice. Within traditional healthcare settings, like hospitals and long-term care facilities, research suggests that advancements in digital technologies may change and potentially improve clinical workflows, health outcomes and patient and family satisfaction with care (Birnie et al., 2018; Chu et al., 2021a; Jibb et al., 2017a, b; Tanioka et al., 2019). One form of digital technologies changing nursing practice is clinical decision support systems (CDSSs) that integrate best practice knowledge and use machine learning (ML)-driven prediction models to inform clinical decision-making, reduce nursing documentation time and allow more time for patient care (Bail et al., 2021; Buchanan et al., 2020b). Robotic devices are another type of advanced digital technology that can complete tasks like seeking and retrieving supplies as well as stocking storerooms (Servaty et al., 2020) and minimizing nurse exposures to infectious agents (Freeman et al., 2020). Further, humanoid robots may facilitate transactive and therapeutic relationships, enhance engagement in rehabilitation, provide patient education and support pain management (Ali et al., 2021; Buchanan et al., 2020b; Kriegel et al., 2019; Tanioka et al., 2019).

Digital technologies are also expected to reflect the attributes of compassionate care—a core value of the nursing profession reflected in theory, education and practice (Buchanan et al., 2020a; Luxton, 2014). Virtual nursing care models are at the intersections of technology and compassionate care. An example would be the virtual chatbot software applications that use natural language processing (NLP) to conduct online conversations with humans to provide mental health resources and to support clients (Buchanan et al., 2020b; Luxton, 2014). Other examples are nurse-engaged mobile device applications and text-messaging solutions that enable nurses to remotely monitor patients and virtually provide clinical advice that led to improved patient-reported health outcomes and satisfaction (Jibb et al., 2017b; Zhang et al., 2018).

The potential, positive effect of virtual nursing care models on health outcomes and system strain has been highlighted in a recent consensus statement (Lewinski et al., 2021). However, nurses need to carefully consider local contextual factors during technology implementation and create mechanisms to support the integrated reporting, evaluation and associated process changes related to new systems. Future research in this area includes: (1) the core components of successful virtual care practices (e.g., healthcare professionals, stakeholders, infrastructure needs), (2) the resources needed to support the nurses delivering virtual care, (3) determine which patients or clients might benefit the most and (4) seek out the optimal mode of virtual delivery for each patient or client.

Data Analytics and Its Impact on Delivery of Nursing Care

The systems and devices that nurses interact with daily, from the electronic health record (EHR) to physiological monitoring systems, store data in an accessible format. Such 'routinely collected' information about patients through the healthcare system can leverage new insights through data analytics. Importantly, these technologies cast light on the previously invisible work of nursing within healthcare organizations, such as the frequent and detailed collection of data on nursing actions like clinical assessments and communication with the team. In doing so, the important impact of nurses on patient and system outcomes is captured and can be quantified (Bergey et al., 2019).

There are three broad categories in which data analysis of routinely collected healthcare data will prove particularly useful in the future: organizational performance, resource allocation and the integration of local data into clinical decision support systems (CDSS). At the organizational level, presentation of *performance* metrics in real time is a feature of analytics used in current nursing practice, for example, the creation of dashboards containing data visualizations to communicate real-time performance metrics. The analyses of routinely collected healthcare data like 30-day hospital readmissions and patient falls are common markers used to judge healthcare quality (Lambert et al., 2016). Predictive data analytics can also be applied for *resource allocation,* for example, predictive data analytics can provide insights into the optimal composition of nursing teams to improve the quality of care (Spetz, 2021). Lastly, Rajkomar and colleagues demonstrate how state-of-the-art, deep learning methods were able to integrate local data into the CDSS to predict mortality risk from raw EHR records. Such advancements can produce highly accurate insights and improve quality of care (Rajkomar et al., 2018).

Artificial Intelligence and Its Impact on the Delivery of Nursing Care

A defining feature of our current digital world is the ubiquitous nature of data collection whereby virtually every Internet connected device is collecting data throughout our daily lives. These data can enable healthcare professionals to gain insights about conditions, illness trajectories and treatments, as well as how we practice (and should practice) in technology-enabled care settings. The digitalization of health-related records and specialized datasets, among other factors, has accelerated the uptake of artificial intelligence (AI) in healthcare and nursing (Naylor, 2018). As nurses often complete the most documentation in healthcare systems (Collins et al., 2018), they generate a significant amount of EHR data that is used to build and train AI models. The nature and quality of nurses' documentation directly impacts accuracy and robustness of AI-driven applications in healthcare (Ronquillo et al., 2021).

There are many examples of emerging AI technologies impacting nursing practice and patient outcomes that are based on data entered by nurses.

Examples of AI models based on EHR data include the following algorithms: those that pre-emptively predict delirium in patients undergoing cardiac surgery (Mufti et al., 2019); that identify patients at high risk for falls in real time to alert care staff (e.g., nurses) (Moskowitz et al., 2020); that predict suicide risk (Walsh et al., 2021) and hospital length of stay (Ma et al., 2020; Daghistani et al., 2019). AI is also being used to advance symptom science research using natural language processing (NLP) techniques on unstructured clinical notes entered by nurses and allied health professionals (Topaz et al., 2019). One study identified up to 11 times more additional synonym words or expressions compared to the baseline Unified Medical Language System synonym lists, and unique multi-word combinations used in the clinical notes to describe constipation, depressed mood, disturbed sleep and fatigue (Koleck et al., 2021). Thus, AI can impact nurses and their practice by helping extract symptom information from EHR notes in an accurate and scalable manner for lexicon enrichment and discovery

As the role of technology continues to influence our clinical decisions, questions regarding the accuracy emerge. Current challenges in AI relate to possible unintended consequences of AI on care or the patient–nurse relationships, as well as ethical and social implications—including the potential for AI to perpetuate bias and the lack of transparency and explainability of algorithms (Cutillo et al., 2020). Applying AI-driven systems outside of the populations represented in the training and validation of datasets (Matheny et al., 2020) can be problematic. The role of nurses as data producers is especially crucial in the context of AI, as societal biases can be embedded into AI algorithms when they use missing, incomplete or inaccurate data (Reddy et al., 2020). As data producers and enablers of data quality, nurses will require new skills and knowledge to ensure that AI and digital technologies can optimally serve patients, communities and healthcare systems. In the next section, we outline five roles and capacities for nursing practice in the 21st century.

Part 2: New Skills and Knowledge Nursing Need in the 21st Century

Nurse as Advocate

The nursing profession espouses the value of advocacy for the needs of patients, families, communities and populations, as expressed in professional codes of nursing practice (Kalaitzidis & Jewell 2020). Broadly, patient advocacy by nurses relates to providing support and representation for patients to protect patient autonomy, preferences and well-being, while empowering valuing and respecting patients (Abbasinia et al., 2020; Kalaitzidis & Jewell, 2020). In the context of digital technologies and AI, the advocacy role of nurses is particularly poignant. In the following sections, we relate the issues of nursing advocacy to equity and access, suitability of technologies, and privacy, confidentiality and data ownership. We draw from a concept analysis by Abbasinia et al. (2020) that identifies five key attributes of patient advocacy in nursing in the context of digital technologies: safeguarding, apprising, valuing, mediating and championing social justice in healthcare provision.

Advocacy for Equity and Access for Patients, Communities and Populations

Not all individuals and populations can currently benefit from the use of digital technologies. The digital divide—the gap between those who have access to the Internet and digital technologies and those who do not—is a substantial barrier (Van Dijk, 2020). Inequities fuel most contributors to the digital divide including: basic access to the Internet and information technology infrastructure (e.g., poor Internet connectivity in rural areas), access to hardware (e.g., computers are not affordable or accessible) and digital literacy skills (i.e., inability or ineffective use of technologies and the Internet) (Van Dijk, 2020).

A basic understanding of the digital divide and how it translates to inequities in health service delivery and outcomes is needed to effectively advocate for equitable access to digital health (Van Dijk, 2020). Nurses can leverage their knowledge of health equity toward application in the digital technologies sphere. For example, nurses are well positioned to recognize that the increasing shift toward virtual care impacts certain groups differently because of the digital divide, potentially exacerbating existing health inequities. Such impacts were apparent during the COVID-19 pandemic where those who were already most vulnerable suffered disproportionately as their access to technology and virtual care was impeded (Chu et al., 2021a; Weiss et al., 2018).

Advocacy for equitable access to digital technologies will need to consider the attributes of *valuing*, *mediating* and *championing social justice*. *Valuing* relates to nurses' support for patients' maintenance of autonomy and self-control, and recognition of a patient's individuality, humanity, values and beliefs, and preferences (O'Connor & Kelly, 2005). In the context of digital technologies, *valuing* involves supporting patient preferences for how their care is delivered. This may sometimes mean advocating for patients' preferences to *opt out* of the use of digital health tools or decline virtually delivered health services. Until digital health technologies are routinely developed for universal abilities and based on user-centered design approaches, nurses need to be able to recognize when in-person alternatives may be more appropriate for a patient.

Mediating relates to nurses as a liaison between patients and the healthcare team in which nurses amplify and provide a voice for the patient (Abbasinia et al., 2020; Waterman et al., 2020). In the context of digital technologies, nurses' mediating role resembles their existing roles as facilitators and communicators. Mediating involves liaising between the requirements to support health services delivery (e.g., use of specific tools) and the preferences of patients. Where patients' needs may be in opposition of desired technologies (e.g., installation of remote monitoring devices in a patient's home that the patient does not want), mediating will involve coordinating care between the team and patients to find acceptable solutions.

Crucially, an understanding of the potential for AI to amplify existing societal biases and the ways that data shape AI are necessary knowledge bases for nurses. *Championing social justice* in the context of digital technologies requires identifying potential blind spots. For example, a system may require that all patients be registered into an electronic system or that digital health tools are used to track patients. Nurses can apply an equity lens and critically examine how the use of such technologies may be worrisome and influence help-seeking behaviors for some patient populations (e.g., undocumented migrants, older people).

Advocacy for Privacy, Confidentiality, Data Ownership, Patient Representation

We refer to the patient advocacy attributes of *safeguarding*, *apprising* and *mediating* (Abbasinia et al., 2020) in the following discussion about nurses engaging on issues related to patient privacy and confidentiality. *Safeguarding* refers to nurses' actions to protect patients from misconduct or incompetency of other healthcare professionals or the healthcare system (Abbasinia et al., 2020; Sundqvist et al., 2016). *Apprising* refers to actions taken to ensure that patients are aware of their rights to be involved in their care and well-informed about all aspects of their health status and care provision. This right extends to knowing one's diagnosis, treatment options, prognosis and post-discharge plans and care (Sundqvist et al., 2016). Ensuring data quality is an important, although often overlooked, part of nurses' safeguarding patients. Nurses' documentation can impact clinical decision-making among the interdisciplinary team by virtue of the nature and quality of data that are recorded. In digitalized health systems, a complete and accurate representation of the patient is an important way of affording protections: technology solutions should be informed by patient data that are as accurate, complete and up to date as possible. Thus, *safeguarding* and *apprising* patient data are important ways that nurses can advocate for patients. Informed consent in the context of digitalized health systems extends current requirements to ensure that patients understand the legal and ethical considerations relating to data management. The informed consent process requires the ability to explain to patients how their data are protected, who has access to their data and the various ways that their data may be used (i.e., for immediate care and re-use in predictive risk algorithms) within policies that will vary by organization, jurisdiction and country.

Nurse as Explainer

AI is often described as a 'black box' that lacks explainability, meaning a lack of transparency about how variables are integrated into models, and which has hindered clinical translation (Topol, 2019). For example, deep neural networks which power machine learning (ML) and AI are incredibly complex involving learnable values (weights) and hundreds or thousands of dimensions of data. The inability for clinicians and patients to understand the logic behind the predictive factors can diminish trust in the output.

Nurses have an ethical duty to ensure basic principles of informed consent are met as part of professional standards and practices (College of Nurses of Ontario, 2017). Nurses as 'explainers of AI' for patients require the knowledge and critical reflexivity to address key questions related to consent and ethics. For example, how can patients give informed consent for clinical decisions from a machine if neither the nurse nor the patient understand how the decisions were made? And, to what extent does the nurse need to understand the processes involved in an AI system to be able to effectively communicate to a patient? One of nurses' greatest ethical responsibilities is non-maleficence (i.e., avoid causing harm in all care delivery), which requires an awareness and knowledge about the tools used to provide care. As such, nurses must ensure that patients understand what is *being explained*.

Looking to data privacy, confidentiality and protection regulations can provide guidance as to what may be required of nurses as explainer. For example, the European Union General Data Protection Regulation (GDPR) requires that companies give users an explanation for decisions ('must provide meaningful information about the logic involved') that are made by 'automated' systems. Legal debates over how 'meaningful information' is defined and the types of law that apply to AI like contracts and tort law are ongoing (Hacker, 2020). As indicated in Article 22 of the GDPR related to automated, individual decision-making, the 'right to explanation' gives patients the human right to understand critical issues about their health or disease management if the decision is 'based solely on automated processing.' However, the practical problem posed is one of the liabilities for clinicians, hospitals and healthcare systems that would be held accountable for predictions/decisions made by AI in the 'black box.' The need to explain becomes more pressing as AI becomes more sophisticated and accurate, beyond human capabilities. It is plausible that to avoid liability for medical malpractice, clinicians may soon be mandated to rely on AI if new standards of care based on AI are created (Froomkin et al., 2019). In the realm of research, resultant movements toward 'explainable artificial intelligence' (XAI) and 'responsible AI' have been established (Gunning et al., 2019). These movements seek to develop systems that can maintain privacy and are more inclusive, fair, safe and transparent—and importantly have accountability mechanisms that are understandable to humans.

Nurse as Implementer

The fields of information science and implementation science provide frameworks and models to better understand nurses' substantial influence in the success or failure of digital health technologies. The Technology Acceptance Model (TAM) and its various iterations (Davis, 1989; Davis et al., 1989) and the Unified Theory of Acceptance and Use of Technology (UTAUT; Venkatesh & Bala, 2008; Venkatesh, 2015) are among commonly used models that nurses can use to examine individual-level factors (e.g., attitudes toward technologies, perceived usefulness of technologies, perceived computer self-efficacy), as predictors of individuals' acceptance and adoption of digital health technologies. Meanwhile, implementation science models can identify the structural and contextual factors that influence technology implementation such as the Consolidated Framework for Implementation Research (Damschroder et al., 2009) and the Reach, Efficacy/Effectiveness, Adoption, Implementation and Maintenance (RE-AIM) framework, among others (Minichiello et al., 2013). Theoretical understanding requires upstream approaches, including technology-focused education in undergraduate and graduate programs to promote digital professionalism and literacy (O'Connor et al., 2020; O'Connor & LaRue, 2021).

Nurses from clinical practice to the administration can influence digital technology implementation in health systems. Their ability to interpret findings within the context of person-centered care is critical to this function (Dowding et al., 2018; Konttila et al., 2019). Nursing leaders must ensure that nurses can recognize cultural and social cues and then advocate for equitable and person-centered care when technology is integrated into care delivery. Nurses must utilize critical thinking skills, turn to evidence, and consider how each intervention can be applied (or not) to a specific patient, for example, how compassionate and culturally sensitive care can be provided to a diverse population (Bail et al., 2021; Buchanan et al., 2020b).

Nurse as Co-creator

Nurses are often viewed as passive end-users of technology and thus are not actively engaged in healthcare technology codesign and evaluation: this non-involvement has negative impacts on implementation and user- and patient experience (Dykes & Chu, 2020). Yet, nurses are the backbone of most healthcare systems. Nurses constitute the majority of the healthcare workers in most of the OECD (Organization for Economic Co-operation and Development) countries and can be found working in many different care sectors (e.g., acute, home, community; public, private). Nurses have in-depth knowledge about patients, the illness trajectory, social determinants of health and the communities in which their patients live, as well as the clinical context and workflow in these settings. This expertise is often ignored, much to the detriment of successful technology implementation and adoption. Research shows that when it comes to developing technology, clinicians were key to identifying the clinical need, informing the development and helping determine the optimal places for intervention while minimizing disruption to workflow (Watson et al., 2020).

Nurses can play a critical role as a creator of technology solutions by participating in the design, development and implementation of technologies and by developing the policies and processes that sustain their adoption. User-centered design approaches (Chu et al., 2021b; Greenhalgh et al., 2016; Unertl et al., 2016) centralize the users' needs and contexts in an iterative design process, and ideally, will result in technologies that can better cater to diverse digital literacies and abilities. It is widely accepted that co-created health technologies will be more acceptable with a higher likelihood of implementation (Nielsen, 1994). Nurses can work closely with vulnerable patient populations to create solutions that work for the patient and their caregivers. One example is an exergaming platform (e.g., games that promote physical activity) for older adults living in long-term care homes. The platform development involved a user-centered, design approach that included older adults, their family and home staff as participants (Chu et al., 2021b; Sultana et al., 2018). User testing showed increased moods and enjoyment, and the technology is being evaluated in a nurse-led, multiple-centered site, randomized controlled trial. Another example is the Pain Squad+ smartphone application (app) developed by nurses to support real-time cancer pain treatment for adolescent patients (Jibb et al., 2017a; Jibb et al., 2020). Preliminary effectiveness results showed improvements in pain intensity and health-related quality of life for the adolescent cancer patient. Currently, the app is being evaluated in a randomized controlled trial (Jibb et al., 2020).

Nurse as Analyst

Providing nurses with the data analysis skills and education needed to leverage ML and AI technologies may help advance integrated care. For instance, central to ML applications in healthcare research are the concepts of *prediction* and *classification*. Put simply, prediction in ML means that we use what we can 'learn' from data drawn from one sample of the population, and then use that information to make a 'guess' about what will be observed in a different sample from the same population. Simple 'statistical' models can be used for just this purpose. We can quantify the relationship between the outcome and predictor variables using linear regression by finding a line of best fit. By fitting the 'line' and determining the intercept and slope coefficients, all we need to make a 'guess' about what the outcome will be for a person not included in the original sample are the predictor variables that were used to fit the regression model. The other major approach to ML is called 'classification.' This is when instead of predicting what a numerical score will be given the predictors included in the model, the goal is to predict which 'class' the outcome should be assigned. Image classification is one example of this type of approach to ML. For classification, we are interested in determining how often the classification predicted by the model was correct and incorrect. This last portion of the chapter demonstrates the nurse as analyst role using a public dataset as a case study.

Building and Evaluating the Accuracy and Usefulness of Predictive Models: Case Study

---

BOX 4.10.1   PREDICTOR VARIABLES

- Age
- Sex
- Severity of dementia (from Mini-Mental State Examination)
- Length of stay in hospital
- Pittsburgh Agitation Scale score
- Barthel score

Having information about patients' quality of life (QoL) would be useful in clinical practice. However, additional time and resources are required to undertake validated QoL scoring procedures. Being able to accurately 'predict' QoL score from other information that is already routinely collected would mean additional resources are not required. This section uses a publicly available dataset of 526 hospitalized patients with dementia (Lüdecke, 2019) to demonstrate how ML can be used to predict QoL. In the study, each patient's QoL was rated using a validated scale called the QALIDEM (Ettema et al., 2007). QALIDEM scores range from 0 to 100 with higher scores indicating better QoL. For this prediction problem, QUALIDEM score is the 'outcome' that we are interested in being able to predict. The predictor variables selected were those we considered as part of routine clinical practice for this population (Box 4.10.11).

Training and Test Sets

The first step is to partition our dataset into components called the 'training' and 'test' sets. The 'training' set will contain 75% of the participants and this is the data we will use to train or 'fit' our model. The 'test' set containing the remaining 25% of the data will be set aside so that we can use it to determine how accurately our model can predict the QoL scores on unseen data. The proportion of data held out for the test set is a somewhat arbitrary choice and will depend on the overall size of the sample. For example, for large sample sizes, it may be more appropriate to use a 90/10 split, because 10% of the data would provide a large enough sample with which to estimate generalizability with satisfactory precision. Only the training set is used for the next step, model selection, which is described below.

Candidate Models and Cross-Validation for Model Selection

It is typical in ML to evaluate several different 'candidate models' and determine which one yields the best predictions. We build and evaluate predictive models using a basic linear regression model in the sections below; 'random forest' and 'xgboost' models are also used.

It is recommended to use an approach known as 'cross-validation' for model selection. Figure 9.1 shows the process of cross-validation. Each row, comprising 20 squares, represents the training data. The lighter-shaded squares indicate the portion of data used to 'train' the model and the darker-shaded squares indicate the portion of data used to 'test' how well the model performed. The key takeaway is that several models must be evaluated to determine the most accurate model RMSE stands for 'root mean square error,' and it measures how accurately a model predicts the outcome. Calculating RMSE is a way that we can determine how well the model

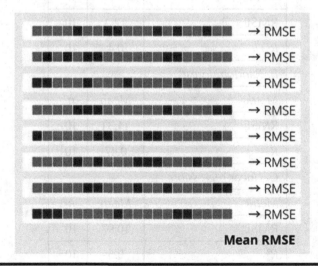

Figure 9.1   (Chu) Visual description of cross-validation.

Table 9.1   Predictions from the XGBoost Model

ID	Observation	Prediction	Truth
Fold01	29	61.79	40
Fold01	66	37.80	41
Fold01	68	56.42	62

performs by getting the average of the differences between the predicted and the true values (i.e., the error) for each patient.

Table 9.1 displays some results from our training of the xgboost model to predict QoL. The 'ID' column shows which step of the cross-validation process this result was produced from, the 'Observation' column is an identification for the patient, the 'Prediction' column is the QoL score predicted by the model (i.e., the 'predicted' value) and the 'Truth' column was the actual quality of life score (i.e., the 'true value') measured in the study for that patient. The 'predicted' value is sometimes quite close to the 'true' value and sometimes it is quite different.

The 'n' column of Table 9.2, A. XGBoost, indicates the number of 'cross-validation' iterations from which the RMSE was calculated. In this case, ten iterations were used. The RMSE for the xgboost model was 12.3

Table 9.2   Performance of the Models

A. XGBoost		
Metric	Mean	n
RMSE	12.3	10
R^2	0.4	10
B. Random forest		
Metric	Mean	n
RMSE	11.31	10
R^2	0.47	10
C. Linear regression		
Metric	Mean	n
RMSE	10.97	10
R^2	0.5	10

RMSE, root mean square error.

and is presented below. Note that the *lower* the RMSE, the *better* the predictive ability of the model. It is important to evaluate several different candidate models to determine which one is best. Thus, the same approach can be done using cross-validation for the 'random forest' and 'linear regression' models (Table 9.2, B. Random forest; C. Linear regression).

Readers should be aware that the way 'accuracy' of predictions is evaluated differs between 'prediction' and 'classification.' For prediction, we used the RMSE as shown in this case study. There are a variety of different ways to present this information for classification, including the sensitivity and specificity of the model and the area under the receiver operating characteristics curve (AUROC or AUC for short).

Making Predictions with 'New' Data

The linear regression model performed the best out of our selection of candidate models because it had the lowest RMSE score (Table 9.2, C. Linear regression). Now that the best model has been selected, one can go ahead and see how well it performs on unseen data. This 'unseen' data is the 'test' set partition we made in the first step of the process described above. Saving data for validation of the model is a very important part of ML because it allows for the ability to determine the extent to which 'overfitting' may be a concern with the model developed. Overfitting of a model is indicated by an RMSE that is much higher in the test set than what was found during training. For example, if it was found that the RMSE for predicting QoL score was 11 in cross-validation but 20 in the 'test' set, this would indicate that our model did not 'generalize' well to unseen data. This would mean the model is an overfit and not suitable for use in clinical practice.

The following section evaluates whether the linear regression model fitted to the training data performs well on the remaining data (i.e., the 'test' set). There were 131 participants in our test set. Table 9.3 displays predictions for the first five patients. The first column is the predicted value for QoL using the linear regression model. The second column is the actual QoL score, manually scored for the patient. The last column, 'Error,' is the difference between the predicted and manually scored values.

RMSE in the test set was 11.9, which is similar to what was observed in the training data, indicating that the model was not an 'overfit.' Note that it is important now to determine if a model that on average is 'off' from the true value by about 12 points is accurate enough to be useful in clinical practice. This decision and judgment should be informed by strong empirical science,

Table 9.3   Predictions on Test Set Using the Linear Regression Model

Prediction	Truth	Error
54	69	15
48	38	−10
62	61	−1
45	46	1
51	44	−7

while balancing the risks and benefits, and consider the ethical and social implications. Nurses and patients have an important voice in these types of decisions.

Conclusion

The advent of new digital technologies requires nurses to acquire news skills and knowledge and to develop new aspects of nursing that are steadfast in the tradition of providing compassionate and person-centered care. Nurses can integrate these new aspects of the nursing role into their practice and be at the forefront of not only the design and adoption of technologies but also playing a critical role to ensure there is careful consideration of the ethical and social implications of technologies in the 21st digital century.

References

Abbasinia, M., Ahmadi, F., & Kazemnejad, A. (2020). Patient advocacy in nursing: A concept analysis. *Nursing Ethics*, 27(1), pp.141–151. https://doi.org/10.1177 /0969733019832950

Ali, S., Manaloor, R., Ma, K., Sivakumar, M., Beran, T., Scott, S. D., Vandermeer, B., Beirnes, N., Graham, T. A., Curtis, S., & Jou, H. (2021). A randomized trial of robot-based distraction to reduce children's distress and pain during intravenous insertion in the emergency department. *Canadian Journal of Emergency Medicine*, 23(1), pp.85–93. https://doi.org/10.1007/s43678-020-00023-5

Bail, K., Merrick, E., Fox, A., Gibson, J., Hind, A., Moss, C., Strickland, K., & Redley, B. (2021). Ten statements to support nurse leaders implement e-health tools for nursing work in hospitals: A modified Delphi study. *Journal of Clinical Nursing*, 30(9–10), pp.1442–1454. https://doi.org/10.1111/jocn.15695

Bergey, M. R., Goldsack, J. C., & Robinson, E. J. (2019). Invisible work and changing roles: Health information technology implementation and reorganization of work practices for the inpatient nursing team. *Social Science & Medicine*, 235, p.112387. https://doi.org/10.1016/j.socscimed.2019.112387

Birnie, K. A., Kulandaivelu, Y., Jibb, L., Hroch, P., Positano, K., Robertson, S., Campbell, F., Abla, O., & Stinson, J. (2018). Usability testing of an interactive virtual reality distraction intervention to reduce procedural pain in children and adolescents with cancer. *Journal of Pediatric Oncology Nursing*, 35(6), pp.406–416. https://doi.org/10.1177/1043454218782138

Buchanan, C., Howitt, M. L., Wilson, R., Booth, R. G., Risling, T., & Bamford, M. (2020a). Nursing in the age of artificial intelligence: Protocol for a scoping review. *JMIR Research Protocols*, 9(4), p.e1749. https://doi.org/10.2196/17490

Buchanan, C., Howitt, M. L., Wilson, R., Booth, R. G., Risling, T., & Bamford, M. (2020b). Predicted influences of artificial intelligence on the domains of nursing: Scoping review. *JMIR Nursing*, 3(1), p.e23939. https://doi.org/10.2196/23939

Chu, C. H., Biss, R. K., Cooper, L., Quan, A. M. L., & Matulis, H. (2021b). Exergaming platform for older adults residing in long-term care homes: User-centered design, development, and usability study. *JMIR Serious Games*, 9(1), p.e22370. https://doi.org/10.2196/22370

Chu, C. H., Ronquillo, C., Khan, S., Hung, L., & Boscart, V. (2021a). Technology recommendations to support person-centered care in long-term care homes during the COVID-19 pandemic and beyond. *Journal of Aging & Social Policy*, 33(4–5), pp.459–473. https://doi.org/10.1080/08959420.2021.1927620

College of Nurses of Ontario. (2017). *Practice guideline: Consent*, College of Nurses of Ontario [online]. Available at: https://www.cno.org/globalassets/docs/policy/41020_consent.pdf (Accessed 10 May 2021).

Collins, S., Dykes, P., Bates, D. W., Couture, B., Rozenblum, R., Prey, J., O'Reilly, K., Bourie, P. Q., Dwyer, C., Greysen, S. R., & Smith, J. (2018). An informatics research agenda to support patient and family empowerment and engagement in care and recovery during and after hospitalization. *Journal of the American Medical Informatics Association*, 25(2), pp.206–209. https://doi.org/10.1093/jamia/ocx054

Cutillo, C. M., Sharma, K. R., Foschini, L., Kundu, S., Mackintosh, M., & Mandl, K. D. (2020). Machine intelligence in healthcare: Perspectives on trustworthiness, explainability, usability, and transparency. *NPJ Digital Medicine*, 3(1), pp.1–5. https://doi.org/10.1038/s41746-020-0254-2

Daghistani, T. A., Elshawi, R., Sakr, S., Ahmed, A. M., Al-Thwayee, A., & Al-Mallah, M. H. (2019). Predictors of in-hospital length of stay among cardiac patients: A machine learning approach. *International Journal of Cardiology*, 288, pp.140–147. https://doi.org/10.1016/j.ijcard.2019.01.046

Damschroder, L. J., Aron, D. C., Keith, R. E., Kirsh, S. R., Alexander, J. A., & Lowery, J. C. (2009). Fostering implementation of health services research findings into practice: A consolidated framework for advancing implementation science. *Implementation Science*, 4(1), p.50. https://doi.org/10.1186/1748-5908-4-50

Davis, F. D. (1989). Perceived usefulness, perceived ease of use, and user acceptance of information technology. *MIS Quarterly*, 13(3), pp.319–340. https://doi
.org/10.2307/249008

Davis, F. D., Bagozzi, R. P., & Warshaw, P. R. (1989). User acceptance of computer
technology: A comparison of two theoretical models. *Management Science*,
35(8), pp.982–1003. https://doi.org/10.1287/mnsc.35.8.982

Dowding, D., Merrill, J. A., Onorato, N., Barrón, Y., Rosati, R. J., & Russell, D.
(2018). The impact of home care nurses' numeracy and graph literacy on com-
prehension of visual display information: Implications for dashboard design.
Journal of the American Medical Informatics Association, 25(2), pp.175–182.
https://doi.org/10.1093/jamia/ocx042

Dykes, S., & Chu, C. H. (2020). Now more than ever, nurses need to be involved in
technology design: Lessons from the COVID-19 pandemic. *Journal of Clinical
Nursing*, 30(7–8), pp.e25–e28. https://doi.org/10.1111/jocn.15581

Ettema, T. P., Dröes, R. M., de Lange, J., Mellenbergh, G. J., & Ribbe, M. W. (2007).
QUALIDEM: Development and evaluation of a dementia specific quality of
life instrument-validation. *International Journal of Geriatric Psychiatry*, 22(5),
pp.424–430. https://doi.org/10.1002/gps.1692

Freeman, W. D., Sanghavi, D. K., Sarab, M. S., Kindred, M. S., Dieck, E. M., Brown,
S. M., Szambelan, T., Doty, J., Ball, B., Felix, H. M., & Dove, J. C. (2020).
Robotics in simulated COVID-19 patient room for health care worker effec-
tor tasks: Preliminary, feasibility experiments. *Mayo Clinic Proceedings:
Innovations, Quality & Outcomes*, 5(1), pp.161–170. https://doi.org/10.1016/j
.mayocpiqo.2020.12.005

Froomkin, A. M., Kerr, I., & Pineau, J. (2019). When AIs outperform doctors:
Confronting the challenges of a tort-induced over-reliance on machine learning. *Arizona Law Review*, 61, p.33. https://doi.org/10.2139/ssrn.3114347

Greenhalgh, T., Jackson, C., Shaw, S., & Janamian, T. (2016). Achieving research
impact through co-creation in community-based health services: Literature
review and case study. *The Milbank Quarterly*, 94(2), pp.392–429. https://doi
.org/10.1111/1468-0009.12197

Gunning, D., Stefik, M., Choi, J., Miller, T., Stumpf, S., & Yang, G. Z. (2019). XAI:
Explainable artificial intelligence. *Science Robotics*, 4(37), p.eaay7120. https://
doi.org/10.1126/scirobotics.aay7120

Hacker, P., Krestel, R., Grundmann, S., & Naumann, F. (2020). Explainable AI under
contract and tort law: Legal incentives and technical challenges. *Artificial
Intelligence and Law*, 28, pp.415–439. https://doi.org/10.1007/s10506-020
-09260-6

Jibb, L., Nathan, P. C., Breakey, V., Fernandez, C., Johnston, D., Lewis, V., McKillop,
S., Patel, S., Sabapathy, C., Strahlendorf, C., & Victor, J. C. (2020). Pain Squad+
smartphone app to support real-time pain treatment for adolescents with
cancer: Protocol for a randomised controlled trial. *BMJ Open*, 10(3), p.e037251.
https://doi.org/10.1136/bmjopen-2020-037251

Jibb, L. A., Cafazzo, J. A., Nathan, P. C., Seto, E., Stevens, B. J., Nguyen,
C., & Stinson, J. N. (2017a). Development of a mHealth real-time pain

self-management app for adolescents with cancer: An iterative usability testing study. *Journal of Pediatric Oncology Nursing*, 34(4), pp.283–294. https://doi.org/10.1177/1043454217697022

Jibb, L. A., Stevens, B. J., Nathan, P. C., Seto, E., Cafazzo, J. A., Johnston, D. L., Hum, V., & Stinson, J. N. (2017b). Implementation and preliminary effectiveness of a real-time pain management smartphone app for adolescents with cancer: A multicenter pilot clinical study. *Pediatric Blood & Cancer*, 64(10), p.e26554. https://doi.org/10.1002/pbc.26554

Kalaitzidis, E., & Jewell, P. (2020). The concept of advocacy in nursing: A critical analysis. *The Health Care Manager*, 39(2), pp.77–84. https://doi.org/10.1097/HCM.0000000000000079

Koleck, T. A., Tatonetti, N. P., Bakken, S., Mitha, S., Henderson, M. M., George, M., Miaskowski, C., Smaldone, A., & Topaz, M. (2021). Identifying symptom information in clinical notes using natural language processing. *Nursing Research*, 70(3), pp.173–183. https://doi.org/10.1097/NNR.0000000000000488

Konttila, J., Siira, H., Kyngäs, H., Lahtinen, M., Elo, S., Kääriäinen, M., Kaakinen, P., Oikarinen, A., Yamakawa, M., Fukui, S., & Utsumi, M. (2019). Healthcare professionals' competence in digitalisation: A systematic review. *Journal of Clinical Nursing*, 28(5–6), pp.745–761. https://doi.org/10.1111/jocn.14710

Kriegel, J., Grabner, V., Tuttle-Weidinger, L., & Ehrenmüller, I. (2019). Socially Assistive Robots (SAR) in in-patient care for the elderly. *Studies in Health Technology and Informatics*, 260, pp.178–185. https://doi.org/10.3233/978-1-61499-971-3-178

Lambert, L. J., Madan, M., Gong, Y., Forsey, A., Galbraith, D., Gill, N., Oakes, G. H., Lavoie, A., Carere, R. G., Welsh, R. C., & PCI Quality Indicator Working Group (2016). Quality of care for percutaneous coronary intervention: Development of Canadian Cardiovascular Society quality indicators. *Canadian Journal of Cardiology*, 32(12), pp.1570–1573. https://doi.org/10.1016/j.cjca.2016.07.511

Lewinski, A. A., Sullivan, C., Allen, K. D., Crowley, M. J., Gierisch, J. M., Goldstein, K. M., Gray, K., Hastings, S. N., Jackson, G. L., McCant, F., & Shapiro, A. (2021). Accelerating implementation of virtual care in an integrated health care system: Future research and operations priorities. *Journal of General Internal Medicine*, 36(8), pp.2434–2442. https://doi.org/10.1007/s11606-020-06517-3

Lüdecke, D. (2019). Dataset: Quality of life of patients with dementia in acute hospitals. *Zenodo* [online]. https://doi.org/10.5281/zenodo.3351450

Luxton, D. D. (2014). Recommendations for the ethical use and design of artificial intelligent care providers. *Artificial Intelligence in Medicine*, 62(1), pp.1–10. https://doi.org/10.1016/j.artmed.2014.06.004

Ma, X., Si, Y., Wang, Z., & Wang, Y. (2020). Length of stay prediction for ICU patients using individualized single classification algorithm. *Computer Methods and Programs in Biomedicine*, 186, p.105224. https://doi.org/10.1016/j.cmpb.2019.105224

Matheny, M. E., Whicher, D., & Israni, S. T. (2020). Artificial intelligence in health care: A report from the National Academy of Medicine. *Journal of American Medical Association*, 323(6), pp.509–510. https://doi.org/10.1001/jama.2019.21579

Minichiello, V., Rahman, S., Dune, T., Scott, J., & Dowsett, G. (2013). E-health: Potential benefits and challenges in providing and accessing sexual health services. *BMC Public Health*, 13(1), p.790. https://doi.org/10.1186/1471-2458-13-790

Moskowitz, G., Egorova, N. N., Hazan, A., Freeman, R., Reich, D. L., & Leipzig, R. M. (2020). Using electronic health records to enhance predictions of fall risk in inpatient settings. *The Joint Commission Journal on Quality and Patient Safety*, 46(4), pp.199–206. https://doi.org/10.1016/j.jcjq.2020.01.009

Mufti, H. N., Hirsch, G. M., Abidi, S. R., & Abidi, S. S. R. (2019). Exploiting machine learning algorithms and methods for the prediction of agitated delirium after cardiac surgery: Models development and validation study. *JMIR Medical Informatics*, 7(4), p.e14993. https://doi.org/10.2196/14993

Naylor, C. D. (2018). On the prospects for a (deep) learning health care system. *Journal of the American Medical Association*, 320(11), pp.1099–1100. https://doi.org/10.1001/jama.2018.11103

Nielsen, J. (1994). *Usability engineering*. Elsevier [online]. Available at: https://uweb.engr.arizona.edu/~ece596c/lysecky/uploads/Main/Lec9.pdf (Accessed: 3 May 2021).

O'Connor, S., & LaRue, E. (2021). Integrating informatics into undergraduate nursing education: A case study using a spiral learning approach. *Nurse Education in Practice*, 50, p.102934. https://doi.org/10.1016/j.nepr.2020.102934

O'Connor, S., Chu, C. H., Thilo, F., Lee, J. J., Mather, C., & Topaz, M. (2020). Professionalism in a digital and mobile world: A way forward for nursing. *Journal of Advanced Nursing*, 76(1), pp.4–6. https://doi.org/10.1111/jan.14224

O'Connor, T., & Kelly, B. (2005). Bridging the gap: A study of general nurses' perceptions of patient advocacy in Ireland. *Nursing Ethics*, 12(5), pp.453–467. https://doi.org/10.1191/0969733005ne814oa

Rajkomar, A., Oren, E., Chen, K., Dai, A. M., Hajaj, N., Hardt, M., Liu, P. J., Liu, X., Marcus, J., Sun, M., & Sundberg, P. (2018). Scalable and accurate deep learning with electronic health records. *NPJ Digital Medicine*, 1(1), p.18. https://doi.org/10.1038/s41746-018-0029-1

Reddy, S., Allan, S., Coghlan, S., & Cooper, P. (2020). A governance model for the application of AI in health care. *Journal of the American Medical Informatics Association*, 27(3), pp.491–497. https://doi.org/10.1093/jamia/ocz192

Ronquillo, C. E., Peltonen, L. M., Pruinelli, L., Chu, C. H., Bakken, S., Beduschi, A., Cato, K., Hardiker, N., Junger, A., Michalowski, M., & Nyrup, R. (2021). Artificial intelligence in nursing: Priorities and opportunities from an international invitational think-tank of the Nursing and Artificial Intelligence Leadership Collaborative. *Journal of Advanced Nursing*, 77(9), pp.3707–3717. https://doi.org/10.1111/jan.14855

Servaty, R., Kersten, A., Brukamp, K., Möhler, R., & Mueller, M. (2020). Implementation of robotic devices in nursing care. Barriers and facilitators: An integrative review. *BMJ Open*, 10(9), p.e038650. https://doi.org/10.1136/bmjopen-2020-038650

Spetz, J. (2021). Leveraging big data to guide better nurse staffing strategies. *BMJ Quality and Safety*, 30(1), pp.1–3. https://doi.org/10.1136/bmjqs-2020-010970

Sultana, A., Biss, R., & Chu, C. H. (2018). Designing an exergaming device for older adults residing in long-term care homes. In Workshop on Designing Interaction for Aging Populations, SIGCHI Conference on Human Factors in Computing Systems (CHI), Montreal, QC.

Sundqvist, A. S., Holmefur, M., Nilsson, U., & Anderzen-Carlsson, A. (2016). Perioperative patient advocacy: An integrative review. *Journal of Perianesthesia Nursing*, 31(5), pp.422–433. https://doi.org/10.1016/j.jopan.2014.12.001

Tanioka, T., Yasuhara, Y., Dino, M. J. S., Kai, Y., Locsin, R. C., & Schoenhofer, S. O. (2019). Disruptive engagements with technologies, robotics, and caring: Advancing the transactive relationship theory of nursing. *Nursing Administration Quarterly*, 43(4), pp.313–321. https://doi.org/10.1097/NAQ.0000000000000365

Topaz, M., Murga, L., Bar-Bachar, O., McDonald, M., & Bowles, K. (2019). NimbleMiner: An open-source nursing-sensitive natural language processing system based on word embedding. *CIN: Computers, Informatics, Nursing*, 37(11), pp.583–590. https://doi.org/10.1097/CIN.0000000000000557

Topol, E. J. (2019). High-performance medicine: The convergence of human and artificial intelligence. *Nature Medicine*, 25(1), pp.44–56. https://doi.org/10.1038/s41591-018-0300-7

Unertl, K. M., Schaefbauer, C. L., Campbell, T. R., Senteio, C., Siek, K. A., Bakken, S., & Veinot, T. C. (2016). Integrating community-based participatory research and informatics approaches to improve the engagement and health of underserved populations. *Journal of the American Medical Informatics Association*, 23(1), pp.60–73. https://doi.org/10.1093/jamia/ocv094

Van Dijk, J. (2020). *The digital divide*. Cambridge, UK and Medford, MA: Polity Press.

Venkatesh, V. (2015). Technology acceptance model and the unified theory of acceptance and use of technology. *Wiley Encyclopedia of Management* [online]. https://doi.org/10.1002/9781118785317.weom070047

Venkatesh, V., & Bala, H. (2008). Technology acceptance model 3 and a research agenda on interventions. *Decision Sciences*, 39(2), pp.273–315. https://doi.org/10.1111/j.1540-5915.2008.00192.x

Walsh, C. G., Johnson, K. B., Ripperger, M., Sperry, S., Harris, J., Clark, N., Fielstein, E., Novak, L., Robinson, K., & Stead, W. W. (2021). Prospective validation of an electronic health record–based, real-time suicide risk model. *JAMA Network Open*, 4(3), pp.e211428–e211428. https://doi.org/10.1001/jamanetworkopen.2021.1428

Waterman, A. D., Gleason, J., Lerminiaux, L., Wood, E. H., Berrios, A., Meacham, L. A., Osuji, A., Pines, R., & Peipert, J. D. (2020). Amplifying the patient voice: Key priorities and opportunities for improved transplant and living donor advocacy and outcomes during COVID-19 and beyond. *Current Transplantation Reports*, 7(4), pp.301–310. https://doi.org/10.1007/s40472-020-00295-x

Watson, J., Hutyra, C. A., Clancy, S. M., Chandiramani, A., Bedoya, A., Ilangovan, K., Nderitu, N., & Poon, E. G. (2020). Overcoming barriers to the adoption and implementation of predictive modeling and machine learning in clinical care: What can we learn from US academic medical centers? *JAMIA Open*, 3(2), pp.167–172. https://doi.org/10.1093/jamiaopen/ooz046

Weiss, D., Rydland, H. T., Øversveen, E., Jensen, M. R., Solhaug, S., & Krokstad, S. (2018). Innovative technologies and social inequalities in health: A scoping review of the literature. *PloS one*, 13(4), p.e0195447. https://doi.org/10.1371/journal.pone.0195447

Zhang, Q., Li, F., Zhang, H., Yu, X., & Cong, Y. (2018). Effects of nurse-led home-based exercise & cognitive behavioral therapy on reducing cancer-related fatigue in patients with ovarian cancer during and after chemotherapy: A randomized controlled trial. *International Journal of Nursing Studies*, 78, pp.52–60. https://doi.org/10.1016/j.ijnurstu.2017.08.010

Chapter 10

The Future of Nursing in a Digital Age: Planning for Rapid Change

Victoria L. Tiase and Marcus D. Henderson

Contents

Introduction

Over the last several years, we have witnessed not only the proliferation of digital health technologies and their potential to transform access to care, but also how their use in conjunction with nursing practice has the potential to reshape the healthcare ecosystem.

Digital health puts consumers at the center of their own care, transforming the way care is accessed and delivered. The growth of virtual visits has

DOI: 10.4324/9781003281047-10

also accelerated the change to new care settings and use of remote patient monitoring that enable nurses to manage patients from their home environment. As digital tools and platforms mature and become more available, they will also support an increased focus on wellness and preventative care. With added visibility into care processes and control over their health data, patients will be supported to make health-related decisions that may normally require a clinician. However, patients and families will have questions and need guidance that calls for discussion with a clinician.

Digital health technologies will generate big data. The capture of patient generated health data and patient-reported outcomes, including sensors and environmental data, means that more information will be available to provide a greater understanding of the patient care journey and potential to improve longitudinal care. Also, there will be opportunities for nurses to use new data sources to accelerate nursing research and test new care models. This applied research in turn can inform nursing education, impact nursing practice and transform health policy.

However, the anticipated technical advances and innovations in healthcare will occur juxtaposed to evolving societal changes and ethical challenges. Healthcare continues to be faced with difficult equity questions and approaches to care for the low-income, the uninsured, people of color and homeless: even when they do get care, these individuals may face serious financial problems from the incurred medical expenses. When care is delivered and at transitions of care, there are known biases and discrimination in terms of provision and quality of care. Ongoing challenges with technical literacy and general health literacy can further widen gaps between the individual and health providers, especially with vulnerable populations. As the most trusted care providers (The Commonwealth Fund et al., 2019; Saad, 2020), nurses are in a position to confront and address inequities, including digital intervention-generated inequity—a situation in which well-intentioned interventions may worsen existing health inequities by benefiting the more privileged over disadvantaged groups (Grossman et al., 2019).

The National Academy of Medicine's (NAM) recent report, *The Future of Nursing 2020–2030: Charting a Path to Achieve Health Equity*, presents a conceptual model that depicts the key areas to strengthen within the nursing profession to meet the challenges of addressing health equity in the next decade (National Academies of Sciences, Engineering and Medicine, 2021). One trend identified in the report's model is technology advances. Nurses are key to the adoption of new technologies within practice, especially related to the collection and use of social determinants of health (SDOH) data elements. The report's conceptual model also underscores the informaticist as an example of a nursing role in acute care, community and public health settings that will impact and address inequities in healthcare access and delivery. Nurse informaticists must consider diverse populations and settings alongside other evolving trends in the design and deployment of new digital tools and technologies combined with the judicious use of data to support all individuals in achieving optimal health. In this chapter, we use the report's conceptual model to highlight the areas in which digital health advances will shape and strengthen nursing roles (Figure 10.1).

To begin, we look at the near future use of digital innovations in nursing practice and associated advances in nursing education that will be needed to optimally function in a digital age. Next, we envision the impact of technology and data on the nurse–patient relationship including new paradigms for communication. Considering the leadership potential of nurses, we then discuss the role of nurses as entrepreneurs as well as industry and community leaders. This section also includes the nurse's leadership role in using digital tools and SDOH data to address care gaps and inequities. Finally, we conclude with an outline of what is needed to plan and prepare nurses for the anticipated future of leveraging data and technologies to provide personalized care, address population needs and advocate for equitable care for all.

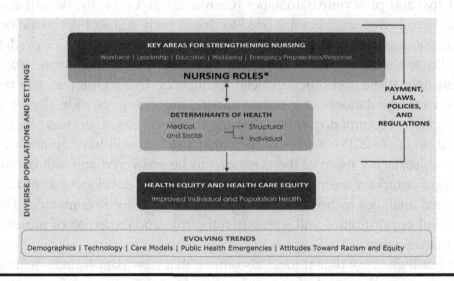

Figure 10.1   Conceptual framework presented in Future of Nursing 2020–2030 Report.

Reimagining Nursing Practice

Using technology, nursing practice will continue to expand beyond the walls of the hospital and other traditional healthcare settings. Technology and data availability are the necessary levers that allow nurses to individualize care longitudinally while addressing the needs of populations. Technology includes arming every nurse with a smartphone or tablet device to create efficiencies and enable the intelligent use of data for real-time insights. With increased data availability, we can expect all stages of the nursing process, especially diagnosis and intervention, to undergo substantial change. In the section below, we discuss the new and emerging technologies used in clinical analytics, connected devices, virtual care and robotics that will continue to expand and be important components to advancing nursing practice in a digital future.

With over a decade since the passing of the HITECH Act (Health Information Technology for Economic and Clinical Health Act) (Adler-Milstein & Jha, 2017), there is a plethora of electronic health record (EHR) data available for gathering, extraction and analysis. For these capabilities to be helpful, data must be discovered quickly and then efficiently delivered to nurses at the point of care in a way that minimizes the burden on nurses and reduces time to treatment. Although some sophisticated data views may be available today, going forward nurses will be involved in the expansion of dashboards that move beyond descriptive data and advance to predictive and prescriptive analytics (Carroll, 2019). Currently, pattern analyses and predictive analytics are used to detect early signs of deterioration in ICU patients, determine a patient's likelihood of readmission or predict mortality to guide end-of-life discussions (O'Dowd, 2017; Ferguson, 2018). Increasingly, these and other artificial intelligence (AI) techniques will be applied to large datasets to generate nursing diagnoses, provide alerts and intervention recommendations—all using evidence-based, decision support tools (Liao et al., 2015). Nurses in the clinical setting will have greater participation in surfacing more of the questions to be answered and will be able to inform computer scientists and digital technology developers as to how advanced analytics techniques can augment clinical decision-making. These expanded opportunities will strengthen the role and expertise of nurses in data management.

Increasingly, new digital tools also mean that new data sources will be used as a routine part of care processes. One data source of growing importance is SDOH data used to screen and identify social needs (NASEM,

2021). With the integration of SDOH data into clinical workflows, nurses will actively address social needs in longitudinal care planning and expand teaming across settings into communities—both rural and urban. One successful example is the Camden Coalition core model which uses healthcare *hotspotting* through the Camden Coalition Health Information Exchange (Camden Coalition of Healthcare Providers, 2021). With the strategic use of data from multiple hospitals, emergency rooms and correctional facilities, the Coalition is able to reallocate resources to a small subset of high-needs, high-cost patients. In addition, patients are strategically connected to community-based providers, such as community health workers and school nurses. As opportunities for data collection and exchange expand, nurses will be able to plan and respond to future public health issues in the community.

The integration of real-time data sources requires a mobile device in the hand of every practicing nurse—much like a stethoscope. These devices are needed to expedite communication with other members of the care team, especially important in-home health and hospice, and additionally, in acute care to ensure that nurses are digitally connected at all times to patient and unit status. Not only do we expect a future where all nurses have data at their fingertips in every care setting, but nurses will also obtain synchronous data from patients and families from wearables and sensors in the form of patient-generated health data. As connected devices become more common for all individuals, nurses will be able to obtain real-time data to better monitor patients' health statuses and to intervene as the need arises, making interventions timelier and more context aware. These novel data flows will chart a path toward greater health prevention and promotion led by nurses.

As the ability to provide care from a distance improves across all settings and geographies, nurses will require expertise in virtual care. Aging in place initiatives, data from smart homes and patient preferences, coupled with a looming nursing shortage, will influence new virtual care delivery models using virtual care consultations, assessments and remote patient monitoring (Fritz & Dermody, 2019). These models will require careful consideration as to which nursing care activities must be performed in person and which can be conducted virtually. Opportunities will be created for nurses to practice in new settings and Mercy Virtual Care Center is one example (Klingensmith & Knodel, 2016). The Mercy facility serves as a hub for telehealth services staffed by nurses, physicians and technical personnel, but lacks traditional hospital beds. Patients can be monitored from home, have virtual visits and be referred to in-person treatments when needed. This type of virtual care supports rural populations and is an effective way for those to obtain care who would not be able to otherwise. We also expect to see the development of a virtual nursing subspecialty that effectively uses technology to provide remote access to individualized, tailored care while addressing patient needs and preferences.

Across the globe, digital health experts anticipate future trends that include using robotics, chatbots and other AI software to simulate conversations as part of routine nursing care. We also expect a growth in the use of virtual and augmented reality to treat chronic pain, anxiety and other mental health disorders (Li et al., 2011). In acute care settings, nurses currently experience interactions with surgical robots, hospital-cleaning robots and robots that deliver supplies, linens and medications. However, new applications are on the horizon. Personal care robotics perform activities and tasks, such as support for social isolation, monitor falls in the home and collection of data on medication adherence (Sharts-Hopko, 2014). Socially intelligent robots or chatbots, enabled with artificial intelligence, can be expected to augment care delivery in a way that supports both nurses and patients. A number of health systems are already exploring the use of smart speakers and voice-assistant platforms to help patients communicate with providers (Drees, 2021).

Virtual reality (VR) technology, also not new to nurses, is commonplace in surgery and simulation training. Moving forward, VR is expected have increased utility in pain management and mental health interventions for a wide variety of conditions, leading to the incorporation of these tools into nursing care plans (Pourmand et al., 2018). As with virtual care, nurses will have access to new data sources and new practice models will evolve as nurses administer care that includes robotics and virtual reality applications. Nurses will also be able to encourage safety, quality and ease of use by assisting patients and families with technology selection and ongoing education on how to use their new technology devices and solutions.

In addition, new evidence continues to emerge related to EHRs, nurse satisfaction and patient outcomes (Moy et al., 2021). Since the advent of the EHR and rise of technology use in healthcare, there has been concern about the burden being placed on healthcare providers contributing to a more stressful and demanding work environment (NASEM, 2021). By learning from these past mistakes, we can ensure that the new technologies are designed with a full understanding of impact on clinical workflow, and a reduction in documentation burden that gives back time to nurses to spend on patient care.

Novel Education Modalities

The Future of Nursing (FON) 2020–2030 report renews the call to action for transformational change within the nursing profession to achieve health equity. Importantly, the FON report calls out nursing education as essential to achieving this foundational shift. The FON 2020–2030 Committee recognized that the future of nursing will not exist without the use of data, technology and digital health tools to augment nursing practice. The Institute of Medicine's landmark 2011 report, *The Future of Nursing: Leading Change, Advancing Health*, raised the issue of nurses requiring enhanced education and training in technology given the rise of electronic health records (Institute of Medicine, 2011). However, the FON 2020–2030 report indicates that little progress has been made in integrating technology use into nursing education and practice, and concluded that nursing programs must develop students' technical competencies in the following areas: patient-facing tools, clinician-facing tools and data analytics (Table 10.1).

The rise in technology use, such as telehealth, will continue to be essential for the provision of care, especially for nurses to address access to care and other gaps for underserved communities. For nursing to meet the demands of the current and continually emerging digital age, nursing education must continue to pivot in order to upskill the nursing workforce.

Table 10.1 Technical Competency Areas

	Technology/Tool	Required skill
Patient-Facing Tools	Remote patient monitoring Mobile health applications Wearable devices Virtual visit platforms Robotics Virtual reality	Empathetic communication Digital literacy assessment Patient education Virtual therapeutic nurse–patient relationship Person-centered care
Clinician-Facing Tools	Electronic health records Mobile documentation Communication devices Screening/referral tools	Collect new data sources Data security Leverage data in decision-making
Data Analytics	Artificial intelligence Information exchange Clinical decision support	Data management Data science Informatics

The FON 2020–2030 report describes the transformational shift needed, for both students and faculty, to incorporate technology throughout the curriculum instead of a separate course. To further incentivize schools of nursing, the American Association of Colleges of Nursing revised *The Essentials: Core Competencies for Professional Nursing Education* with a shift toward competency-based, nursing education that emphasizes informatics, digital health and technology (American Association of Colleges of Nursing, 2021).

The COVID-19 pandemic has shown that traditional approaches to nursing education struggled to meet the needs of graduates entering the workforce during a pandemic (Morin, 2020). The abrupt transition to online and distant learning challenged the traditional modalities of brick-and-mortar education due to restrictions placed on in-person learning and clinical training. This shift exposed the need for increased use of alternative and virtual methods (e.g., simulation, virtual reality), which are effective teaching modalities, to supplemental traditional clinical learning moving forward (Aebersold & Dunbar, 2021). More importantly, nurse faculty must be adept at training the basic use of such technologies and be comfortable with the technical demands related to all aspects of nursing practice.

For sustained change, a multi-level, interprofessional approach is needed to support students, faculty and schools of nursing (SONs). Students will require equitable access to the technology necessary to engage in simulation-based and virtual reality learning. SONs must seek out and collaborate across professions with academic–practice partners that can instruct topics concerning patient-facing tools, clinician-facing tools and data analytics (Smart et al., 2020). This would allow for students to be trained by highly skilled experts in the use of these technologies rather than by nurse faculty who may lack the technical skills. Also, investments by SONs in resources and infrastructure will be critical to support such efforts. But traditional pedagogy will not be sufficient moving forward. Simulation centers that incorporate EHR documentation, in addition to real-world experiences, to provide empathetic care through technology must be the norm.

Coupled with general technical skills for all nurses, the nursing workforce of the future will demand a substantial growth of nursing informatics specialists. New data sources will require an understanding of information needs, standards and terminologies that are needed to advance interoperability. Nurses with requisite informatics expertise will continue to be in high demand for the adoption, implementation and evaluation of new technologies.

Transforming Nursing Research

The speed of digital transformation will demand new ways of conducting nursing research in the future. Expedited approaches to generating evidence must be developed to translate research into practice before new data sources are generated or technologies outdated. Digital data collection, greater interoperability and remote connections to other researchers will yield easier access to large datasets that can be shared across organizations and create a foundation for new research collaborations. In addition, new types of data, novel care settings and workflows will require nurse researchers knowledgeable in data science and informatics.

Sustained focus and funding in digital technology research is critical to unleashing the potential of the nursing workforce. Nursing will need to examine the gaps related to knowledge on the effective use of technology in nursing practice. The impact of technology interventions on workflow redesign, care models and patient outcomes should be a part of research agendas. Across populations, telehealth visits and the utilization of other telehealth services must be examined related to the experiences of patients with limited English proficiency, with varied health or technical literacy, and disabilities. Focusing on public health and extending care into the communities, research should explore the role of nurses in teaming across settings leveraging technology. This is especially important as we rethink the role of nursing and the judicious use of data to respond to disasters and public health emergencies.

Recognizing the need for a transformative shift to enable the next generation of nurses, the American Nurses Foundation convened a group of nursing, health, business and technology leaders to launch the *RN Initiative to Reimagine Nursing* (American Nurse Foundation, 2021). The initiative seeks to support the transformation of nursing practice to improve access to care and population health outcomes by funding pilot projects that set out to achieve the program's priorities and goals. Starting in 2021, projects that evaluate ways to accelerate change in nursing education, regulation and practice will be funded for three years. Specifically, the initiative calls attention to the need for a *digitally enabled nursing practice* in the future and for nurses to be integral in design and testing of tools and other technologies used to augment their practice. Similar funding will be crucial for future advances.

Additional research is required to understand the capabilities of a digitally connected nursing workforce. A thorough exploration of how nurses use technology and data in practice along with the skills that are lacking can be used to inform education improvements. There are gaps in evidence related to the preparation of nursing instructors to incorporate robotics, virtual reality and simulation in nursing education. It is also unclear as to how digital technology can be used to provide nursing education at scale. Finally, but most importantly, large-scale studies will be required to understand the impact of digital technology on the nursing workforce, especially its impact on nurses' well-being.

Partnership with Patients

As consummate patient advocates, nurses are positioned to leverage the new digital landscape for improved communication with patients and families. Digital technologies will be called upon to connect with hard-to-reach populations and facilitate contact between in-person patient visits. However, maintaining the human connection through digital means is critical. Nurses will be expected to project a caring relationship through technology, using their empathy skills to build rapport.

Given the anticipated increase in national, digital health portals and the promise that patient-facing, digital health apps will be covered by health insurance, patients will be generating and sharing more and more data. Wearables, sensors and other devices have been shown to increase patient engagement in their care (Bayo-Monton et al., 2018). Moreover, patient expectations require that patient-generated health data (PGHD) are acted upon and feedback provided. Nurses will be using PGHD to partner with patients, keep communication channels open and facilitate shared decision-making. Considering health equity, nurses will also incorporate patient preferences and access suitability of technology solutions to meet patient needs. Nurses will help to empower patients by teaching them how to use the data they produce.

As the most trusted health profession, nurses are uniquely positioned to leverage technology to advocate for and communicate with the public. Nurses can harness the power of social media to educate patients and advance promotion and prevention efforts. Given the impact of COVID-19 on health behaviors, it will be important for nursing to approach communication strategies in a systematic way. This includes streamlining evidenced-based care recommendations to avoid misinformation. Nurses will also use technology platforms to support and advocate for communities to address health disparities (Ross & Cross, 2019). This includes advocating for user technology needs and individual access to health data, considering principles of security and privacy.

Digital Leaders, Innovators and Entrepreneurs

The expansion of digital health technologies throughout all business sectors has created new positions for nurses as leaders outside of the traditional healthcare space. By utilizing civic engagement, elected office and roles within community organizations, nurses will influence digital health from new perspectives. Nurse leaders can advocate for sustained collection of SDOH data sources and ensure they are used in a way that improves the safety, quality and affordability of healthcare.

By forging alliances with technology companies or working within such companies, nurses can advocate for the judicious use of nursing workflows and consider patient-centered care models in the design and development of solutions. These roles position nurses to disrupt, design and innovate new tools and devices. The future will also require more nurses in technology development, moving new processes, models and products into practice and as entrepreneurs, leveraging their knowledge to create their own healthcare businesses. However, to accelerate this change, nursing participation in innovation activities is critical. Nurses in all roles must have the space and permission to drive innovation (Fuller & Hansen, 2019).

Digital Health Equity

As technological advancements aimed toward improving quality, cost and efficiency continue to enter the market, nurses must ensure that the focus is centered on equity and population health outcomes to reduce disparities. While the use of technology can help to improve clinical care and outcomes, it can also worsen disparities, exacerbate inequities and perpetuate structural racism (Ibrahim et al., 2020; Knight et al., 2021). When introducing patient-facing tools, nurses should assess for reliable access to broadband. Many Americans, especially those in underserved, disadvantaged and rural communities, do not have adequate access (Arcaya & Figueroa, 2017). This also is true for nursing students engaged in online or distant learning. During the COVID-19 pandemic, many nursing students did not have access to reliable Internet or necessary technologies, thus impacting their engagement in learning (Morin, 2020). These technologies will only be effective if nurses and patients alike are able to independently access and realize their benefits.

Furthermore, clinician-facing, data analytic tools have the potential to worsen disparities (Knight et al., 2021). For example, clinical algorithms have been found to reinforce racial bias, thus perpetuating inequities and racism (Obermeyer et al., 2019; Vyas et al., 2020). The creation of algorithms based on artificial intelligence should be tested in a way to ensure that they are safe, fair, transparent and free of bias. Nurses should be a part of evaluating such algorithms to ensure their use is in the best interest of patient care.

Nurses are often left out of the conversations concerning the development and design of new technologies. Simply educating current and future nurses about the potential consequences of technology use for patients and providers is not enough. To mitigate these possible effects, nurses and patients must be involved in the development and evaluation process of new technologies. This involvement would allow for possible adverse consequences to be identified and potentially prevented. Community engagement and transparency are foundational to building trust, ensuring the development of patient-centered technologies and promoting health equity (Brewer et al., 2020; United States Food and Drug Administration, 2021).

Given the rise in technology use during the COVID-19 pandemic, and the ability for technology to reduce disparities in access, nurses must have the technology competencies necessary to support collective efforts in advancing health equity. To address social needs, nursing informatics specialists will take the lead in initiatives for the systematic collection, analysis and use of SDOH data within clinical workflows. Initiatives should also focus on ways to expand interoperability to community settings and redesign clinical documentation to leverage new data sources. The FON 2020–2030 committee emphasized the integration of SDOH data in one of its recommendations (Table 10.2).

New Possibilities

Not only will virtual care be a new specialization within nursing, but we expect the digital transformation of healthcare to usher in a host of other new sub-specialties within nursing. The capacity to leverage environmental datasets and advanced technology devices in healthcare will advance the specializations of aerospace nursing, genomic nursing and environmental nursing. Our vision is that nurses will be viewed as data experts, divergent

Table 10.2   FON 2020–2030 Report Recommendation 6

Using Technology to Integrate Data on Social Determinants of Health into Nursing Practice

All public and private healthcare systems should incorporate nursing expertise in designing, generating, analyzing and applying data to support initiatives focused on social determinants of health and health equity using diverse digital platforms, artificial intelligence and other innovative technologies.

- Integrate data on SDOH and build a nationwide infrastructure.
- Ensure that health equity data collaboratives improve visualization of data on SDOH.
- Employ nurses with expertise in informatics to improve individual and population health.
- Give nurses in clinical settings responsibility and associated resources to innovate and use technology.
- Provide resources to facilitate telehealth by nurses.

thinkers and business owners. The overall shift from less illness to more prevention and wellness promotion will provide opportunities for nursing yet to be realized.

Conclusion

The digital age has the potential to not only transform equitable healthcare, but it will also afford opportunities to amplify nursing practice and create new roles for nurses. In 2030, nurses will have a drastically different practice environment from what they have today. Nurses should have the educational opportunities to advance their technical knowledge and keep pace with evolving trends (Risling, 2017). Moreover, to strengthen the role, expertise and capacity of nurses, research must be accelerated to unveil how digitally enabled, nursing practice will create efficiencies, engage patients and reduce inequities. With the required planning and preparation, nurses will rise to the challenge of meeting technical advances with the human touch in a way that advances health for all.

References

Adler-Milstein, J., & Jha, A. K. (2017). HITECH Act drove large gains in hospital electronic health record adoption. *Health Affairs*, 36(8), pp.1416–1422.

Aebersold, M., & Dunbar, D. M. (2021). Virtual and augmented realities in nursing education: State of the science. *Annual Review of Nursing Research*, 39(1), pp.225–242.

American Association of Colleges of Nursing. (2021). *The essentials: Core competencies for professional nursing education* [online]. Available at: https://www.aacnnursing.org/Portals/42/AcademicNursing/pdf/Essentials-2021.pdf (Accessed 31 May 2021).

American Nursing Foundation. (2021). *Reimagining nursing initiative* [online]. Available at: https://www.nursingworld.org/foundation/programs/rninitiative/ (Accessed 31 May 2021).

Arcaya, M. C., & Figueroa, J. F. (2017). Emerging trends could exacerbate health inequities in the United States. *Health Affairs*, 36(6), pp.992–998.

Bayo-Monton, J. L., Martinez-Millana, A., Han, W., Fernandez-Llatas, C., Sun, Y., & Traver, V. (2018). Wearable sensors integrated with Internet of Things for advancing eHealth care. *Sensors*, 18(6), p.1851.

Brewer, L. C., Fortuna, K. L., Jones, C., Walker, R., Hayes, S. N., Patten, C. A., & Cooper, L. A. (2020). Back to the future: Achieving health equity through health informatics and digital health. *JMIR mHealth and uHealth*, 8(1), p.e14512. https://doi.org/10.2196/14512

Camden Coalition of Healthcare Providers. (2021). *Camden core model* [online]. Available at: https://camdenhealth.org/care-interventions/camden-core-model/ (Accessed 31 May 2021).

Carroll, W. M. (2019). The synthesis of nursing knowledge and predictive analytics. *Nursing Management*, 50(3), pp.15–17. https://doi.org/10.1097/01.NUMA .0000553503.78274.f7

Commonwealth Fund, New York Times, Harvard T. H. Chan School of Public Health. (2019). *Americans' values and beliefs about national health insurance reform* [online]. Available at: https://cdn1.sph.harvard.edu/wp-content/uploads /sites/94/2019/10/CMWF-NYT-Harvard_Final-Report_Oct2019.pdf (Accessed 2 July 2021).

Drees, J. (2021). *'Alexa' finds a voice in healthcare: 4 systems that have built skills for Amazon's digital assistant* [online]. Available at: https://www.beckershospital review.com/digital-transformation/alexa-finds-a-voice-in-healthcare-4-systems-that -have-built-skills-for-amazon-s-digital-assistant.html (Accessed 22 August 2021).

Ferguson, R. (2018). Care coordination at end of life: The nurse's role. *Nursing*, 48(2), pp.11–13.

Fritz, R. L. Dermody, G. (2019). A nurse-driven method for developing artificial intelligence in "smart" homes for aging-in-place. *Nursing Outlook*, 67(2), pp.140–153.

Fuller, R. Hansen, A. (2019). Disruption ahead: Navigating and leading the future of nursing. *Nursing Administration Quarterly*, 43(3), pp.212–221.

Grossman, L. V., Masterson Creber, R. M., Benda, N. C., Wright, D., Vawdrey, D. K., & Ancker, J. S. (2019). Interventions to increase patient portal use in vulnerable populations: A systematic review. *Journal of the American Medical Informatics Association*, 26, pp.855–870.

Ibrahim, S. A., Charlson, M. E., and Neill, D. B. (2020). Big Data analytics and the struggle for equity in health care: The promise and perils. *Health Equity*, I(1), pp.99–110.

Institute of Medicine. (2011). *The future of nursing: Leading change, advancing health*. Washington, DC: The National Academies Press. https://doi.org/10 .17226/12956

Klingensmith, L., & Knodel, L. (2016). Mercy virtual nursing: An innovative care delivery model. *Nurse Leader*, 14(4), pp.275–279.

Knight, H. E., Deeny, S. R., Dreyer, K., Engmann, J., Mackintosh, M., Raza, S., Stafford, M., Tesfaye, R., & Steventon, A. (2021). Challenging racism in the use of health data. *The Lancet Digital Health*, 3(3), pp.144–146.

Li, A., Montaño, Z., Chen, V. J., & Gold, J. I. (2011). Virtual reality and pain management: Current trends and future directions. *Pain Management*, 1(2), pp.147–157.

Liao, P. H., Hsu, P. T., Chu, W., & Chu, W. C. (2015). Applying artificial intelligence technology to support decision-making in nursing: A case study in Taiwan. *Health Informatics Journal*, 21(2), pp.137–148.

Morin, K. H. (2020). Nursing education after COVID-19: Same or different? *Journal of Clinical Nursing*, 29(17–18), pp.3117–3119. https://doi.org/10.1111/ jocn.15322

Moy, A. J., Schwartz, J. M., Chen, R., Sadri, S., Lucas, E., Cato, K. D., & Rossetti, S. C. (2021). Measurement of clinical documentation burden among physicians and nurses using electronic health records: A scoping review. *Journal of the American Medical Informatics Association*, 28(5), pp.998–1008.

National Academies of Sciences, Engineering, and Medicine. (2021). *The future of nursing 2020–2030: Charting a path to achieve health equity*. Washington, DC: The National Academies Press.

Obermeyer, Z., Powers, B., Vogeli, C., & Mullainathan, S. (2019). Dissecting racial bias in an algorithm used to manage the health of populations. *Science*, 366(6464), pp.447–453.

O'Dowd, E. (2017). IoT devices significantly lower nurse response times. *HIT Infrastructure*. Available at: https://hitinfrastructure.com/news/iot-devices-sig-nificantly-lower-nurse-response-times (Accessed 31 May 2021).

Pourmand, A., Davis, S., Marchak, A., Whiteside, T., & Sikka, N. (2018). Virtual reality as a clinical tool for pain management. *Current Pain and Headache Reports*, 22(8), p.53. htts://doi.org/10.1007/s11916-018-0708-2

Risling, T. (2017). Educating the nurses of 2025: Technology trends of the next decade. *Nurse Education in Practice*, 22, pp.89–92.

Ross, P., & Cross, R. (2019). Rise of the e-nurse: The power of social media in nursing. *Contemporary Nurse*, 55(2–3), pp.211–220.

Saad, L. (2020). U.S. ethics ratings rise for medical workers and teachers. *Gallup*. Available at: https://news.gallup.com/poll/328136/ethics-ratings-rise-medical -workers-teachers.aspx (Accessed 2 July 2021).

Sharts-Hopko, N. C. (2014). The coming revolution in personal care robotics: What does it mean for nurses? *Nursing Administration Quarterly*, 38(1), pp.5–12.

Smart, D., Ross, K., Carollo, S., & Williams-Gilbert, W. (2020). Contextualizing instructional technology to the demands of nursing education. *Computers, Informatics, Nursing: CIN*, 38(1), pp.18–27. https://doi.org/10.1097/CIN.0000000000000565

United States Food and Drug Administration. (2021). *Artificial intelligence/machine learning (AI/ML)-based software as a medical device (SaMD) action plan* [online]. Available at: https://www.fda.gov/media/145022/download (Accessed 31 May 2021).

Vyas, D. A., Eisenstein, L. G., & Jones, D. S. (2020). Hidden in plain sight: Reconsidering the use of race correction in clinical algorithms. *New England Journal of Medicine*, 383(9), pp.874–882.

Chapter 11

Envisioning Digital Health and Nursing's Call to Lead Unparalleled Transformation of Person-centered, Connected and Accessible Care

Connie White Delaney, Charlotte A. Weaver,
Joyce Sensmeier, Lisiane Pruinelli and Patrick Weber

Contents

DOI: 10.4324/9781003281047-11

Introduction

Since the planning for this third edition of *Nursing and Informatics for the 21st Century* four-book series began in late 2019, numerous earth-moving, sea-changing events have occurred. A perusal of these four books captures a sense of these seismic changes, creates a foundation for reflection and invites us to dare to commit to bold transformation of advancing the health of people, societies and the planet.

The worldwide impact of the COVID-19 pandemic has exposed profound vulnerabilities in our national and global public health systems. We continue to witness the inequities within and among institutions, organizations and countries related to access to care, critical supplies, resources, health personnel and vaccines with a disproportionate amount of the human suffering endured by low-income populations (see Wright et al., Book 1, Chapter 10; Rosenthal et al., 2020).

We have also seen the power of social media's counter-messaging to compete with the explanations and recommendations from science, government leaders and public health officials. Cha and Park (Book 4, Chapter 5) address these issues with examples of various social media strategies and messages that public health and healthcare entities used to proactively counter misinformation and give examples of nurse-led initiatives at community and national levels. Worldwide, we have experienced quarantines and lockdowns with healthcare facilities having to separate COVID-19 patients from their families and loved ones at the door. Nurses responded with creative solutions, such as using mobile phones, iPads and laptops with face-to-face apps, to make family visits possible for desperately needed connectedness and final goodbyes. For those not familiar with these technologies, the young taught the less experienced. As we go to press with this four-book series, the outcome of the pandemic is still largely unknown. In many countries, including large parts of the world, vaccines are still not available, and even where they are available, we continue to see high incidence and death rates related to COVID-19 due to variants emerging from unvaccinated populations. Consequently, public health officials warn that the possibility of novel, vaccine-resistant, variants emerging is still a threat that looms over our world.

On the policy front, prior regulatory and payment restrictions for use of telehealth visits were quickly removed, and globally healthcare systems expanded their use of technologies to accommodate virtual access to care. Broadband capacity was expanded within health systems as well as communities to enable expansive work from home. Concurrently, in the US, a federal statute enacted in 2020 (45 CFR 170) as part of the *21st Century Cures Act: Interoperability, Information Blocking, and the Office of the National Coordinator (ONC) Health Information Technology (HIT) Certification Program* placed the consumer in control of their health data as owner with total data access and control rights (ONC, 2020). In Book 4, Chapter 6, Moon walks us through the technical requirements detailed in this 2020 statute and the common mechanisms that must be used for easy consumer access, as well as for the controlling and sharing of individual health data. Similarly, Moen et al. in Book 1, Chapter 6, present the European perspective on the 'voice of the consumer' as full partners in their healthcare decisions with ownership of their health data. Additionally, Flemming and Ellßel in Book 4, Chapter 8, outline Europe's regulatory and legal aspects of data access and control.

Taken together, these policy changes and the disruptive impact of the COVID-19 pandemic opened a wide door for large numbers of technology innovators to enter the global markets. Additionally, in the US, to stay competitive and in compliance with the 21st Century Cures Act, healthcare systems are rapidly implementing digital applications integrated into their electronic health records (EHRs). In turn, consumers are increasingly adopting digital tools, sensing and mobile monitoring devices as part of everyday life (Clancy, Book 3, Chapter 4; PIH, 2021), and initiating data exchanges with providers. Individuals are continuing to use the options of virtual visits and communications in place of in-person clinic or office visits as discussed by Krupinski and Shea, in Book 3, Chapter 9. Numerous chapters throughout this series address how these digital technologies and extended healthcare settings carry new dimensions of advocacy, mentoring, digital literacy and protection from harm into nurses' roles (Michalowski and Park, Book 3, Chapter 7; Cha and Park, Book 4, Chapter 5; Moon, Book 4, Chapter 6). The majority of the 44 chapters comprising this third edition book series illustrated in Tables 11.1, 11.2 and 11.3 speak to the need for higher levels of digital literacy of our nursing workforce and student graduates (Wilson, Book 2, Chapter 7; Perezmitre et al., Book 2, Chapter 8). Furthermore, Chu et al. in Book 4, Chapter 9, and Tiase and Henderson in Book 4, Chapter 10 discuss the increased knowledge and skills that nursing informatics specialists will need for implementing patient (person)-centered design methods in new applications and systems. The application of machine learning, including artificial intelligence, in health information technology (IT) systems will require transparency and the ability to explain the underlying rules, methods

Table 11.1   Third Edition of *Nursing and Informatics for the 21st Century–Embracing A Digital World*, Book 1—Realizing Digital Health—Bold Challenges and Opportunities for Nursing, Table of Contents

Introduction
1. Digital Health Ecosystems: A Strategy for Transformation of Health Systems in the Post-Pandemic Future
2. Digital Health and New Technologies
3. Opportunities and Challenges for Digital Health Advancement
4. Ethical Considerations in Digital Health
5. US Health and Healthcare Current State: Nurse Executives
6. Engage the People: Health Informatics and Personal Health Management
7. Information Management in Nursing Leaders' Operational Decision-Making
8. Informatics in Large Health Systems: Organization, Transformation and Nursing Informatics Leadership Perspectives
9. Nursing Informatics within Health Systems: Global Comparison
10. South Africa's Healthcare Systems, Technology and Nursing
11. Teamwork and Informatics: Capturing the Work of Nurses as Team Members

and cautions to providers and consumers (see Risling, Book 3, Chapter 6; Iqbal, et al., Book 3 Chapter 8).

The explosive pace at which consumer health technologies are entering the marketplace is unprecedented. These technologies include the EHR integrated, patient-facing applications, mHealth and social media. The implication for nurses is one of an ever-increasing rate of innovation that will

Table 11.2   Third Edition of *Nursing and Informatics for the 21st Century–Embracing A Digital World*, Book—2 Nursing Education and Digital Health Strategies, Table of Contents

Introduction
1. Nursing Informatics Educational Programs in Academia and in Practice
2. International Health and Healthcare Education Current State
3. Health and Healthcare Education Current State
4. Using Digital as a Tool, Not Being the Tool of the Technology Giants
5. Learning from Clients/Patients to Advance Education and Scholarship
6. Cultivating a Workforce of Nurse Disruptors: An Academic–Practice Innovation Hub
7. Nursing Education and Digital Health Strategies
8. Nursing Informatics Competencies for the Next Decade
9. Interprofessional Practice and Education: Interrelationship with Knowledge Generation, the IPE Core Data Set and National Information Exchange Infrastructure
10. The use of the IMIA Education Recommendations and the IMIA Knowledge Base as a Foundation for Competencies in Health Informatics in Africa
11. Simulation-Based Learning from across the Globe

Table 11.3   Third Edition of *Nursing and Informatics for the 21st Century–Embracing A Digital World*, Book 3—Innovation, Technology and Applied Informatics for Nurses, Table of Contents

Introduction
1. Top Informatics Trends for the Next Decade
2. Canadian Health Outcomes for Better Information and Care: Making the Value of Nursing Visible through the Use of Standardized Data
3. Consumer-Generated Whole-Person Health Data: A Structured Approach
4. Sensors and the Internet of Things
5. Applied Data Science
6. Understanding the Foundations of Artificial Intelligence: Data, Math and Machine Learning
7. Artificial Intelligence for Nursing and Healthcare: Potentials and Cautions
8. Artificial Intelligence-Based Model for Monitoring Pressure Ulcer Changes in Bedridden Patients: A Case Study from Taiwan
9. Telehealth and Virtual Care
10. Simulations-Based Care Delivery
11. Case Studies in Applied Informatics during COVID-19

require agility in learning new tools, care delivery modes, digital literacy and management of patient-owned data (see Moon, Book 4, Chapter 6; Austin, et al., Book 3, Chapter 3).

Within this context, the US National Academy of Medicine's Committee on the Future of Nursing 2020–2030 published a consensus study report that charts a path to achieving health equity in the US over the next decade (NAM, 2021). This vision of a more highly skilled, educated professional nursing workforce with health equity as a core mandate is a foundational and necessary roadmap for nursing's future. However, the report comes at a challenging time for it to be received by the largest segment of the nursing workforce in the US (2.2 million) that work in acute care and connected facilities (NAM, 2021 p. 66). Chief nursing officers of large, integrated delivery systems are reporting high nurse turnover rates, staff burnout and experiences of trauma due to the impact of the extended COVID-19 pandemic. The nurse executives are warning that the pandemic's impact will require a re-evaluation of care delivery models, empowerment of nurses and nursing, and discernment of the import and visibility of nursing.

Importantly, the NAM report asserts the need for a national nurse identifier to facilitate recognition and measurement of the value of services provided by nurses (NAM, 2021 p. 366). Further, it states that an identifier is important for performance metrics to incentivize nursing roles and functions that advance population health and health equity. To realize the benefits of a unique nurse identifier, the Policy and Advocacy Workgroup of the Nursing Knowledge: Big Data Science multi-year initiative began an advocacy campaign in 2020 to increase awareness and use of the unique nurse identifier. This Policy and Advocacy workgroup developed the following policy statement that is foundational to this campaign:

> The National Council of State Boards of Nursing (NCSBN ID) should be used by key stakeholders as a nurse identifier to help demonstrate the value of nursing through research and enhance individual care and health outcomes via more comprehensive documentation in *the Electronic Health Record* (EHR), Enterprise Resource Planning (ERP) systems and other technologies and systems.

(Alliance for Nursing Informatics, 2020)

A groundswell of support for the use of a unique nurse identifier is being realized. The Alliance for Nursing Informatics (ANI) has published a board endorsed, unique nurse identifier policy statement as well as reference and educational materials which are informing policy development (Alliance for Nursing Informatics, 2020). The use of a unique nurse identifier, such as the NCSBN ID, will be able to detect identifiable and actionable events in disparate health IT systems and technologies (Carroll & Sensmeier, Book 4, Chapter 4). Adoption of a unique nurse identifier will help distinguish the importance of nurses and nursing in continuously improving nursing care, outcomes and transforming systems, delivering evidence-based practice and increasing nurse visibility to quantify value-based care.

Moreover, the Future of Nursing 2020–2030 report calls for nursing to embrace the goals of health equity and equal access to care with a focus on the social determinants of health, following in the footsteps of the World Health Organization's 2008 roadmap charge (WHO, 2008). In its report, entitled 'Closing the Gap in a Generation: Health Equity through Action on the Social Determinants of Health,' the WHO delivers a clarion call for equity and equality in access and care services using a social determinants of health framework. This charge was further supported by the United Nations 2015 report 'UN Sustainable Development Goals (UN, 2015).' This UN report provides a planetary health perspective, translating to the goal of ensuring healthy lives and the promotion of well-being at all ages. Potter and colleagues in chapter Book 4, Chapter 1, address this planetary health perspective in relation to nursing's role in this arena.

To emphasize nurses' essential role in healthcare delivery, prevention and general health, WHO published a 2020 report, 'State of the World's Nursing' (WHO, 2020a), detailing gaps, opportunities and recommendations. Expanding emphasis on prevention is a key concept in the future. Nurses have a strategic role in the domain of prevention. With the help of the evolving technologies with the capacity of multiple data analyses, nurses will help the people to evaluate early on how to advance people's health status. Nurses should become the architects of the new health-related technologies taking into account the population needs and the capacity of the healthcare system. Countries that are empowering the nurses (education, leadership, decision-making) will measure better health status outcomes.

Further, in April 2020, the WHO published a bulletin in partnership with the International Council of Nurses and Nursing Now identifying a global shortage of 5.9 million nurses and asked all countries to increase their annual number of nurse graduates by 8% (WHO, 2020b). Additionally, the American Nurses Association (ANA) published an alert in September 2021 asking the Department of Health and Human Services to declare the current nurse staffing shortage a national crisis (ANA, 2021). As we continue into the 2020–2030 decade, we must acknowledge that we stand on a threshold of a severe nursing shortage. These challenges invite us to consider how nursing can most effectively and efficiently address the challenges and opportunities proposed by the WHO, the Future of Nursing report and the demands of our societies.

Partnerships as Our Way Forward

How do we most effectively enable the rapid cultural changes called for within our profession, schools of nursing, professional organizations, and healthcare systems? The accomplishments resulting from the foundational 2011 Future of Nursing report included the unparalleled increase in Doctor of Nursing Practice (DNP) programs and graduates. However, according to the 2020–2030 Future of Nursing report, very little progress, if any, has been made since the 2011 report in getting informatics embedded in curricula, addressing increased need for PhD graduates, and improving faculty and workforce informatics knowledge and competencies. Thus, we are recommending that nursing organizations actively collaborate with other disciplines and health provider entities and organizations to enable rapid progress with infusing informatics skills, nimbleness and literacy for our workforce, our faculty and, most importantly, nursing graduates at all levels.

Further, the complexity of digital technologies, data science and computer science is dramatically raising the bar for nursing informatics specialists as well. Presently, nurse informaticists are specializing within informatics in specific areas of expertise, e.g., standards/terminology, modeling, machine learning/artificial intelligence (ML/AI), analytics, and development and implementation science. In this specialty evolution, we recognize that it is essential to expand informatics training while also expanding generalist informatics education for all nurses. While many incentives are in place, further awareness, empowerment and local to international strategies and partnerships are essential to achieve this vision and address this urgent crisis.

Academic–practice partnerships (APP) have the power to lift up and synergize organizations' engagement in leadership, education and research. These APP partnerships can make it possible for clinical practice to inform research questions and for the latest science to be rapidly adopted into clinical practice. As illustrated in the Emory APP example (Book 2, Chapter 6), these partnerships can also provide access to big data to support learning analytics skills, optimum clinical practice placements with exposure to current technologies, and the creation of healthy, thriving nursing communities of innovators. As another APP instance, the University of Minnesota School of Nursing formed a tightly integrated faculty/nurse leader partnership with Fairview Health System beginning in 2013. Consisting of 10 hospitals and 48 clinics and led by a strong collaboration between the Dean and the Fairview's corporate chief nurse/chief operations officer, participants from each organization serve on each other's councils, committees and other joint appointments. This Minnesota collaboratory is designed to be a 'think-tank' and an incubator for creativity and innovation to enhance nursing education, research, practice and ultimately patient care. Example outcomes include empowered joint leadership, extensive partnership with DNP projects, collaboration on the Nursing Knowledge Big Data Science initiative, convening the annual Nursing Research Day, Grand Rounds, celebration/recognition for Nurses Week, and most recently multiple COVID-19 and workforce studies.

Building on the Minnesota collaboratory's national recognition of excellence by the American Association of Colleges of Nursing (AACN)/American Organization for Nursing Leadership (AONL), this model has been further expanded to embrace additional academic–practice partnerships, including the Minneapolis Veterans Administration Healthcare System, Essentia Health, and Faith Community Nurse Network.

Similarly, the Emory Academic/Practice Partnership was forged by a committed handshake between the Emory School of Nursing's Dean and the Emory

Health System's Chief Nurse Office. As described in McCauley and Pappas (Book 2, Chapter 6), this partnership extends to joint research initiatives and clinical practice settings that include home, community, Advance Practice Registered Nurses (APRN) and DNP-led practices and 11 medical centers. As mentioned above, the Emory partnership also offers an EHR-fed database with resources to support staff nurses and students at all levels in building queries, assessing their clinical practice and developing sophisticated research studies. Important to the following recommendations, Emory's School of Nursing data analytics and technology faculty and staff resources come from multiple disciplines, including a nationally renowned AI research team, and all are dedicated resources to the school as well as to Emory Health's nurses. Similarly, the simulation lab in the new Emory Nursing Learning Center has been planned collaboratively with a commitment to support and maintain skills for Emory Health nurses and other personnel, including midwives, nurse anesthetists, and acute and primary care nurses from Bachelor of Nursing (BSN) to DNP levels. Planning for the Emory Nursing Learning Center building was a shared project between McCauley and Pappas and reflects their commitment to nursing being a part of multidisciplinary teams that function in every setting from homes to intensive care units, with deliberate outreach to the surrounding local Atlanta communities. The efficiencies and excellence resulting from this partnership are reflected in the School of Nursing's growth in student enrollment, faculty and grant monies, and improved national rankings. For Emory Health, the benefits of this partnership influence their joint clinical governance and practice councils, joint research projects, injection of practice-informed research questions, feedback into data-based and evidence-based practices throughout their nursing workforce, competitiveness for nurse recruiting and low nurse turnover. Additionally, academic–practice partnerships support accelerated changes by leveraging collective expertise. The pathways for new graduates reflect a more diverse nursing workforce, which is essential in addressing long-standing racial and ethnic health disparities. Ongoing collaboration between these groups can lead to continuous improvement and evolution toward creating a competent and resilient workforce.

Partnerships with Other Disciplines and Organizations

A fast and efficient way to infuse informatics into nursing curricula is to engage experts from disciplines such as data science, informatics, biostatistics/epidemiology and computer science to work in tandem with nursing faculty. This approach would provide needed 'hands-on' guidance and skills training to nursing faculty, as well as accomplish rapid transformation of curricula and support simulation lab exercises. Evolution of a new discipline, such as informatics, follows a predictable pathway, including drawing upon related disciplines to foster advanced education in a specialty. PhD education in nursing is an example. Initially, nurses obtained PhD degrees in other fields, such as sociology, anthropology and education, until the profession had sufficient numbers of PhD prepared faculty to develop doctoral programs in nursing. Including faculty and/or consultants from the social sciences who have specialized in medical/health systems and can bring needed cultural expertise into schools of nursing, and encourage their engagement in curricula empowers the synergy across education, practice and industry. Inherent biases occur within all professions and disciplines, including nursing. Opportunities to study and engage in other cultures, experience diverse care settings, engage with different cultural backgrounds of teammates will help develop the compassion and humility goals called for in the Future of Nursing report. This multidiscipline/partnership approach invites us to transition from competition and resource scarcity to a world of collaboration and resource abundance.

There is also a pressing need in nursing education for further evolution of informatics degree programs, as well as specialties within the field for data science, AI/ML applications and design/implementation methodologies in mHealth solutions. Until nursing has the needed informatics resources and skill sets within its own faculty ranks, we should not hesitate to include informatics faculty from other disciplines to help us quickly accomplish curricula upgrades and upskilling of nursing faculty. Informatics resources, including financial support within dedicated budgets, must be available to teach new technologies to students, especially for ML/AI, and data analytics.

Partnering with community organizations, healthcare systems, companies and extended non-acute settings, including home health and hospice, is essential. Nurse entrepreneurs' businesses and practices provide vibrant opportunities for student rotations and projects. Opportunities to participate in team projects in diverse cultural settings (multidiscipline) are important to foster recognition of social determinants of health and awareness of one's own culture and biases. These partnerships open doors for guest lectures, participation in simulation laboratories and other beneficial collaborations that are commonly used in business and computer/data science degree programs. For example, the University of Minnesota School of Nursing is a charter member in the Optum Labs Research Collaborative, a novel network that brings together new partners, data and analytic techniques to implement research findings in healthcare practice.

Simulation Labs and Advantages of Partnerships

In response to changing technologies and skills training needs, simulation as an active learning pedagogy has proliferated across academic and practice settings to teach clinical skills, as well as to improve the skills of individual care providers and clinical team performance (Bradley et al., Book 3, Chapter 10). Consequently, healthcare organizations and schools of nursing are facing a need to invest in simulation laboratories that provide technology used in all settings and for all patients. Simulation labs can easily be multi-million-dollar investments and thus present another opportunity to partner. Partnerships may be with other schools in the health disciplines, with practice partner organizations, community colleges, as well as with equipment and software vendors.

The goal is to have sustainable simulation laboratories that include state-of-the-art technologies encountered in all clinical environments, including individuals' homes. As described by Muro Sans and colleagues in Book 2, Chapter 11, simulation, AI, virtual reality and other digital approaches have expanded and enabled greater degrees of immersion and interactivity in virtual environments globally. Importantly, nurses who have an understanding of the principles underlying AI are better prepared to support the safe adoption and use of these digital technologies. Educational tools supported by AI, such as virtual reality by which novel situations can be generated for simulated patient care experiences and robotics (British Broadcasting Company, 2020, paragraph 26), will further support the nursing process. Additionally, because a best practice is to support data querying in the context of care planning and evaluation, nurses need data analytic skills as well as keen understanding of the difference between evidence-based practice and care based on data. Hands-on, experiential approaches including those offered through simulation labs, clinical settings selected for their technologies, and paired with informaticians/data science partners for learning would demonstrate how to look at clinical practice/research questions from practice databases. Engaging students from multiple disciplines within complex case studies that cross all care settings reflects the realities of healthcare and helps bridge the transition from education to practice.

Despite numerous safety initiatives, preventable medical error is esti-mated to remain the third leading cause of death (Johns Hopkins Medicine, 2016). As discussed by Bradley and colleagues in Book 3, Chapter 10, simulation training has demonstrated positive outcomes and supports the need for continued exploration of innovative strategies to reduce prevent-able errors throughout care delivery organizations. Positive care outcomes, whether individual or team based, have promoted the adoption of simula-tion-based activities in patient care delivery settings. The evidence obtained through simulation training strengthens healthcare organizations dedicated to improving patient safety and quality of care. As the pedagogy of simula-tion matures, refining best practices will continually improve the process through which individuals and organizations prepare for simulation, use it within organizations and evaluate its outcomes. Ongoing empirical testing is needed to further investigate innovative uses of simulation to improve the delivery of healthcare at all levels, from individual provider care to team care, to across organizational system processes.

Expanding Landscape of Digital Health

Social injustices, inequities in distribution of resources and healthcare access have all been painfully exposed by the pandemic. Globally, the pandemic gave urgency to the need for new digital solutions, including virtual, tele-health and mHealth solutions to manage public health imperatives, as well as to deliver care unrelated to COVID-19. Telehealth is an example of digi-tal technology that has been available for years, but with the pandemic, it became widely used by all types of healthcare providers to effectively deliver care at the patient's location and avoid physical contact with the health system. Realizing the necessity of digital health is palpable, as is the pivotal role of nurses in advancing the transformation of health sys-tems toward the digital health ecosystems of tomorrow (Snowdon, Book 1, Chapter 1).

Notwithstanding challenges and barriers, emerging technologies includ-ing AI, the Internet of Things (IoT), virtual and augmented reality and cloud computing are transforming how nurses deliver patient, family and community care and manage system operations across the care continuum spanning local to global contexts. It is essential that nurses understand and embrace these new digital technologies (Sensmeier, Book 3, Chapter 1). The value of the innovations that they make possible is established for clinical practice and health outcomes. Personalized healthcare, telehealth, AI, voice enabled technology, predictive analytics and mobile device integration are key technologies already used in healthcare today.

Likewise, the IoT, defined as the networking capability that allows information to be sent to and received from objects and devices on the Internet (Merriam-Webster Dictionary, 2021), is rapidly changing how and where care is provided. As Clancy details in Book 3, Chapter 4, advances in sensor technology, wired and wireless networks and commercial acceptance of standards are accelerating health systems adoption of the IoT. Data captured by sensors on medical devices and sent via networks to large databases in the cloud are being analyzed to discover new knowledge, as well as to create AI for a variety of clinical activities. The IoT is enabling the transformation of health systems from a hospital-centric model to patient-centered care through its capacity to provide access anywhere along the continuum of care. Nurses have a key role in this transformation as they mediate information flow between patients and providers throughout their various levels of care.

Data Analytics and Nursing

Let us boldly prioritize and advance applied data science. Data science has a broad definition, including all the processes needed to extract meaning from big data for a specific knowledge domain. Pruinelli and Topaz explain in Book 3, Chapter 5 that a better understanding of data science concepts and skill sets is needed to move this discipline and its impact on healthcare forward, including frameworks and resources available to conduct real world analytics projects that have the potential to improve health outcomes. Although several conceptual frameworks have been adapted from various specialties to support data science, only a small number are focused on healthcare data. Additionally, these frameworks are not widely adopted nor are they readily available to stakeholders, including researchers, clinicians and the public. The Applied Healthcare Data Science Roadmap (Pruinelli and Topaz, Book 3, Chapter 5) was developed with the goal of educating healthcare leaders on the use of data science principles and tools to inform decision-making, thus supporting research and approaches in clinical practice that will improve healthcare for all.

Data analytics for nursing data is empowered by nursing's use of terminology standards in nursing documentation and data. A powerful example is Canada's C-HOBIC initiative, a multi-decade journey to achieve a national standard for nursing documentation described by White, Nagle and Hannah in Book 3, Chapter 2. The authors describe their methodology and detail the benefits gained. By using international terminology standards for nursing measures and outcomes in clinical documentation within their EHR systems, the C-HOBIC undertaking allowed individual clinicians to evaluate their own outcomes, as well as nurse managers and executives to look across their departments and systems to better understand the components of operations that influenced outcomes (White, 2016).

Nurses' essential role in health and healthcare requires a solid knowledge of emerging technologies, incorporation of related ethical practices and an innovative spirit. An example of ethical practices is the European Union's (EU) adoption of the FAIR principles for all future research concerning health data. The concept defines the data to be: Findable, Accessible, Interoperable, Reusable (FAIR). When data is FAIR compatible, the structure, definitions and meaning of the data are known, and thus enable standard uses (Willems et al., 2020). The FAIR principles or similar practices enable the expansion and integration of data. Enabled by sound ethical principles, the vast amount of data, that is big data, allows the AI concept to be adopted and implemented. Moreover, expanding the reuse and analysis of health data, largely collected by nurses, empowers nurse researchers to discover new interpretations of clinical data (O'Connors, 2020). Nurses should take a proactive role in the development of new and updated systems incorporating data analyses and interpretations with the assistance of computing power (Chu et al., Book 4, Chapter 9). A number of chapter authors urge nurses to actively contribute to the development of AI capabilities (Michalowski & Park, Book 3, Chapter 7; Risling, Book 3, Chapter 8; Ronquillo et al., 2021) to have these applications developed from nurses expertise. From all of these perspectives, we anticipate that the availability of big data will increasingly affect how nurses learn, practice, conduct research, develop policy and maximize promotion of human health and well-being (Topaz & Pruinelli, 2017).

Nursing Leadership in a Digital World

The importance of this digital transformation has powerful implications for health and healthcare, nursing and leadership. The role of nurse executives in this transformation is essential for empowering patient-centered care. As addressed by Begley and fellow nurse executive authors in Book 1, Chapter 5, nurse leaders do understand the need to shift toward non-traditional care delivery models that enable more convenient, on-demand care that is connected, engages health informatics and extends responsive services. Combined with the evolving roles in nursing and changes in care delivery, operational leaders face a steep learning curve. Thus, Begley and colleagues stress that there is an urgent need for nurse leaders to be prepared to meet expectations encompassing a visionary future and the necessary executive and leadership competence, including informatics, for leading into this future.

Nursing and systems leaders clearly recognize that it is essential to integrate nursing informatics into everyday operations and care delivery to create future organizational excellence, achieve exemplary patient outcomes and develop extraordinary care teams supported by digital technologies. Moreover, nurses will play a critical role on healthcare teams to facilitate teamwork processes, communication and coordination, and the need to abandon traditional methods and strategies that have kept integral members of the healthcare team hidden. The EHR and digital technologies are rich sources of big data for nurses and serve as a tremendous resource for capturing team member attribution, value and their impact on clinical outcomes.

Informatics and Nursing Education

The rapid evolution of healthcare into a digital system requires nurses to have the knowledge, skills, competencies and capabilities to participate in and lead this transformational change. To do this, educators, faculty, mentors and preceptors must also possess these skills. We know this is not always the case. The 2021 AACN Essentials with its ten core domains provide the foundational competency roadmap for our future. The HIMSS TIGER Global Interprofessional Competency Synthesis provides additional guidance details. However, the digital health evolution will require an understanding of more complex topics such as AI, robotics and genomics and modifying the workflows that are needed to make this work efficiently and effectively for clinicians, patients, consumers and populations. Additionally, technology advances are also rapidly expanding the knowledge and expertise that nurse informaticists must have to stay current with clinical practice. Against this backdrop, we offer the following considerations for immediate nursing education transformation.

While nursing education in general has been developing and improving for over 100 years, training in the specialty of informatics is still relatively new. Maximizing digital technologies, big data and decision support including AI requires nursing informatics competencies driven by responsive training structures, expertise and processes. Global and even national consensus on the appropriate competencies to include in informatics curricula continues to be a challenge despite the availability of several models. There is currently a lack of consensus on a single model or supporting evidence for (1) a specific informatics competency list, (2) an effective method of delivery (in-person, simulations, virtual or in combinations) or (3) where to place the informatics content into nursing academic programs. It is time to resolve this inert stance so that foundational competencies addressing technological competency, information literacy and information management to advance successful nursing practice can be applied to prepare faculty, students and clinicians.

Nursing faculty in academic institutions are confronted with the need to address informatics education at multiple levels. First, the integration of core informatics competencies into baccalaureate nursing programs is foundational. Second, the development of graduate level informatics curricula that use one of the available competency models is needed. Third, the development of doctoral-level programs that prepare nursing informatics leaders of tomorrow will benefit the entire profession. Finally, the development of competent faculty in the field of informatics will help infuse the core competencies across the curricula. Consistent with our recommendations to leverage partnerships to achieve rapid upskilling of faculty as well as curricula transformation, we offer the following recommendations.

Faculty professional development is mandatory and the existing informatics specialty organizations could provide valuable assistance. Faculty teaching in nursing informatics graduate specialization programs should be knowledgeable and experienced informaticians with the academic background to address essential content. In the US, the growth in DNP programs has placed considerable pressure on faculty resources, as programs have worked to assure that they were meeting *the essentials of doctoral education for advanced nursing practice* including the requirement of a final DNP project (AACN, 2006). In addition, the advanced practice registered nurse programs have to meet the requirements of the various specialties. All of the DNP curricula, including BSN-to-DNP and post-master's DNP, are currently being revised to comply with the 2021 AACN Essentials (American Association of Colleges of Nursing, 2021). Courses that simply provide an overview of informatics as a specialty are no longer sufficient. Courses directed at successfully incorporating informatics and information and communication technologies must align these skills and best practices to care delivery, best communication processes and operational workflows.

We urgently recommend normalizing an educational curriculum for nursing informatics and practice competencies. Globally, this goal would have to take into consideration the technological maturity, healthcare system structure and the specific needs of a given country or geographic environment of adoption (Wright et al., Book 2, Chapter 10). Emphasis needs to include programs in rural areas and middle- and lower-income regions. The goal would be to reduce the variability and confusion on the education and competencies required to prepare informatics nurses. It would also clarify the variations in nurse's role functions cross-culturally and allow for better-informed planning among developed and developing countries in nursing informatics education requirements.

A helpful approach would be to develop partnerships to bridge the gap in nursing informatics education between developed and developing countries with two-way exchanges, such as by committing to and developing virtual educational conferences for faculty and students. These exchanges would enhance and inform current knowledge through updates and requirements for education and competencies of informatics nurses from each organizational/country participant so that learning happens bilaterally. The value of these exchanges would enrich students and faculty by learning healthcare delivery variations and the innovative digital technologies used so that the partnerships honor and benefit all.

The second priority is aligning the nursing informatics education curriculum, which is based on a well-developed framework, such as the ten core competencies for professional nursing education described by AACN in 2021 with three most common nursing informatics competencies that focus on knowledge, skills and attitudes. This alignment would clearly outline both the education and practice-based competencies required to produce graduates that are knowledgeable, skilled and prepared for dynamic and technology-intensive healthcare systems. In addition, the outcome measures for each competence in the three main domains should be linked to curricula on all levels.

A third priority to be considered is to re-evaluate and standardize the tools used to assess nursing informatics competencies to meet the needs of the rapidly evolving working environment of nurses in both academia and practice. Finally, it is essential to develop frameworks for leadership competencies in nursing informatics. Preparing nurse informaticists with the appropriate leadership skills may improve nursing involvement in informatics projects from development to implementation across settings and potentially improve the resulting outcomes.

Closing Summary

Consider how much nursing has evolved and changed from its inception under Nightingale or the various religious orders in the 1800s. Is there a more profound testament to the strength of nursing's resiliency and its openness to constant learning, role expansion, and our impact on the health of people, families, communities, and organizations? It is essential for the 21st century nurse is to be comfortable with having power: assured by their expertise, rights and obligations. In turn, nurse leaders' need to focus on supporting these empowered frontline nurses, and be ever ready to mentor, acknowledge and reward the innovators and disruptors. We are not yet there.

We shine a spotlight on the fact that AI and ML are driving and influencing significant societal change around the world with healthcare as one of the key focal points. There is little doubt that AI and ML will forever change healthcare systems spanning the full continuum of care and delivery, including nursing practice. Are nurses prepared to co-create and participate in this future? Understanding the basic building blocks that contribute to the complexity of AI is an essential first step. For nurses to be able to monitor, advocate and collaborate on the integration of this technology into healthcare systems, we must increase our professional knowledge of this technology.

AI has been transformative for many public and private industries, and we are currently observing an AI-led revolution in healthcare. While this transformation is occurring, recognizing the potentials and cautions is paramount. The use of AI is a fundamental paradigm shift in healthcare that is already affecting nurses in their everyday work, and its impact will be even more pronounced in the future. AI is embedded in nurses' daily lives as algorithms in smart systems within mobile phone apps for banking, purchasing, finding directions, etc., as well as in their education applications. Even though AI applications in healthcare date back to the late 1970s, technological advances in robotics and computing and the right social climate have created ideal conditions to take full advantage of what AI can contribute to improving the provision of care. Yet healthcare constitutes a complex system that presents many challenges to AI's adoption. Ethics, the ability to explain and justify models' inputs and outputs, education of patients and providers, inherent biases, fairness and social equity are some of the technical and non-technical issues that need to be addressed for AI solutions to be safely integrated into care delivery (Michalowski and Park, Book 3, Chapter 7). Outstanding questions are: what are the adoption priorities for robotics, machine learning, mobile technology and virtual and augmented reality? Moreover, what are the cautions that need to be considered in their implementation?

In this book series we explore the impact that digital technologies will have on how care is delivered, the expanding care settings into the community and the home, virtual monitoring and patient generated data, and ultimately the numerous ways that nursing roles and digital health skill sets are needed to support the global goals of equal access to health and care.

We have welcomed two defining works informing nursing's future: NAM's *Future of Nursing 2020–2030* report and AACN's *Essentials*. Together, these two publications offer a potent mandate for nursing, greatly expanding our advocacy role to address healthcare inequity, bias and access. These valuable, visionary resources also detail the skills and competencies that our nursing workforce will need to be able to effectively navigate and inform our highly complex technical and cultural healthcare system. This book series highlights educational strategies embedded in schools of nursing and the actual and potential synergies needed with practice to afford full availability to these resources for the nursing workforce. The message is clear, bold and inviting—nursing in partnership with our transdisciplinary colleagues are called to lead and create an unparalleled transformation toward person-centered, connected and accessible care anchored in digital health. We must invest in developing the necessary knowledge and skills to propel nursing into the future. This advancement for nursing will take a united and committed effort in a world forever changed by recent global events that have accelerated technology agendas in many countries.

References

Alliance for Nursing Informatics. (2020). *Demonstrating the value of nursing care through use of a unique nurse identifier policy statement* [online]. Alliance for Nursing Informatics. Available at: https://www.allianceni.org/sites/allianceni.org/files/ANI%20Unique%20Nurse%20Identifier%20Policy%20Statement%20FINAL4%20Approved%20071620.pdf (Accessed 6 June 2021).

American Association of Colleges of Nursing. (2006). *The essentials of doctoral education for advanced nursing practice* [online]. Washington, DC: American Association of Colleges of Nursing. Available at: https://www.aacnnursing.org/ DNP/DNP-Essentials.pdf (Accessed 24 May 2021).

American Association of Colleges of Nursing. (2021). *The essentials: Core competencies for professional nursing education* [online]. Available at: https:// www.aacnnursing.org/Portals/42/AcademicNursing/pdf/Essentials-2021.pdf (Accessed 2 November 2021).

American Nurses Association. (2021). *ANA urges Dept of Hlt and human services to declare nurse staffing shortage a national crisis* [online]. September 1. Available at: https://www.nursingworld.org/news/news-releases/2021/ana-urges -us-department-of-health-and-human-services-to-declare-nurse-staffing-short- age-a-national-crisis/ (Accessed 21 October 2021).

British Broadcasting Company. (2020). *What the world can learn from Japan's robots*. [online]. Available at: https://www.bbc.com/worklife/article/20200205 -what-the-world-can-learn-from-japans-robots (Accessed 24 May 2021).

Johns Hopkins Medicine. (2016). *Study suggests medical errors now third leading cause of death in the U.S.* [online]. Available at: https://www.hopkinsmedicine .org/news/media/releases/study_suggests_medical_errors_now_third_leading _cause_of_death_in_the_us (Accessed 29 October 2021).

Merriam-Webster Dictionary. (2021). [online]. Available at: https://www.merriam -webster.com/dictionary/Internet%20of%20Things (Accessed 5 March 2021).

National Academy of Medicine. (2021). *Future of nursing 2020–2030: Charting a path to achieve health equity* [online]. Available at: https://nam.edu/publications /the-future-of-nursing-2020-2030/ (Accessed 26 May 2021).

O'Connor, S. (2020). Secondary data analysis in nursing research: A contemporary discussion. *Clinical Nursing Research*, 29, pp.279–284. https://doi.org/10.1177 /1054773820927144

Office of the National Coordinator for Health IT (ONC). (2020). *21st century cures act final rule: Interoperability, information blocking, and the ONC health IT certification program* [online]. Available at: https://www.healthit.gov/curesrule/ (Accessed 2 November 2021).

PIH Health. (2021). PIH health begins remote patient monitoring initiative. *PIH Health: Healthy Living*, Fall issue, pp.8–9.

Ronquillo, C. E., Peltonen, L., Pruinelli, L., Chu, C. H., Bakken, S., Beduschi, A., Cato, K., Hardiker, N., Junger, A., Michalowski, M., Nyrup, R., Rahimi, S., Reed, D. N., Salakoski, T., Salanterä, S., Walton, N., Weber, P., Wiegand, T., & Topaz, M. (2021). Artificial intelligence in nursing: Priorities and opportunities from an international invitational think-tank of the nursing and artificial intelligence leadership collaborative. *Journal of Advanced Nursing*, 77(9), pp.3707–3717. https://doi.org/10.1111/jan.14855

Rosenthal, B. M., Goldstein, J., Otterman, S., & Fink, S. (2020). Why surviving the virus might come down to which hospital admits you. [online]. *New York Times*, July 1 (updated September 22, 2021). Available at: https://www.nytimes.com/2020/07/01/ nyregion/Coronavirus-hospitals.html (Accessed November 2, 2021).

Topaz, M., & Pruinelli, L. (2017). Big Data and nursing: Implications for the future. *Studies in Health Technology*, 232, pp.165–171.

United Nations. (2015). *UN sustainable development goals*. United Nations [online]. Available at: https://sdgs.un.org/goals and https://www.un.org/sustainabledeve lopment/health/ (Accessed 21 September 2021).

White, P. (2016). The case for standardized data in nursing. *Nursing Leadership*, 28(4), pp.29–35.

Willems, M., Herczog, E., Russell, K., & Stall, S. (2020). FAIR data maturity model: Specification and guidelines – draft. https://doi.org/10.15497/RDA00045

World Health Organization (WHO). (2020a). *State of the world's nursing 2020: Investing in education, jobs and leadership: Web annex. Nursing roles in 21st-century health systems* [online]. Geneva: World Health Organization. Available at: https://www.who.int/publications/i/item/9789240007017 (Accessed 21 October 2021).

WHO. (2020b). *WHO and partners call for urgent investment in nurses* [online]. Available at: https://www.who.int/news/item/07-04-2020-who-and-partners-call -for-urgent-investment-in-nurses (Accessed 2 November 2021).

WHO CSDH. (2008). *Closing the gap in a generation: Health equity through action on the social determinants of health*. Final Report of the Commission on Social Determinants of Health [online]. Geneva: World Health Organization. Available at: http://apps.who.int/iris/bitstream/handle/10665/43943/9789241563703_eng .pdf;jsessionid=455C4B5EBE5F4D6533FBC1A8FB92F239?sequence=1 (Accessed 1 January 2022).

Index

Printed in the United States
by Baker & Taylor Publisher Services